'Chalkie' White

Leicester Tigers Legend

‘Chalkie’ White

Leicester Tigers Legend

Martin Whitcombe

ST DAVID’S PRESS
Cardiff

Published in Wales by St. David's Press, an imprint of

Ashley Drake Publishing Ltd
PO Box 733
Cardiff
CF14 7ZY

www.st-davids-press.wales

First Impression – 2025

ISBN
Limited Edition Hardback 978-1-904609-26-1
Paperback 978-1-904609-27-8
eBook 978-1-904609-28-5

British Library Cataloguing-in-Publication Data.
A CIP catalogue for this book is available from the British Library.

Typeset by Prepress Plus Technologies, www.prepressplustechnologies.com
Cover designed by the Welsh Books Council, Aberystwyth
Colourised image on cover courtesy of Jez Holdsworth & James Stockton

CONTENTS

To Doris Gwendoline White

INTRODUCTION

Aged 19, on July 12 1981, I qualified as a Physical Training Instructor, a PTI, and received my first posting, to RAF North Luffenham near Oakham. At the station gymnasium I was handed a letter inviting me to join training sessions at Leicester Tigers. I phoned Jerry Day straight away and accepted his offer. "Good. Training starts next week," he replied, "introduce yourself to our coach Chalkie White when you get there."

I didn't know anyone at Leicester Tigers so walking through the main gates on Aylestone Road for the first time was very intimidating. Up to this point I had played most of my rugby at Keighley RUFC on the iconic 'Tip Top', the old corporation rubbish dump which had been turned into playing fields; I hadn't played for a club with stands before, let alone a stadium.

One of the first people I met that day was Brian Hall, the former Leicester captain, who welcomed me warmly. I asked Brian where I could find Chalkie White, and after a short wander through the ground, Chalkie was introduced to me. It was a simple greeting; he looked me in the eyes before extending his right hand and said: "Welcome to Leicester Football Club."

Brian then took me to the Tigers training ground, the Welford Road Recreation Ground – the 'Rec' – which is known today as Nelson Mandela Park. It had just played host to Billy Smart's Circus and one of my first tasks was to help my teammates clear the elephant dung from the field, exemplifying that whether a new recruit or a regular England international, we were all equal and expected to lend a hand when required.

"What's Chalkie White like," I asked Brian, and his reply told me all I needed to know about Leicester's coach. Brian explained that not only did the two men share a lift to training three times a week, but that Chalkie was always blunt but honest. During one of their many journeys Brian had once asked 'coach' if he was good enough to play for England. "No Brian," he replied, "you're not good enough, but you're the yard stick by which the ones that do will have to measure themselves against."

That was the first time I heard one of his famous sayings, and the anecdote about the lifts to training was another insight into the club's culture, as I was later to discover when asked by Ray Needham the then youth team coach, to give Tony Cliff – one of his players who lived in Uppingham – a lift to training. I willingly did, and it became a tradition that continued for many years as Tony progressed into the senior teams, resulting in us being life-long

Martin Whitcombe

friends. The values and principles of the club ensured that all players, at whatever level, supported each other – we were all Tigers together.

I hadn't met anyone like Chalkie White before and I haven't met anyone like him since. A man fiercely dedicated to coaching rugby. Often outspoken, he had little time for players who didn't share his enthusiasm. He was a hard taskmaster in training who demanded the highest standards on the field of play, and his vision as Head Coach inspired a generation. He was also compassionate and understanding and helped me adjust to living away from home for the first time. He also helped other players deal with disappointments, setbacks and tragedies in a caring and fatherly way.

The very mention of some of the great players associated with Leicester Tigers evokes a host of memories, but not only has Leicester given great players to the game, the club also owes much to the excellence of their administrators. Leicester had two exceptional club Secretaries – Tom Crumbie, who served for 33 years, and Eric Thorneloe MC* who held the position for 29 years. In 1966, Jerry Day became the club's Secretary. A local businessman who was not afraid to voice his opinion, Day and White formed a formidable partnership over the following 16 years, which took Leicester to the pinnacle of the game in England.

Chalkie seized every opportunity to benefit Leicester. He once visited Dave Phillips at Hoylake RFC on the Wirral to take a coaching session and enjoyed the surroundings so much he chose the location as a training camp venue in the 1970s. Perfectly typifying the amateur era, the changing rooms were used as the players' accommodation and the clubhouse was where the lads socialised, and where Chalkie spent his evenings sharing his views on coaching with the local Hoylake players.

A significant number of those who nurtured and supported Chalkie as he built the club to dominate English rugby over these years, as well as those who reported and commentated on the club's progress, had unmistakable Welsh accents. The post-War exodus of predominately young, talented, rugby-playing teachers from their homeland to the East Midlands certainly worked to Leicester's advantage. Known to all as 'Van', Sidney Ifano Hopkins, Headmaster at Lancaster Boys School and a committee member at Welford Road for over 20 years, introduced future Swifts, Extras and then 1st XV Secretary, club President, Honorary Secretary, stadium announcer and stalwart of 50 years' loyal service to Leicester, John Tudor Thomas, to the club in 1963. Hopkins also pioneered the BBC's local radio commentary at Tigers games from 1967 until he retired in 1987, when he was succeeded by former Tigers fly-half and fellow Welshman Bleddyn Jones, from Brynamman. The key Welsh connections continued with former 1st XV player Dave Lyons, the Cardiff-born PE teacher at Roundhill High School who founded the youth team; Bill, the classic old school 'magic sponge' physio, known to all as 'Taffy', who created his own high-octane liniment to keep injured players on the pitch; and renowned rugby correspondent Martin Johnson, born in Newport and educated at Monmouth School, who heralded the onward march of the Tigers to cup glory in the pages of the *Leicester Mercury*. Wales' loss was Leicester's gain, and with their love of rugby being matched by that of Cumbrian Chalkie White, they together proved to be an unstoppable and irresistible combination.

After serving his apprenticeship at Camborne RFC, in the cauldron of Cornish club rugby, Chalkie White found a new teaching opportunity in 1957. The move to Nottingham High School also enabled him to continue his rugby playing career by joining Leicester Tigers. His impact on the club over the next 26 years as a player, committee member and coach would have a profound influence on the Leicester club which he would change forever.

Martin Whitcombe
July 2025

GET BUSY LIVING!
The Matt Hampson Foundation

Matt Hampson was living out his boyhood dreams, a member of the Leicester Tigers first team squad and starting tight head prop for the England under-21s during their Six Nations campaign in 2005. Then on 15th March at Franklins Gardens during a scrummaging session his life changed in the blink of an eye.

A freak injury left Matt paralysed from the shoulders down and breathing via the aid of a ventilator. After 18 months in Stoke Mandeville hospital he returned home. After much soul searching and adjusting to his new life he made the decision he was going to do something positive with his life, focus on the things he could do rather than those he couldn't – he was going to 'Get Busy Living'!

Former Leicester Tigers forward Matt "Hambo" Hampson

And by God has he done that, Matt has packed more into the last 18 years than most would in a whole lifetime. He has set up a successful charity along with his good friends Roy Jackson (Chairman of Trustees) and Tommy Cawston (CEO): the Matt Hampson Foundation, a charity to inspire and support young people seriously injured through sport. This led to the construction of the unique and inspiring Get Busy Living Centre, an incredible rehabilitation facility in the heart of the Leicestershire countryside.

Matt is more passionate about rugby and the Leicester Tigers now than before his accident. The players and club have been so supportive over the years and it's that grounding and mental toughness, forged on the grass at both Oval Park and Welford Road, that gave him the determination to make something of his life despite all the challenges he faced. He's never happier than being around the boys, and his knowledge of rugby particularly the scrum is second to none.

The Foundation and the Tigers are forever linked; it is one of the club's chosen charities each year, and the support of players, staff and fans has been incredible and something that Matt treasures. The joint venture of setting up the first wheelchair rugby team with a professional rugby club came from Matt's passion for Leicester to be pioneers and to set a precedent for others to follow.

As time passed, Matt's former teammates retired and with Covid it was difficult to keep up a relationship with the current crop of players. A tragic accident to young Taylor Gough has changed all that. Taylor, an academy graduate, suffered life-altering injuries in a serious car crash in 2020.

The Foundation stepped in from the beginning and supported both Taylor and his family and helped them navigate a traumatic period. Taylor had actually visited the centre on a number of occasions, to help decorate some walls before it had even opened, and to cook a meal for the beneficiaries with the academy lads, so he knew he had a familiar and welcoming haven where he could continue his rehab, and a support network to help guide him through this new challenge he faced.

Taylor, like Matt, is a Tiger through-and-through, and the Foundation took him under their wing and will continue to support him and his family. Tigers, both current and former players, have been brought together by Taylor's courage, enthusiastically volunteering for fundraising activities and started to meet at the centre to provide support for one of their own. Taylor is now playing wheelchair rugby for the Leicester Tigers – the first to represent both teams – and we are all so proud of him.

The centre provided the venue where the values of the Foundation could flourish, to compliment the Leicester Tigers ethos of supporting former players in times of need – once a Tiger, always a Tiger. This partnership of principles has resonated across the generations at Leicester, and Matt's innovative and inspirational efforts to assist others in their time of need was recognised in 2021 when he was awarded an OBE in the New Year honours.

The Get Busy Living Centre, Melton Mowbray, Leicestershire

Taylor's accident has also meant a new crop of talented young players are now ambassadors for the Matt Hampson Foundation. A group who can speak with authority about what the Foundation has done for their friend. They are exceptional and articulate young men and the club should be incredibly proud of them all.

Rugby is important, winning trophies is important, but the true beauty of what rugby offers and what is truly important is the brotherhood, the friendship, and knowledge that people you care about have your back. The real success of Leicester Tigers isn't the amount of Premiership titles or the two European cups it's the quality of the men who have worn the shirt and continue to look after former players, way after the boots have been hung up.

Martin Whitcombe continues that proud tradition and is a good friend to the Foundation. We were thrilled when he informed us that his proceeds from this tribute to Chalkie White will be donated to the Matt Hampson Foundation.

As Martin's book brilliantly illustrates, Chalkie's Leicester legacy is immense and all those connected to the club owe him a huge debt of gratitude. His legacy is not only the on-field success of the club, but the values we all hold dear and it lives on through the deeds of those he inspired.

Tommy Cawston
Chief Executive Officer
The Matt Hampson Foundation

ACKNOWLEDGEMENTS

This biography of Chalkie White has been a long, seven-year journey of discovery and I couldn't have achieved it without the support of a huge number of amazing people to whom I owe so much.

The relative abundance of archive material available on Chalkie's period as coach of Leicester Tigers is contrasted by the scarcity of publicly-available information about his early and family life, his career in teaching and his period as a rugby player.

Fortunately, he touched the lives of so many and made such an impression on several generations of rugby players he'd coached, former pupils he'd taught, and colleagues he'd worked alongside that they, alongside his devoted family, willingly shared their memories and experiences for this book. Such was the depth of respect for Chalkie that not one person refused to participate in the project or contribute their recollections, and the full list of interviewees are listed in the Bibliography. I cannot thank you all enough for your support and your patience as the research for the book took on a life of its own. I am delighted and honoured to be able to share your combined contributions in this book.

In addition to the personal testimonies, I am also indebted to all those who helped me curate the impressive array of photographs and rugby memorabilia that adorn this book. My heartfelt thanks are offered to the following: Peter and Margaret Wheeler, Garry Adey, John Allen, Nick Youngs, Wayne and Sylvia Richardson, Ged and Diane White, Steve Kenney, Paul Dodge, Dusty Hare, Malcolm Foulkes-Arnold, Dave Thomas, Duncan Black, Clive Galloway, Mike Beason, Sam Swift, Dominic O'Sullivan, John Duggan, Sean Cussack, Philip 'John' Collins, Marcia Able-Smith, Simon Bennett, Adam Lubbock, Phil Horrocks-Taylor, Stuart Farmer, John Dewhirst, Gary French, Bleddyn Jones, Ian 'Dosser' Smith, Steve Johnson, Chris Goddard, Arthur Hazlerigg, Gwynne Day, Mick Newton, Tudor Thomas, Mike Davis, Andy Key, Chris Thau, Simon Cohen, Jez Krych, Kelvin Wilford, Jack Forfar, Josef Jedlicka, Mike Poulson, Bob Reeves, Will Feebery, Paul Hull, Dave Lyons and Leicester FC.

I'd also like to express my appreciation for the assistance received from Bruce Barritt, Harry Roberts and Andy Tucker who helped me with information about the 1982 tour to Zimbabwe. Thanks also to John Allen for helping me identify many of the players in old photographs. I formed a most unlikely friendship with John when I was a player, which we continued during the research for and writing of this book. His knowledge of Leicester Tigers was unrivalled, and I was fortunate to be able to cross-reference much of the information I gleaned with him – I also benefited greatly from his unique knowledge of the inner workings at Welford Road. John, more than any other, encouraged me to record Chalkie's story, and in true John Allen style he asked for neither acknowledgement or recognition.

Thank you to former Leicester Tigers players, Peter Wheeler for writing the Foreword, Martin Johnson for his Afterword and David Matthews for the Preface. David was not in the best of health and his much-valued contribution would not have been possible without the considerable assistance of Ian Smith. A special mention must also go to Roger Grove, Steve Kenney, Dusty Hare, Les Cusworth, John Kaye and Will Feebery who went way above and beyond what could have been reasonably expected.

Two sports writers also deserve a special mention for their encouragement and support over the years – Leicester Tigers historian Stuart Farmer and the journalist and author Huw Richards. Thank you both for your assistance and valuable insight as the book has been transformed from a dream into reality. Thank you both.

I would like to thank my publisher, Ashley Drake of St. Davids Press – a man I consider to be a good friend. He consistently inspires me with his detailed vision for every book, his dedication to achieving excellence and for the personal support he gives to his authors. Without him this book would not have been possible.

The Matt Hampson Foundation has a special place in the hearts of all Leicester Tigers, and I'd like to thank Tommy Cawston, Roy Jackson and, of course, Hambo for so generously supporting the publication. This has always been a labour of love and as such it will be my pleasure to donate all of the royalties generated by the sale of this book to the Foundation.

It is a matter of great personal sadness that several of those named above have not lived to see the publication of this book. I treasure the contributions they made and take solace that their words live on through the memories and anecdotes they kindly shared with me.

The love and support of my family – wife Carron, daughter Natasha and son-in-law Harrison, and son James – while writing this book has been truly magnificent and I am so very grateful and lucky to have you in my life.

Apologies are unreservedly offered to anyone I've inadvertently omitted from these words of thanks, and for any errors or misinterpretations I may have made whilst writing this book. Publishing this book has been a team effort but, as the captain, I take responsibility for any mistakes.

Finally, a word of sincere thanks to Chalkie's family, particularly his daughter-in-law Diane and son Ged, for your assistance and generosity – no words of thanks can adequately reflect my huge debt of gratitude to you. I hope I've done your father proud – he deserves nothing less.

Martin Whitcombe
July 2025

PREFACE

It is a great honour to contribute to Martin Whitcombe's book about Chalkie White – a man I probably knew better than most, having played alongside him, encouraged him into coaching, then watched him flourish, innovate and lead the club I love.

A very intelligent, knowledgeable and hard-working man, Chalkie was a rugby visionary who set the highest standards in everything he did. The most important quality he brought to Leicester, with his schoolmaster background, was discipline.

I played in the same Tigers team with Chalkie when he made his debut. He was a born leader, famous for his trade mark dive pass, and always played well against some good scrum-halves, including Dickie Jeeps. Chalkie had the same philosophy as the Harlequins centre and captain Joe McPartlin: if he got an awful ball, he'd pass it on and say to the recipient, "make your own arrangements!" He is also the only player I have seen who would, on occasion and out of the blue, punch one of the opposing team. When I once asked why he did that, the reply typified the man: "because we were playing like pussy cats and weren't putting enough effort in." He wanted to stir the opposition up and get a reaction, and it worked. As a coach he would provoke his players in training, and sometimes the opposition coach during a game, to see how they would react. He very quickly discovered what made people tick, it was a great strength he had. He wanted to get inside the players' minds and know what he was working with.

David Matthews – scored 119 tries and served as the club's President (2001-03)

I wasn't surprised when he became Tigers coach. Colin Martin, Leicester's New Zealand captain was the first coach of any note. I remember the players were helping prepare the pitch for the Barbarians

David Matthews – 502 appearances for Leicester Tigers (1955-74) and Coach (1988-91)

game, which was the following day, after we had adverse weather. When we had finished, Chalkie came charging over to me. He wasn't very happy as I had put his name forward to start coaching, but his credentials were way in advance of anyone else. When he started coaching in the late 1960s, he had already been teaching rugby at Nottingham High School for several seasons, and his practice at school prepared him for this. I was captain sometimes when Chalkie was coach and we always had frank and open conversation with each other, exchanging honest and forthright views, but we never fell out and very much enjoyed each other's company.

He had a new vision for training and how a team should play. For some players, who were used to having some power, didn't want change, this meant he wasn't always the easiest bloke to get on with. Graham Willars, Chalkie and I spent more time discussing the future direction of Leicester Tigers than any other set of players I've ever known – we spent hours talking about rugby and the two of us supported Chalkie during the transition.

He was always prepared to accept change and he would never turn his back on a new idea. Ultimately, he had the respect of everyone at Welford Road, but it wasn't always plain sailing in the early days of his coaching. In the early 1970s, the committee did, at one stage, consider replacing him with me. Jerry Day approached me and asked me if I was interested in getting involved with training and coaching; I wasn't. Instead, I continued to support Chalkie.

He was sharp enough, as times changed and rugby evolved, to move forward with the game and he came up with new ideas like the shortened line-out which, at the time was unheard of. He was always looking for new players to strengthen the team. His attention to detail was second to none.

I remember when he flew to South Africa in 1980 to watch Paul Dodge, Peter Wheeler and Clive Woodward play for the British and Irish Lions against South Africa. He was very proud that three of his players had made the Lions Test team.

I believe Chalkie should have been England coach and would have done a good job. He knew the game upside down and inside out and he could handle the players. Leicester Tigers undoubtedly benefited from him being overlooked because he had a point to prove to the RFU. His determination to show his coaching quality had a long-lasting and positive influence on the club and drove him to success with Tigers season after season.

When I think about the coaches of the modern – professional – era, I can only think of one who compares to Chalkie, a very shrewd man who was clever enough to move on and keep up with the game: Ian McGeechan.

Beyond rugby matters, when players had problems or ups and downs at home, Chalkie White was someone they could talk to and trust. He had a good knowledge of many things and it would be unusual for him not to 'hit the nail on the head', whatever it was.

His impact at Leicester Tigers was as significant as anybody's in the club's history, but he couldn't have achieved anything without the support of his wife Doris, she was his rock.

By the time he left Welford Road, in 1983 to take up a post with the RFU, Chalkie had the respect and good wishes of everybody at Leicester Tigers. Over his twenty-six years of service he had earned a unique position in world rugby and it is doubtful whether his record will ever be equalled, let alone surpassed.

David Matthews
(17 April 1937 – 19 June 2019)

FOREWORD

I am delighted that Martin has given me the opportunity to say a few words about Chalkie. I first met Martin in 1981 during his RAF days, when he came to play at Leicester as a budding young prop. Who would have known then that he was to become such an accomplished author. He comes from a strong Yorkshire rugby family, which now includes his son James, whom I saw in the England U20 team and am now enjoying watching him playing in Leicester's 1st XV. Congratulations Martin – you must be very proud the dynasty continues!

I joined Leicester Football Club at the start of the 1969-70 season, which was Chalkie's third season as coach of the 1st XV. Chalkie White had a greater influence on me, and on the important parts of my development, than anyone else. He was so much more than just a rugby coach – although he was a very good one at that.

Leicester had all the trappings of a great club. You only had to walk into the Welford Road ground to know that you were somewhere very special. It was a club full of history and tradition. However, as a young player, it wasn't only the two enormous stands, like a replica Twickenham, that filled you with awe, but the way in which the club was run. Everything was always done properly, as it always had been. When playing away at Gloucester, for example, Jerry Day, our Honorary Secretary for many years, would follow tradition and make sure that lunch prior to playing the game was booked at The Royal Hop Pole, at that time a luxury hotel in Tewksbury, for a good steak. We didn't have the nutritional knowledge of what we should be eating pre-match in those days! Or if we were playing away in south Wales, another luxurious hotel would be booked for us to stay overnight. Leicester was certainly famous for doing things in style.

If there had been a league in rugby union at that time, Leicester would certainly have been in the first division, but probably short of challenging for the top spot against clubs like our Midlands rivals Coventry and Moseley, who both had more international players in their teams than us. There were no current England internationals in the Leicester team at that time, Bob Rowell being the last player to be capped by England, in 1964, and Rodger Arneil had played for Scotland and the Lions in 1968.

An exceptional man – serious, philosophical and a deep thinker – Chalkie was dedicated to the game of rugby, and his influence at the club grew steadily. Alongside his professional work as a school-master, he put an enormous amount of time into the physical and psychological preparation for Tigers' games. He worked on the game at home, he took training, he attended committee meetings, he went to matches and gave of himself far more than anyone had the right to expect in an amateur era. He saw the game as an art form and marvelled at the potential that any eighty minutes may bring. He was a visionary, being able to plan the game long-term, not only sketching out how the season would end, but the clarity of his foresight allowed him to identify the pitfalls and rewards the game would throw up during the next five to ten years.

In the early days, if he had a weakness, it was in his man-management. It was his inability to conceal when he was less than pleased with our performance. At first, he would storm into the changing room, tense with emotion, to point the finger for a dropped pass or wayward kick, sometimes literally rapping a player's knuckles or even cracking the touch flag on someone's head. But he progressed quickly and learned to take himself away from the players, perhaps to share a cup of tea with the groundsman, Derek Limmage, and listen to the football results for twenty minutes. His handling of the players then became one of his great strengths. He always treated players as individuals, and was quick to recognise the good qualities a player could bring to the team, but he would never ask a player to perform a skill beyond his capabilities. Indeed, he could be quite frank explaining this to the player. One of his legendary sayings that we former players still quote today was: "Let others tell you how good you are. I'll tell you how to be better." He never suffered fools gladly, but learned to accept weaknesses for the benefit of the good qualities a player brought to the game.

His influence was enormous, not only on the team but on players as individuals because he helped educate us. He took a bunch of young players, like myself, and changed our lives. He didn't lecture us, but he made it very clear that to prosper in your rugby career you also had to do the right things in life. Another of his sayings that has always rung in my ears was: "If you cheat on the training ground, you'll cheat in the game, and you'll cheat in life."

As impressionable young men we stood and listened and learned. Fortunately for us, he was a wise and caring man who understood the responsibilities of his role. With his great passion for the game, he loved to discuss it endlessly. If we stopped at a pub he would always find someone with whom to chat about rugby and it wasn't long before people would come looking for him to discuss every aspect of rugby at Leicester Tigers. On the long away trips to the West Country, Wales or the North of England he would always sit at the front of the coach, holding court. On mid-week nights after training, there was always a group of players sitting with him in deep discussion, soaking up his knowledge for most of the time until we needed to get a beer and have some fun times, when others took our place. Always smartly dressed, always well-prepared, he trained us and taught us and worked us hard. He never gave up on us. Although such a serious man who didn't suffer fools, he would always join in the lighter moments and would often look over at us youngsters with a knowing smile, warming to our individual characters.

We had wonderful times in these days as we embarked on that journey together and gradually life at Leicester changed as we became a more and more successful team.

We always felt fortunate to be the only English club to have a long-standing annual Christmas fixture with the Barbarians. As Leicester improved as a team, the Barbarians needed to turn out an almost full international team, while sticking with their tradition of selecting at least one uncapped player. The crowds grew and grew and it became a sell-out Leicestershire occasion and a hugely important match for us players. It was a great honour to play in such esteemed company and we did not want to let ourselves down. Chalkie geared up fitness and preparation and pushed us to the max. We used the pitch at Loughborough University for one of the final training sessions and, to finish the practice, we did a hundred laps of the training ground. He ran all the laps with us and, afterwards, I remember seeing him completely drained: "I've given everything I have," he told me, "there is nothing more I can give to help us beat the Barbarians."

That fixture, of course, was an ideal proving ground for the John Player Cup games. The administrators became accustomed to dealing with huge crowds and players were able to identify how much work was needed. The large crowds attending so many successive wins leading to our third John Player Cup triumph led to increased club membership, which in turn laid the foundations, some years later, for coping with the game going professional.

Under Chalkie, Leicester were in the final of the John Player Cup in 1978, 1979, 1980 and 1981, winning the Cup outright with three successive wins between 1979 and 1981. These wins, alongside the number of Leicester players now playing at international level, were the highlight of Chalkie's career and the measure of his success. In his sixteen years as Head Coach, he had no serious rival for his position, and by the time Chalkie had reached his most influential phase as club coach, the raw material he had to work with – by 1978, Robin Cowling, Dusty Hare, Paul Dodge and myself had become England internationals – was from a much richer seam.

We could have lost him halfway through our Cup run if England had asked him to coach the national side. As coach to the most successful team in English club rugby, Chalkie was the stand-out candidate. The job would have been absolutely right for him at that stage. He had all the credentials: the track record, had worked successfully with players at all levels and gained their respect, and was ambitious too. In the period after I was capped by John Burgess in 1975, England went through a number of coaches, but instead of giving Chalkie the position, he was packed off to become Technical Administrator for the south west, where he became an over-qualified administrator, and never to become England coach.

Many feel Chalkie was let down by England. However, times were beginning to change. After so many years of the prominence of the County Championship in English rugby, conflicts were arising in the RFU when the clubs, spurred on by the success of the John Player Cup, started to exert their authority and were looking for club leagues – leading of course to rugby going professional. Leicester Tigers were at the forefront of driving the clubs forward and maybe Chalkie's career suffered because of that, and him never having been the greatest diplomat! England missed their opportunity to benefit from what he was capable of achieving.

As a 20-year-old, and living away from home for the first time in my life, it will surprise no one to learn that I was much influenced by Chalkie White. Initially the relationship tended to be that of master and pupil, but it broadened after I became club captain into something more akin to being father and son. He knocked away my immaturity and set standards for me as he did for everyone. I always believed that coaches had to have some special quality, and while there may be coaches as good as he was, I doubt if many of them will encompass the human qualities he also had. He was a great man.

Peter Wheeler – Leicester Tigers (1969-85), England (1975-84), British Lions (1977 & 1980), and RFU President (2019-20)

Peter Wheeler
July 2025

Chalkie White was not a coach who would say "good luck" before a match. He believed that matches were won by teams that had trained hard and prepared meticulously – luck wasn't required. He was also not inclined to say "well done" after a match – even when his team had won – preferring to explain to players how they could improve even further. A professional coach in an amateur era, Chalkie's rugby philosophy and training methods were revolutionary and produced talented players and successful teams. This is his story.

1

Cumbrian Days

As a Cumbrian, Herbert Victor 'Chalkie' White belongs to a great rugby tradition. It includes league giants like Douglas 'Duggy' Clarke and Martin Hodgson, union men like Stuart Lancaster and Steve Borthwick (occupant, until his appointment by England in December 2022, of the Leicester Tigers role Chalkie defined), and those who cover both like Jim Brough. As with Steve Borthwick he came from Carlisle, born to Anne ('Annie') and Albert Victor White at their Raffles Avenue home on January 16 1929.

They were the classic hard-working family. Albert Victor, known to many as 'Vic', had returned to working for the Chance family at Morton Manor after the war service that had cost him an eye. Annie walked to the Carlisle Brewery, famous for having been nationalised along with the city's pubs in 1916, where she worked as a cleaner each morning.

They had met while lodging in Collingwood Street, Denton Holme in Carlisle, and married in 1927. Annie was Albert's second wife; his first wife, Mary Porter, had died very young. Albert and Annie had four children together, but Kenneth, Chalkie's elder brother, sadly died aged five months. Although known as 'Chalkie' from an early age, he was always 'Herbert' to his parents and younger siblings, Margaret and David.

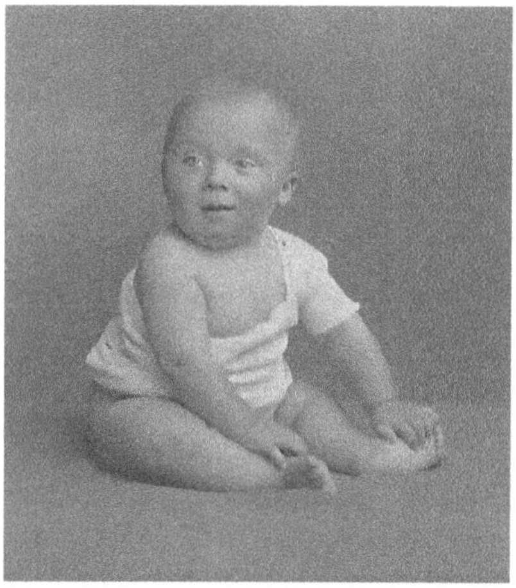

Herbert Victor 'Chalkie' White as a baby

Albert had been born at The Globe Hotel, Cockermouth, Cumberland in 1897 and had three younger siblings: Norman Ashley, Hugh Herbert ('Bert') and Martha ('Mattie') Elizabeth. After school he worked for the Chance family at Morton Manor for three years as a Page Boy and Footman, before joining up for the First World War.

He enlisted as a Private in the $2/4^{th}$ (Cumberland and Westmorland) Battalion

Albert White (standing, right) – Page Boy and Footman

Albert and Annie with Chalkie (aged 6) and Margaret (aged 3)

of the Border Regiment, which was formed at Kendal in September 1914, then moved to billets in Blackpool. On March 7 1915 the regiment sailed from Avonmouth to India, where it remained until 1919, on *HMT* (Hired Military Transport) *Tunisian*.

From March 1916 the battalion was stationed in and around Peshawar, and then took part in the Mohmand Blockade from February to May 1917. Service continued, with serious consequences for Albert, for a year after the European armistice of November 1918. He was wounded in action, losing an eye, in the Third Anglo-Afghan War of 1919, while 45 men from his battalion died in battles fought in brutal heat. Memories of seeing the Khyber Pass and the award of the British War medal and the Indian General Service medal with the clasp 'Afghanistan NW Frontier 1919' were limited compensation.

Annie was five years younger than Albert. She had been born out of wedlock and never lived with her mother, carrying with her the secretiveness that accompanied the then stigma of illegitimacy. She had been brought up as a step-relative by the Shipley farming family in Bewcastle, a large civil parish in Carlisle where they still farm today.

Chalkie's childhood, and most of his parents' married life, was spent at Raffles Avenue, Carlisle, a council house with an outside toilet and wash house which local historian Stephen White dates to 1928, adding: "Albert and Annie White appear at Raffles Avenue on the electoral register for 1930, so one suspects they may have been the first tenants."

Albert again left the Chance family, this time to drive ambulances for the medical services while volunteering in the Civil Defence Service during the Second World War. Annie juggled two jobs and childcare. She would return home from work and make lunch for David while still wearing her hat and coat, then go on to her afternoon job at Teasdale sweet factory, Denton Holme, on the production line making throat lozenges. After the

Chalkie jumping his way to success

war Albert was increasingly afflicted by bronchitis, but still spent over 17 years with Border Oil garage, cycling to his work as a forecourt attendant.

After first attending Ashley Street School, from 1940 Chalkie was a pupil at Creighton School in Strand Road. He was no slouch in Creighton's classrooms, opened in its new buildings in 1940. Six passes were needed to obtain the School Certificate, that era's equivalent of GCSEs. In 1945 Chalkie obtained a distinction in Maths, a credit in Geography and passes in English Language, English Literature, History and Physics, but he made his greatest mark on the playing fields. A boy's school, Creighton had initially played football but had joined the post-war shift to rugby union in 1921 and developed a strong tradition. Three boys, R.S. Lancaster and John Paisley (who captained the team) in 1935 and Neil Ferguson in 1938 had played for England Schools.

Chalkie excelled in three of the school sports: rugby union, athletics and swimming. He gained the Royal Life Saving Society award of merit and won the 'Campbell' Cup twice as school athletic champion in 1944 and 1945 despite a rule being introduced in 1935 to make it impossible for a boy to be champion in two consecutive years. In 1944 he set school records for both the high jump and throwing the cricket ball. He also played county rugby for Cumberland Schools.

Double school athletic champion, with the 'Campbell' Cup (standing, left)

He was gifted enough as a sprinter to try mixing it with adults. Professional sprints were very popular at this time and their financial rewards hard to resist. On August 25 1944 Chalkie, aged 15 and a half, entered the £125 men's handicap 100 yards sprint. He finished second to the winner of the final heat, R. Bell of Hepburn. Having competed for the first time as a professional he lost his amateur status as an athlete.

Nor was there any chance to emulate his predecessors who had won national honours in rugby, the limits on representative sport just one of many consequences of war. Instead, Chalkie collected waste paper. He was to recall "visiting the up-market parts of Carlisle with a hand cart and appropriately dressed in a Scout uniform, complete with woggle."

Among the waste paper were copies of nudist magazine *Health and Efficiency*, famed for its photographs. "There wasn't a sportsman either on its cover, front or back, or inside. I failed to have my imagination fired in any way by *H & E*," but some of his schoolmates felt differently and swopped up to four comics for one *H & E*. "My contribution to the swop was a funny mag that I never read." Adding, "the *Hotspur* and the *Wizard* were to transport me into a world of real men and scar my imagination forever."

School assemblies doubtless brought regular reminders of the ultimate cost of war as the school war memorial, now maintained by its ultimate successor, Trinity School, records the loss of 81 former pupils.

2

National Service – Royal Navy

Chalkie could, on the basis of his examination results, have stayed on at school, but even had the White family been able to afford it, he had plans of his own. He had developed a love of the sea as a member of the sea cadets.

In May 1944 he had spent a fortnight with them, including several days training afloat. Unit commander Ivan Carr wrote to Albert that his son: "Did very well and appeared to learn quickly. I think he enjoyed himself although

Leading Cadet White (right) spent a few days afloat with Lieutenant Ivan Carr, Officer Commanding, Carlisle Sea Cadet Unit (left)

the weather was somewhat against us," adding a handwritten coda that "I think your son is going to be a fine man. It was a real pleasure to have him with me." In 1946, aged 16, he joined the Royal Navy to do his National Service based at RNAS Culdrose in Cornwall as a Leading Radio Electrical Mechanic (LREM).

Although the war was over, there were still serious demands on the armed forces. In June 1945 the process began of demobilising the thousands of men and women who had served in the forces during the war, now desperate to return to civilian life. There was still an urgent need to keep up a high level military presence in parts of the world where Britain had strong ongoing commitments, which included: the enforcement of the terms of surrender on Germany and Japan, the maintenance of security within the diminishing British Empire, and the re-establishment of British influence in the world, particularly in the Middle East.

Volunteering had important implications for Chalkie. While he probably did not know it, unless he was a close follower of national politics, he retained control over his own fortunes. Had he not joined up, he would, at the age of 18, have been subject to the National Service Act, introduced in 1948, which made all able-bodied men between the ages of 18 and 30 liable for call-up. But very few men did their National Service in the Royal Navy. Unlike the other services it could fulfil most of its manpower requirements from volunteers, and it was also quickly realised that recruits needed more long-term service. So, it is unlikely he would have been able to serve in the Navy, when called up.

His time in the Navy could have started more happily. At the beginning of October 1946 his parents received a letter telling them he had been admitted to the Royal Navy Hospital at Seaforth, Lancashire, with acute appendicitis. He had been operated upon and was making good progress, but was likely to be there for some weeks. Once recovered, his service career took him to Cornwall, which would play an important part in his life, and to the person who would play perhaps the most important part, his future wife.

Culdrose, near Helston on the Lizard Peninsula, had started its life when the Admiralty surveyed the area in 1943 and finally purchased the 750 acres of prime agricultural land formerly known as The Downs in February 1944. It was still RNAS Helston (HMS Chough, after the Cornish bird) when Chalkie arrived, but became RNAS Culdrose (HMS Seahawk) when commissioned by the Lords of the Admiralty on April 17 1947, under the command of Captain Godfrey Dickins.

Chalkie was to recall: "No-one knew where RNAS Culdrose actually was. The more imaginative young sailors who had been drafted to the new Air Station in 1947 had visions of the Arctic or even the South Pole, but the truth was a pleasant surprise. The summer over, we produced a rugby team, and played local sides and Service teams from over the Tamar at Plymouth and Devonport. So well organised were we that we once travelled a week early for a game against the Royal Naval Engineering College. That was my first taste of West Country rugby, and the first Australian tourists I saw were at Camborne."

Chalkie had some memorable days, one report noting: "On Saturday the rugby XV was entertained by St. Ives Harlequins and emerged victorious by 14 points to six. LREM White crossed the line on three occasions. Superior play was also demonstrated by Lieutenant Thomson, who scored a try and added the extras, Petty Officer Giles received an injury to his ankle, while selected to play at short notice, Able Seaman Barber put up a good performance."

The Navy had a formidable rugby history, including players like famed England half-backs William 'Dave' Davies and Cecil Kershaw, and the future Admiral Percy Royds who missed the 1900 international season because he was in action in China putting down the Boxer Rising. Men like Royds became influential rugby administrators and Devonport Services were often among the best clubs in England, but it could have mixed consequences for those outside established circles.

Chalkie was still in his mid-teens and his most demanding previous rugby had been for the Old Creightonians club after leaving school. The Navy could call on copious talent, but historian Geraint Ashton Jones suggests that for Navy rugby administrators, those jokes about nobody knowing where to find Culdrose had a basis in fact.

"The Army, in particular, but also the Royal Navy struggled during National Service to find a system where they could track players and look to select their strongest side. Due in main to the sheer volume of players they suddenly had who in the main were serving for a relatively short period. This may well be a key reason why Chalkie White did not become a capped player, when I look at the teams that the Navy put out post-World War Two.

"For the Navy's matches immediately after the war the team was selected by Surgeon Commander (D) Leslie 'Ginger' Osborne, manager of the 1950 British Lions to New Zealand and a future RFU President. His selections were firmly based around the two service clubs of US Portsmouth and Devonport Services. I would suggest that with the exception of HMS Raleigh, at Torpoint, the Navy Selector struggled to travel west of the Tamar river and the team was very much selected from a London/Portsmouth nucleus with the odd star name from Plymouth. It is very unlikely that the new air station as far West as Culdrose would have been on his itinerary to watch players.

"During the War years the RN Rugby Union in effect disbanded and very little rugby was played by the RN when compared to the RAF or Army throughout World War Two. At the end of the War in Europe the Union was

Leading Seaman 'Knocker' White

WRNS Doris Gwendoline Websdale

re-established under an emergency committee with a primary aim to reignite a RN team and re-start the Inter Service matches. They turned to Osborne, who had selected the side from 1936 to 1938 and under him the team was selected from the familiar rather than looking further afield for potential talent. At this time the Secretary of the Royal Navy Rugby Union was John Forrest the former England international. John, like 'Ginger', had been a Navy Selector (1938-39), he was a former captain of Devonport Services RFC and the Navy, as well as a stalwart of United Services Portsmouth RFC. He would be minded to look at these two clubs first before looking to the other Navy units. It wasn't until 1958 that RNAS Culdrose (HMS Seahawk) provided its first player to a Navy Inter Service side."

While getting established as a rugby player was difficult, Chalkie excelled at athletics. Runner-up in both the javelin and high jump in the Royal Naval Air Command Championships, he was chosen as a reserve for the Royal Navy for the 1947 Inter Service tournament.

He also acquired another nickname. In the Army, he would most likely have remained Chalkie, but in the Navy anyone surnamed 'White' was called 'Knocker', derived from 'knocker white', a miller's assistant. A pen knife marked with 'K', kept as a souvenir of his service, attests to this alternative nickname.

Most importantly of all during his National Service, he met Doris Gwendoline Websdale, from Bexleyheath in Kent, who worked in the stores at Culdrose. To Doris, Chalkie was always 'Vic'. She was to become Chalkie's rock, his soul mate and mother of his three children. Although it was hardly a whirlwind romance as they knew each other for seven years before marrying.

3

Back to Civvy Street in Cumbria

In 1948 Chalkie White was demobilised from the Royal Navy as a Petty Officer and returned to Carlisle. Armed with his School Certificate, he turned his attention to his future and settled upon teaching. To gain experience he worked in a peripatetic role at primary and secondary modern schools under the authority of the Carlisle Education Committee.

Nelson Hewitson JP, Headmaster of Upperby Council School, Carlisle, who had known him since his mid-teens, wrote of him in a reference: "I have watched his career with interest; he is a conscientious teacher, always giving of his best and very willing to assist in the extra duties outside the usual school hours...I have no hesitation in vouching for his moral character. He is a gentleman in every sense of the word and a fine example of the temperate Christian way of life."

Hewitson was equally impressed by his sporting abilities and optimistic about his rugby prospects: "Mr White has played Rugby Union Football in the best of company, understands the game thoroughly and is an excellent performer in track and field events. He is an excellent coach for youngsters in Athletics or Games, and raised the standards of these activities in my school. He undertakes the extra work and match supervision with good heart. I anticipate him gaining County Rugby Honours for Cumberland in the near future."

It was to take a little longer than Hewitson anticipated. Chalkie played in the Cumberland & Westmorland final trials in 1949, 1951 and 1952. In season 1952-53 he was travelling reserve, and finally made it into the county team in the back row in 1955.

County rugby was a hugely important part of English rugby at this time. With no leagues for clubs, the County Championship was its main competition and for ambitious players a vital means of progression towards representative honours, while the organisation of the Rugby Football Union ingrained county unions in its power structures.

Cumbrian legend Jim Brough, a fisher-boy from the coastal village of Silloth who made his England debut at Twickenham against New Zealand in January 1925, aged 21

Cumberland & Westmorland had won the County Championship in 1924, and the following season full backs Jim Brough of Silloth RUFC and Tosh Holliday of Aspatria RUFC both played for England, while Richard Lawson of Workington RFC won a single cap. Brough and Holliday were both lost to rugby league, Brough going on to captain and coach the Great Britain Lions teams in Australia and New Zealand. While the regional basis on which the championship was organised meant a desperate, more often than not unavailing, struggle to get past perennial powerhouses Lancashire – who won the competition in 1947, 1948, 1949 and 1955 and were finalists in 1952 – and Yorkshire, winners in 1953.

Chalkie had rejoined the Old Creightonians, formed in 1930 and recognised since 1932 as a senior club by the Cumberland Rugby Union, where he played in the back row in the Cumberland Cup final against Workington at Keswick RFC's ground, Keswick School Playing Field, on April 1 1950.

The programme notes added: "To-day is Cup Final day, and it is our pleasure to welcome the finalists, Old Creightonians and Workington (in alphabetical order, mark you). We believe we are correct in saying that this is the first time the Old Creightonians have appeared in the Cup Final. Workington have appeared many times before, and won it many times too. Both are teams with a good record this season. Indeed, Workington have carried all before them, and can be justly proud of being a keen, flourishing Club with a wonderful spirit. Old Creightonians are a model, to our mind, for those who like to see a bunch of booties make a way for themselves. In fact, we couldn't be more proud to have any two clubs on our ground."

The old order prevailed, with Workington winning 22-0. Many years later teammate John Graham, later the club's President, would recall Chalkie as being "the clubs most famous ex-player."

His past as a professional athlete was no great problem, as historian Tony Collins points out: "The RFU's amateur regulations were a bit of a minefield, but essentially they were directed against anyone playing rugby league. The regulations forbade anyone from playing any type of rugby for monetary or other reward, so professional athletics was not covered by them. It wouldn't have affected his career in union or teaching one way or another."

It might have complicated athletics for him, but he sought and obtained reinstatement from the Northern Counties Athletic Association in June 1950. At the same time, he was learning to sail at Silloth, taught by his old Sea Scout commander Ivan Carr (one of the owners of Carr's biscuit factory) and in later years would travel up to Cumberland to sail to Scotland or the Isle of Man on Carr's boat.

OLD CREIGHTONIANS (Blue)			WORKINGTON (Black and White Hoops)
J. QUEEN	Full Back	1	J. THOMPSON
D. GRAHAM	Right Wing	2	W. MORGAN
S. HUTTON	Right Centre	3	P. PARSONS
T. RAE	Left Centre	4	K. FAULDER
R. FARISH	Left Wing	5	J. LAWSON
G. IRVING	Stand-off	6	G. McCRACKEN
F. CLIFFORD	Scrum Half	7	E. HOLLIDAY
N. STEWART	Front Row	14	M. KNOWLES
D. GREENE	"	9	A. HARRISON
D. TWEDDLE	"	10	C. SHAW
J. PAISLEY	Second Row	11	B. COPSEY
W. COLLINS	"	12	R. ATKINSON
H. WHITE	Back Row	13	J. EARL
J. SEWELL	"	8	D. WATCHORNE
G. LIGHTFOOT	"	15	A. QUAYLE

Kick-off, 3-15 p.m. | Referee : W. Boustead, Borrowdale

Cumberland Cup Final – Old Creightonians v Workington

The Old Creightonians XV – September 1950
Back Row (L-R): Alan Dixon, Ted Graham, Tony Notman, Jack Sewell, Bill Collins, Billy Stewart, Tom Rae, Geo Lightfoot, Reg Bright
Front Row (L-R): Derek Shipton, Frank Gifford, Jim Faulder, Chalkie White, Doug Greene, John Paisley

4

A New Career – 1950-53

Chalkie worked for Carlisle Education Authority as a relief teacher from January 30 to September 23 1950. The next step was to gain the qualifications needed for a teaching career which, at that time, meant taking a two-year diploma at a training college. Chalkie's obvious talents made it natural to look towards PE as his likely specialism, and he studied for his diploma at Borough Road College, Isleworth.

While not up to the level of St. Luke's and Loughborough, which in good years could challenge strong first-class clubs, Borough Road had a strong rugby tradition, particularly in the seven-a-side game and Chalkie soon became

Chalkie after a match between Borough Road College and University College, February 1951

captain of the college team with sufficient success for it to be noted among the Old Creightonian club notes in the local paper back in Carlisle: "This team playing many of the London clubs, has put up some grand performances."

Funded by a Ministry of Education grant, he entered fully into college life, captaining the boxing team as well as rugby. He also won half-colours for basketball, athletics and swimming, became a member of the Student Union Society Council and the winter sports committee, and took part in the college's Dramatic Society production of *Oedipus Tyrannus* as one of the chorus of Theban Elders.

A still greater attraction was proximity to Doris, who was working as a book-keeper for Selby Shoes in Old Bond Street, Mayfair, located opposite the chocolate shop Charbonnel et Walker, which is credited in family lore for awakening her taste for rum truffles. A sweet tooth was clearly part of her relationship with Chalkie, as noted by college friends – at a time when sugar was still rationed – for his ability to cajole women staff into granting him an extra ration.

Chalkie with Doris at a Borough Road College dance, 1952

'Official' wedding photo

'Unofficial' wedding photo

The sweet-toothed charmer graduated on July 26 1952, achieving a distinction in Physical Education. It was a double celebration as, three weeks previously on July 5, he and Doris had married in Welling, Kent.

He still had another year to come as a student, taking the specialist PE diploma at Carnegie College in Leeds, graduating in 1953 with a distinction for Practical Work which qualified him to enter the profession.

5

Cornwall – 1953-57

Chalkie entered the search for employment armed with a glowing reference from Borough Road. Alongside his sporting accomplishments, college principal Eric Hamilton reported: "Mr White is a man of very good appearance and a quiet, confident, alert manner. He has a strong professional sense and is an energetic and effective teacher of more than average ability. He establishes excellent relations with his pupils, and is highly competent in general teaching, but especially in Physical Education."

Like many young teachers, Chalkie had to travel for his first job, although few journeyed quite as far as he did – more than 400 miles from Carlisle – but while distant, it was hardly unfamiliar, as he had returned to Cornwall. It was news felt worthy of coverage by Carlisle's local paper, which reported: "Mr Herbert Victor White, eldest son of Mr and Mrs A.V. White, 134 Raffles Avenue, Carlisle has been appointed games Master at Truro High School for boys commencing at the September Term. Educated at Ashley Street and Creighton Schools, he was captain and sports champion for two years at the Creighton previous before going to Borough Road College, Isleworth for two years. This was followed by one year at Carnegie College, Leeds, for physical education and he gained his diploma, passing with distinction for practical work."

It also provided his first extended exposure to senior club rugby, starting at Penzance & Newlyn RFC where he found his opportunities at scrum-half restricted by the presence of club, and Cornwall, captain Peter Mitchell. So, in 1953 he moved on to Camborne, where he made an immediate impact

Former Camborne player Brian Smith recalled: "You had to play for the reserves as a new player before you could play for the 1st XV, the Chiefs. I played with Chalkie at Number 8 and he was scrum-half in our game at St. Ives reserves, there were no colts or other teams in those days just the first team and the reserves."

While he had faced stiff competition at Penzance & Newlyn, his arrival at Camborne coincided with established scrum-half Fearnley Caddy being called up to do his National Service. Caddy was not the only player lost to

Philip 'John' Collins won three England caps in 1952

Camborne around this time. John Collins, who had recently become their first and only England player, making his debut at full back in the 19-3 Calcutta Cup victory over Scotland at Murrayfield on March 15 1952, had been forced into retirement by a knee injury and had joined the committee.

Collins, whose 25 appearances for Cornwall followed his father's 44, recalled: "Chalkie came to join Camborne in 1953-54 season during my first year on the committee. Chalkie was a nice chap, straight forward and what you saw was what you got. He was also a very good sevens player. I remember a famous victory at Weston-super-Mare RFC when we lost our second row forward, international trialist Gary Harris, injured, the only time I remember him leaving the field. In those days there were no replacements. Playing with 14 men, Chalkie scored the only try of the game from a scrum to give us a 3-0 away win."

Lifelong Camborne RFC man Merrill Clymo, who made his debut as a full back in 1947 but converted to the pack while doing National Service at RAF Sopley in Hampshire, was playing at Number 8. He remembered: "He was everything you need in a rugby team, a leader, a good team player, and a tactician. As a player he was a great man to have on the field and he was very popular."

His abilities earned representative recognition of a sort. He was still listed as a Truro School player when he appeared at scrum-half and scored for the President's XV which played a Cornwall XV in a match reported as the first floodlit rugby match in the West of England, at St. Austell, in October 1953.

It was the following season, however, when he put his stamp on Camborne, showing qualities that foreshadowed his coaching career. Camborne and Cornwall hooker Brian Eddy recalled the sequence of events that elevated him suddenly to the captaincy: "The club captain at this time was Dick Honeywell who was injured in the first game of the season, so Ted Burt our prop forward was made captain, but was also injured during the game and ruled out for the rest of the season. Chalkie then took over the captaincy of the club, as a newcomer, for the next game against Rosslyn Park. He knew more than most

Camborne RFC players crossing the Tamar on the Torpoint Ferry
Back Row (L-R): Peter Smith, John Collins, Cecil House, Roger James, Terry Symonds
Front Row (L-R): Barry Wilton, Kitto Sampson, Mike Welsh, Chalkie White, Brian Eddy

of us and convinced us of his ability. Camborne beat Rosslyn Park 12-9 at The Recreation Ground on September 21 and he was retained as captain for the rest of the season."

Committee man Collins remembered: "In those days the captain was responsible for training the team as well, and the committee wanted Chalkie to get the team fit. At one practice session, two of our players were kicking the ball to each other when Chalkie advised them they should do their training first, which one player took exception to, and went to join Falmouth RFC for a season!

"In my playing days there was no such thing as a coach, the Camborne forwards used to pack the front row against the changing room wall and the rest of the lads behind to get the scrum right. When I won my first cap at Murrayfield, I spoke to Ted Woodward, the Wasps and England winger, who told me the only coaching advice he'd ever had was 'run towards the corner flag as fast as you can!' Chalkie was the first person I saw comparable to the modern coach."

He made a similar impression on Merrill Clymo, destined to become the club's Secretary and Chairman, earning election to life membership: "It was as a captain that I really remember Chalkie. He was a hard taskmaster and set very high standards. His sessions were enjoyable but we had to work

Chalkie (left) contests the ball, watched by Camborne teammates Reg Carter (left) and Brian Eddy (right). Redruth hooker Bill Bishop (second right) would later become RFU President (1995-96)

hard. He even had us running up and down the stand steps on some training nights."

Returning to the ranks in 1955-56, when Gerald Wakeham was captain, with Caddy also back at the club, 'Cherry and White' of *The Camborne and Redruth Packet* suggested Chalkie might be moved to outside-half: "There is a strong feeling that were Chalkie to agree to play at stand-off, whilst Fernley Caddy fed him from the base of the scrum, the Camborne three-quarters would look a lot stronger. I am inclined to agree that Chalkie would make a fine outside-half, but this is a matter that can only be decided in Chalkie's mind."

There were also good reasons for keeping him where he was, as the same article – a preview of their prestigious fixture against Ebbw Vale, three times Welsh unofficial champions between 1951 and 1957 – acknowledged: "Scrum-half Chalkie White has proved over and over again that he is a potential match winner, and many sides have reflected that if they had paid more attention to him the score might well have been a great deal less...At the moment he is probably the finest scrum-half in the county and I feel that the selectors would do well to leave the choice to him."

Chalkie might have been forgiven for pleading other commitments, sleep deprivation, or both when asked about the captaincy for 1956-57. His and Doris's first child, Gerald, universally known as Ged, was due at the start of

Camborne RFC 1956-57
Back Row (L-R): Jim Milton (linesman), Des Mitchell, Brian Eddy, Gary Harris, Barry Wilton, Reg Carter, Kenny Toy, Trevor Phillips, Vivian Ford, Raymond Harris, Henry Casley, Sidney Dunstan (ambulance officer)
Middle Row (L-R): Dave Lendrum, Eric Rockett, Max Biddick, Chalkie White (captain), Leonard Thomas (Chairman), Peter Smith, Terry Symons, Geoff Harris
Front Row (L-R): Malcolm Harty, Don Bailey

pre-season training but, never one to duck a challenge, he took on the job in the spirit intended, as recalled by Eddy: "As a captain Chalkie knew what he wanted, he was more dictatorial than we were used to. He told us in no uncertain terms what he wanted from the team." Dictatorial he may have been, but Eddy added that he remained: "A nice chap, everyone liked Chalkie. He was always one of the boys."

However, this was to be his last season at Camborne. At the end of the 1956-57 season Chalkie advised the club of his imminent departure for a new teaching job. His final game was at left centre on September 9 1957, in a 3-3 draw against Public School Wanderers, with Trevor Harris positioned at scrum-half.

Chalkie recalled his own warm memories of Camborne in the club's 1978 centenary brochure: "I consider it to be an honour and a privilege to be allowed to contribute to the Centenary programme of the Camborne Rugby Club. My four years with the Camborne club – by kind permission of Truro School – was a vital part of my education, and I must add not only my rugby education.

"I have absolutely no doubt in my mind, and never have had, that the game of rugby football is about people, furthermore it always has been and always will be. The politics and the polemics mean little in the long run of events but the memories linger on – memories of faces, features, deeds and acts by those with whom one shared a common interest.

"My happy time at Camborne was entirely due to Fearnley Caddy joining the R.A.F. He was a grand scrum-half and I was never able to show him how grateful I was for the chance he provided for me. Due to school duties, I could not travel with the team and my first away trip was taken in Ted Burt's car to Paignton – another debt that I owe to a fine club player. Dick Honeywell was very much a force in the club in my first season, 1953-54; an experienced, knowledgeable player with a penchant to stand offside with both hands in the air, as if he was not conspicuous enough, with a somewhat distinctive hairstyle. In the teams I played in, I came to appreciate the talents of Trevor Phillips, Max Biddick, the late Eric Rockett, county hooker Reg Carter, Gerald Wakenham and that man alone, Gary Harris. Trevor played very good soccer when he was either recovering from a rugby injury or mending his injured pride having tangled with the committee. Max was the epitome of steadiness, both on and off the field, a sharp contrast to the very talented and fiery Eric. Reg, with ruddy cheeks and traditional hooker's pride, worked very hard at his game. Lesser men than Gerald have played for England and one can say the same about Gary. Strong men both, Gary immensely so, they were tremendous allies to have in one's side when the going was tough. Of course there were other players, no less valuable to the club but considerably less unsung, Peter and Brian Smith I shall always remember as well as international full back John Collins nearing the end of his injury ridden playing career.

"Then there was the committee! Two Leslies, May and Clymo, and Eric's father Charlie, Jimmy Milton, and a cheerful 'cuts' man Sid Dunstan. Bless them all and especially the Ladies Tea Committee – faithful, tireless and resilient – more debts of gratitude outstanding.

"I frequently had a lift to Camborne from a young man, who worked in a garage in Truro, Ken Trestrail, and I talked rugby for many an hour. I hope his wife forgave him. I can remember as well some of the 'enemy', the late Tony Bidgood of Redruth, a tremendous prop, who taught me a simple lesson – I've forgiven him. And, while some memories remain wonderfully clear others are a little hazy but certainly not forgotten. I wonder how many supporters will remember an Army officer, a big stand-off half from Bodmin, who frightened the life out of the Redruth side one afternoon in the mid '50s. I bet Trevor Phillips would remember a chap called Stephens.

"Quite definitely – how can it be otherwise – rugby is about people. In this, the centenary year with a very good season behind the club and who knows what is to come, please remember the people, all the people."

6

A New Day Job – Nottingham High School

There was no doubt of his affection for Cornwall, but a young man of professional and sporting ambitions from the other end of the country was unlikely to stay there for good. The move he made in 1957 took him to the job and the rugby club which were to define his life. He was to stay with both until 1983.

Chalkie joined Nottingham High School as its first trained PE specialist and was to recall the Headmaster, Ken Imeson, saying on his appointment: "I hope I've made the right decision, we have never had anyone like you before."

It was an independent day school for boys, with 852 pupils admitted on the basis of the school's own examination entry process. Part of the state Direct Grant Grammar School system until 1945, it had gone independent due to cuts in the numbers of city and state scholarships, but continued to accept some pupils on that basis until the 1990s. Notable former pupils included the novelist DH Lawrence and the chemist Jesse Boot.

Well-equipped for sport and games, the school had extensive grounds and pavilion purchased in 1931, and a gym constructed in the 1930s after a donation from cigarette-manufacturers John Player. After rapid growth in the early 1950s, it remained stable in numbers during Chalkie's 26 years there.

Soon after taking up his teaching role at Nottingham High School, Chalkie and Doris' second child, Stella, was born. His sons Ged and Nick both attended the school, but, as it didn't go co-ed until 2015, Stella did not.

Chalkie's time at the school was book-ended by notable politicians from the then three main parties. Future Conservative Chancellor of the Exchequer, Kenneth Clarke, was in the sixth form when he arrived, while Labour Shadow Chancellor-to-be, Ed Balls, and Liberal Democrat leader, Ed Davey, were working their way up the school when he left.

His start was inauspicious, turning up a day late because he had forgotten his starting date, but as games-teaching colleague Geraint 'Geri' Thomas recalled, his belated arrival went into school legend. He immediately startled the staff room when he shinned up a centrally placed metal pole to imprint

Chalkie (in white trousers) in Nottingham High School's gymnasium – "Physical education at its very best" according to Geraint 'Geri' Thomas

feet marks on the ceiling. The Headmaster came in a short while later and the fresh footprints caught his eye. Despite his stern enquires, thankfully no one responded. On another occasion, Chalkie repeated the escapade to write some motivational words on the ceiling.

It was merely the beginning, Thomas recalls in a vivid memoir of his former colleague, of an impact on school life which stretched far beyond the gym and rugby pitch. "He had a marked effect on the school's rugby team and it benefited to an incalculable degree. As countless people came to understand he had the inherent ability to get inside peoples' minds. He could zone in on what a boy was finding difficult and come up with a solution to improve. Many boys will testify that Chalkie gave them more self-belief and that they went on to reach levels of skill that they could not have envisaged.

"He set high and demanding standards and woe betide anyone if they did not comply with his instructions, but all came to understand that he was there for them to be better players and team members. From developing spin passes, complex moves in the backs and getting boys to zone in on opponent's deficiencies, this was a new experience for the boys. His infectious enthusiasm for the game was clear and transferred to his real wish for boys to enjoy the game and play it well.

"Yet, Chalkie's contribution to school life was much more than that of a rugby coach. He was the first professionally trained PE teacher at the school and he built an impressive department, stressing that all were important whether in a team or not and all to work and gain satisfaction from personal best performances.

"Back with the rugby, the Old Nottinghamians RFC circuit training sessions were taken on by Chalkie – they were in shock from the demands initially, but came through and gained from again being taken to heights beyond their expectation.

"Chalkie would amaze and delight new boys at their first lesson in the gym he would walk out on his hands from his office into the gym. When out in the playground exhorting boys participating in athletics standards his stentorian voice would carry into many other parts of the school and raise smiles. Also, in athletics he inspired pole vaulters – technically the most difficult of events – getting them through painful landings and over seemingly impossible heights – he could certainly inspire.

"Chalkie also took charge of the Naval Section of the Combined Cadet Force (CCF) and subsequently became commanding officer of the CCF contingent. He was at the forefront of organising demanding expeditions and endurance activities. He also linked this facet to his work as Nottinghamshire and Derbyshire Secretary for the Outward Bound Trust.

"He became a house tutor in 'Maples', and it was perhaps in this capacity that he did his finest work. Boys in his tutor set would remain in his pastoral care for the duration of their time at the school. He took enormous pains to ensure that the advice and care he gave was thoroughly sound and well advised. He was recognised as a first-class schoolmaster, including teaching mathematics to junior boys. Chalkie was always ready to encourage the weak, to spend time with those in trouble or were in a bad patch. Yet, he was willing to criticise the arrogant or give good advice to those who thought they needed none. Whatever he did, he did efficiently and with good brisk humour.

"He remains a legend amongst the Old Nottinghamians' community and tales still abound including a delayed return to the school from a Leicester Tigers two-game tour of Ireland in November 1958. I had carefully covered up for Chalkie, only to find a half page photo of him scoring a try against Bective Rangers in the *Sunday Times*! Fortunately for both Chalkie and me, the Headmaster chose not to/did not see the photo.

"He impacted massively on Nottingham High School, countless boys and colleagues gained from their contact with him. Memories of him are still treasured and live on. What a man!"

Chalkie's youngest son, Nick, recalls: "Dad and Geri Thomas were always keen for all the boys under their tutelage to exploit their sporting ability to the maximum, and all the better if that could be harnessed for the benefit of the Nottingham High School (NHS) teams. Positive results were obviously

Breakfast on a Combined Cadet Force (CCF) trip to Scotland, as Ged recalls: "The group would have stayed in a 'bothy' on the side of Ben Nevis or near Loch Rannoch in the central Highlands. As head of the Naval section, Dad would have organised this week away and would have enlisted the help of his good friend Eric Tarry. Eric was head of rugby at Nottingham High School before Geri Thomas arrived. Geri tells the family that Eric was respected by Dad more than anyone, and was a steadying influence."

favourable for the sports department (Dad and Geri) but also kept the NHS in the local newspapers. This improved the school's profile beyond the scholastic arena, doubling-up as a subtle marketing campaign in the competitive world of fee-paying schools and promoting the school as a more rounded environment in which boys could excel in a wide variety of ways.

This push to do well manifested in many forms but was nowhere more apparent than with school athletics. Innovations and training drills remembered for: "Encouraging membership of the national AAA 5-star award scheme where boys would score points for times and distances, across their three selected events, contributing to award scheme badges, this fostered a competition and a great range of skills within the athletics team.

"The yard at school was marked out as a 200-metre loop for the boys to sprint in 200-, 400- and 800-metre training races. This often led to the school resonating to Dad's high-volume encouragement with its distracting effect on classroom-bound students. On one notable occasion, Dad's motivational tone caused someone to run so hard, to improve an AAA time, that he ran straight

Leicester scrum-half Chalkie White is engulfed by Harlequins forwards – Twickenham, 1959

through the finish line to the bin in the corner of the yard to shed a couple of pounds of his breakfast. Plenty of people will understand that desire to do well.

"Entries in the less popular or highly technical events, such as hammer and pole vault, enabled additional points gathering – and higher placement of NHS in the overall Track and Field standings – on the occasions when other schools had decided not to enter pupils.

"For this, Dad was always keen to find 'volunteers' willing to take on these outlier events (one step forward for my brother and me for pole vault!) while also keeping the team and the coaching firmly up to date. And this meant the school became an early adopter of the new bendy fibre-glass pole (though only Dad would be able to answer how the purchase of this was sold to the school as a useful expense). The second half of the bendy pole introduction being the adjustment journey needed by coach and pole vault team to move from the old steel poles (the norm back then) to the new technology. However, Dad was always open to a challenge, even if sometimes it was on other people's behalf. I am sure many people may remember him saying that his threshold of our pain was very high when they started to lag in any of his sessions."

7

Earning His Tigers Stripes – Leicester FC

Running parallel through the whole of his 26 years at Nottingham High School was the sporting connection that was to make him famous, with Leicester Tigers.

One of the most distinguished clubs in English rugby, Leicester was founded in 1880, and had been playing at Welford Road, the largest club ground in England, since 1892. Its main stand was named after Tom Crumbie, its guiding force as club Secretary from 1895 to 1928, a period in which it had dominated the Midlands Cup so completely that it withdrew to give other clubs a chance, and hosted five England games including a memorable draw with Wales in 1904. The year previously, Jack Miles had become the first of many Tigers to play for England.

Douglas 'Joe' Kendrew was 20 when he toured New Zealand and Australia with the 1930 British Isles team. Capped ten times by England – twice as captain – Kendrew was one of the most highly decorated officers of the Second World War and was knighted (KCMG) in 1963, then as Knight of St. John in 1964. Kendrew Barracks near Oakham is named in his honour

Not least of Crumbie's talents was recruitment, a skill put to more serious use during the First World War. Leicester ran as an invitation club, with long-remembered giants like Douglas 'Joe' Kendrew, Wavell Wakefield and Alexander Obolensky passing through their ranks, and maintained that tradition into the 1950s.

Obolensky was one of 28 Tigers killed during the Second World War, but left vivid memories with those who had watched him play. Tigers' history points to one highly specific example in Edward Ridgway 'Peter' Bennett, whose life and career typify the continuities running through all storied rugby clubs.

Three years younger than Obolensky, Bennett followed him as a boarder at Trent College, hero-worshipped him as did most of his fellow-pupils, and dreamed of further emulating him by

Wavell Wakefield played 29 times for Leicester between 1921 and 1924, and was club captain from 1923-24. Capped 31 times, he was renowned for being one of England's finest players. Knighted in 1944, Wakefield became RFU President in 1950 and in 1999 became the first English player to be inducted into the International Rugby Hall of Fame

Prince Alexander Obolensky scored two tries on his debut in England's famous win at Twickenham in 1936, their first victory over the New Zealand All Blacks. He was tragically killed while serving with the RAF during the Second World War

becoming a Tiger. Before achieving that, he had to follow the brilliant Russian in another way, becoming a Second World War fighter pilot. Known as 'Peter' although named after his uncle, Capt. Edward Ridgway, recipient of the Croix de Guerre, who was killed at Cambrai in the First World War, he was called up, aged 18, when war broke out and joined the Fleet Air Arm, but unlike Obolensky survived and was still serving as a pilot when hostilities ended in 1945.

His senior rugby career had to wait until he was demobbed, after which he joined Westleigh as a winger and did well enough to be spotted by the Tigers, and was invited to join them in 1948. Nor was he exactly eased in, making his debut at home to Cardiff on November 20. The Welsh giants were at one of the peaks in their history and arguably the strongest club team in Britain, fielding a nearly all-international XV around the genius of Bleddyn Williams. Cardiff

'Peter' Bennett ready for action, like many of this generation his best years were spent in the service of his country

won 6-0, but Bennett did well enough to keep his place as a wing or centre for most of the rest of the season.

Bennett scored tries against Gloucester and Bath and attained the dream cherished since his schooldays a decade earlier – one widely shared among local players – by earning the Leicester Tigers players' tie, awarded for 20 1st XV appearances, at Plymouth Albion on April 18 1949. It could be argued that in this respect he outdid Obolensky, who fell three games short. The following season he dropped a goal at Cardiff Arms Park, but lost his place for a few matches, only to reappear for his thirtieth and final game as late as the Easter tour in 1954, when he turned out at Exeter.

From playing he moved, like many old Tigers, to spectating and was a regular in the Members' Stand, jokingly telling his son Simon: "watch that lot over there in the Crumbie Stand." Simon recalls that "he went whenever he could" until the mid-1990s with the Barbarians match and Twickenham excursions sacrosanct, so that he was present for Chalkie's playing career, all of his coaching triumphs, and beyond. Simon continues to watch, amid "that lot" in the Crumbie Stand.

Bennett, like Obolensky and Chalkie, played all of his rugby for Leicester at a time when they, and England's other leading clubs, played only friendly matches. Opposition to competitive rugby, at least for clubs, had been ingrained from the earliest days of the game. Leagues and cups were, in the eyes of the Rugby Football Union, a harbinger of professionalism.

Within five years of its foundation in 1871 the RFU rejected an offer from the Royal Military Academy, Woolwich, of a trophy worth £150 for a competition along the lines of football's FA Cup, another 1871 innovation. The Calcutta Cup, donated in 1878, might also perhaps have been used, but the RFU felt that the "lasting good for the cause of Rugby Football" specified by its donors was better fulfilled by the annual England v Scotland match.

Events did little to dispel innate distrust of competitive rugby. Wales turned the South Wales Challenge Cup over to its junior members in 1887, concerned that matches had become increasingly violent over its initial ten seasons, during which Newport won five times. It was revived for a single year in 1913-14, but not resumed after the First World War.

County Cup competitions became popular in the 1880s, particularly in Yorkshire and Lancashire, where the large gates attracted by cup-ties enabled the more successful clubs to start compensating their players. Nor did it escape notice that the breakaway Northern Union (later Rugby Football League) formed by those clubs in 1895 had, within a year, created its own Challenge Cup competition.

The Hospitals Cup had been created in 1875, but the competition, held at Oxford University, was later discontinued for 'making college matches too bloodthirsty'. From 1889 the County Championship offered England's best players a national cup, but one which was run and contested by the counties – the units on which the RFU's structures and committees were based – rather than the clubs.

County cups continued after the schism of 1895 and gave Tigers an early chance to assert their status as a leading club, winning eight Midlands Cups from 1898 onwards and 12 in total in the 16 years prior to the First World War. But the competition was discontinued in 1921 after the Midland Counties Rugby Union was dismantled into its constituent counties.

The rugby league breakaway had hardened attitudes in rugby union; turning amateurism from a set of rules into the game's defining ideology, while the county delegates who ran the RFU had a vested interest in the status quo represented by the County Championship as the highest level of competition below the national team. The significant exception was France, but clear evidence of players being rewarded for success in their highly-competitive national league led to its expulsion from the Five Nations Championship in 1931, until 1947.

Phil Judd – the England captain who made 442 appearances for Coventry, and was a great leader for Warwickshire during their successful County Championship winning years in the 1960s

The illogicality of the official stance would be summed up by Irish forward Noel Murphy when he was interviewed in New Zealand during the 1959 Lions tour: "There's no such thing as competitive rugby in our country. It's bad for the game, bad for the spirit of it. Apart from the Munster Cup, the Ulster Cup, the Leinster Cup, the seven-a-side tournaments, the International Championship, the West Wales League and in England, the County Championship, the

'Cuppers' at the varsities and the Hospitals Cup and things like the Yorkshire Cup, the Northumberland Cup and so on, we have no competitive rugby at all. No, it would never do!"

This may have been felt most strongly by Leicester's rivals Coventry – unquestionably the leading English club of this period – among a minority who earned true respect from Welsh opponents and provided almost the whole of the Warwickshire teams who won seven County Championships in eight seasons between 1958 and 1965. Yet, as historian Adrian Smith notes: "Coventry had no league or cup triumphs to underpin the club's reputation and thereby attract support." Down the road from them, Coventry City FC's rise from the Fourth to the First Division over almost the same period added 12,000 to their average attendances in a period of general decline in gates.

The Tigers season was one of annual rituals, with fixtures agreed years in advance. Bedford and Bath were played at the start of the season, with Coventry, Northampton, Gloucester and Oxford and Cambridge Universities in the autumn. Bristol were played just before Christmas, and the crowning moment of the season, against star-studded Barbarians teams, immediately after. Then it was Newport and Northampton in February and a late season incorporating Bristol and Exeter, sometimes as part of the Easter tour which usually went to the West Country, Llanelli and the return against Coventry.

Leicester scrum-half Mike Lubbock

It was one of the strongest fixture lists in English rugby, with the derbies against Northampton, Bedford and Coventry featuring alongside the Welsh fixtures, with Newport and Llanelli regular opponents at this time, and Swansea and Cardiff more intermittent. There is a striking contrast in the historic playing records. The 1993 history by Stuart Farmer and David Hands shows Tigers with a historic edge over most English opponents, other than Gloucester, and parity with Bristol. However, Tigers were very much the underdogs against Newport (W24, L 89), Cardiff (W18, L57), Swansea (W26, L73).

It made wins over the Welsh giants special, but rare, occasions, and gave the matches a distinct atmosphere. The rugby journalist Michael Green, who grew up in

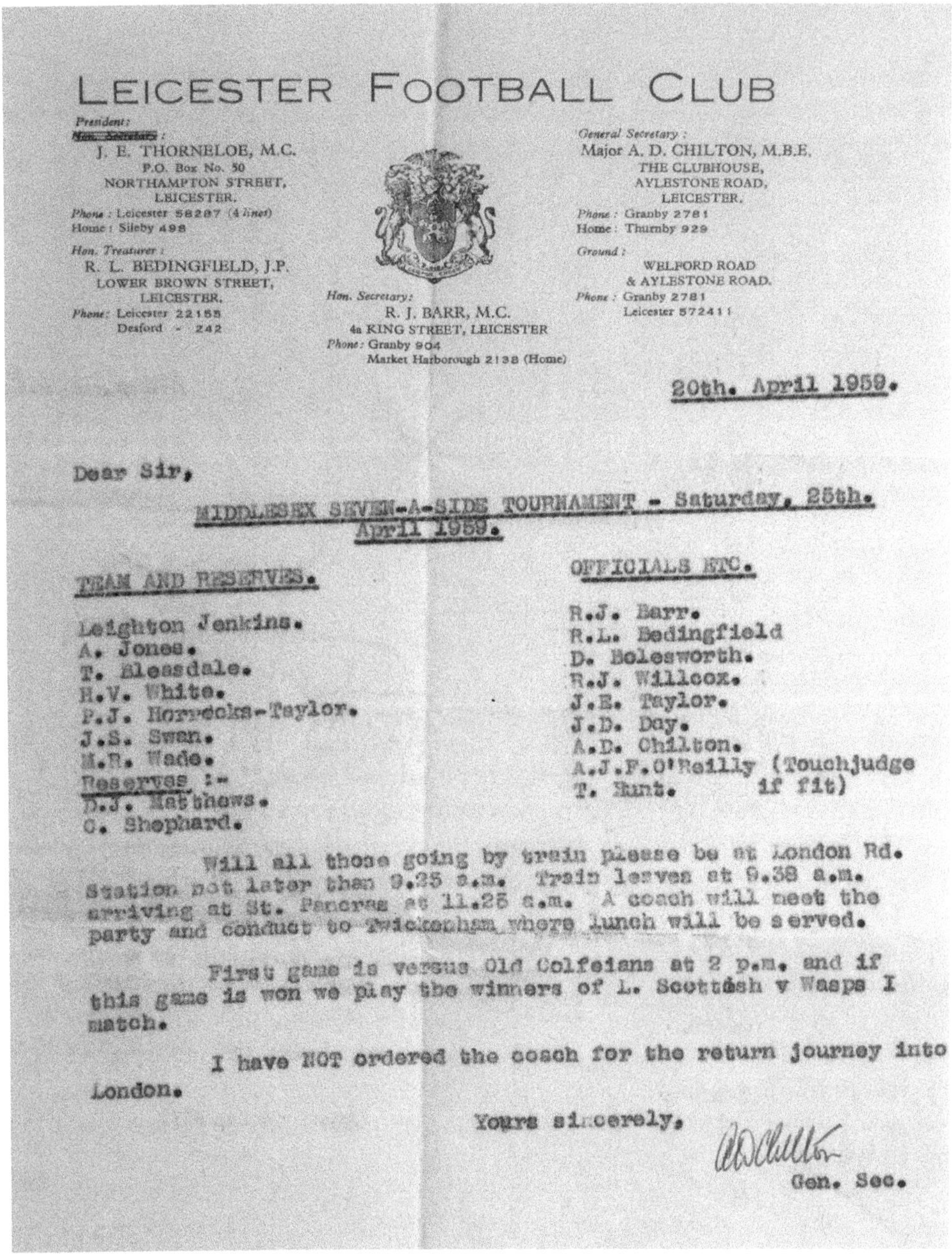

LEICESTER FOOTBALL CLUB

President: ~~*Hon. Secretary*~~:
J. E. THORNELOE, M.C.
P.O. Box No. 50
NORTHAMPTON STREET,
LEICESTER.
Phone: Leicester 58287 (4 lines)
Home: Sileby 498

Hon. Treasurer:
R. L. BEDINGFIELD, J.P.
LOWER BROWN STREET,
LEICESTER.
Phone: Leicester 22155
Desford - 242

Hon. Secretary:
R. J. BARR, M.C.
4a KING STREET, LEICESTER
Phone: Granby 904
Market Harborough 2138 (Home)

General Secretary:
Major A. D. CHILTON, M.B.E.
THE CLUBHOUSE,
AYLESTONE ROAD,
LEICESTER.
Phone: Granby 2781
Home: Thurnby 929

Ground:
WELFORD ROAD
& AYLESTONE ROAD.
Phone: Granby 2781
Leicester 572411

20th. April 1959.

Dear Sir,

MIDDLESEX SEVEN-A-SIDE TOURNAMENT - Saturday, 25th. April 1959.

TEAM AND RESERVES.

Leighton Jenkins.
A. Jones.
T. Bleasdale.
H.V. White.
P.J. Horrocks-Taylor.
J.S. Swan.
M.R. Wade.
Reserves :-
D.J. Matthews.
C. Shephard.

OFFICIALS ETC.

R.J. Barr.
R.L. Bedingfield
D. Bolesworth.
R.J. Willcox.
J.E. Taylor.
J.D. Day.
A.D. Chilton.
A.J.F. O'Reilly (Touchjudge
T. Hunt. if fit)

Will all those going by train please be at London Rd. Station not later than 9.35 a.m. Train leaves at 9.38 a.m. arriving at St. Pancras at 11.25 a.m. A coach will meet the party and conduct to Twickenham where lunch will be served.

First game is versus Old Colfeians at 2 p.m. and if this game is won we play the winners of L. Scottish v Wasps I match.

I have NOT ordered the coach for the return journey into London.

Yours sincerely,

A D Chilton

Gen. Sec.

Chalkie's selection letter to play in the Middlesex Sevens

Leicester Tigers Easter Tour 1958
Back Row (L-R): Denis Bolesworth (linesman), Brian Small, John Thompson, Rob Muddimer, John Elders, Gordon Almey, David Matthews, Michael Wade, Frank Chawner, Maurice Key, Ken Kinder, Eric Lacey, Mike Lubbock
Front Row (L-R): Cliff Shephard, Rex Skelton, John Spence 'Ian' Swan, Tom Bleasdale (captain), Mick Walker, Mike Freer, Chalkie White

Leicester, recalled attending a match at Welford Road before the Second World War. Baffled by his father's purple-faced fury, "Why is Daddy shaking his fist at the man in the white shirt?" he asked his mother. "Because he's a Swansea player, dear," came the reply. As Green wrote: "Since I have discovered more about Welsh rugby, I am also able to appreciate why father was waving his fist."

Tigers were made distinctive by their shirts and their tradition of players wearing lettered rather than numbered shirts. This habit was shared with Bristol, leading to matches in which one writer likened a loose maul to 'a bad hand at scrabble', although Tigers lettered their players from A, B and C in the front row to O at full back, while Bristol ran in the opposite direction.

Chalkie had joined a club which had marked time for most of the post-war years, recording losing records in eight of the 11 seasons before his arrival. There was furious debate about running an A team, with the local clubs happy to release their better players to play for the Tigers' 1st XV – much as Welsh junior clubs would release their stars, under licence, to Newport or Swansea – but unhappy that an A team would weaken them as players took up permanent residence at Welford Road. It was dropped in 1955, leading to an exodus of fringe players now left with no team to play for.

A slightly earlier arrival, in 1956, was Colin Martin, who brought with him the rather harder-edged attitudes prevalent in New Zealand rugby. In 1993 he told David Hands: "My first impression of playing with Leicester was that in spite of vigorous individual training, we had little team training, simply because less than half the squad turned up for practice. My first game, against Newport, soon demonstrated that the Welsh clubs did not suffer from this weakness. We seemed to have many talented individual players to call on, but frequently they were unable to play and often lived miles from Leicester. It was apparent, talking to many of the senior players, that this approach, while extremely successful in the past, was increasingly inadequate for the needs of the day."

A committee of inquiry, formed of Tigers' great and good, including club captain Tom Bleasdale and three former internationals: Tom Berry, Alastair Smallwood and Doug Norman (who also acted as Chairman), that commenced its deliberations in the summer of 1956, reached much the same conclusion.

As Hands records: "the main recommendation was that the Tigers should be a club in the real sense of the word, running three XVs and leaving behind any idea of being an invitation club which, the committee pointed out, had alienated many local players. The second XV was to be known as the Extra First and the third as the Swifts."

Harlequins (18) Leicester Tigers (11) – Twickenham, September 1959
Back Row (L-R): Arthur Jones, Brian Smith, David Senior, Brian Wigley, Harry Constable, George Cherry, Mike Gavins, Cliff Shephard
Middle Row (L-R): Peter Konig, Rex Skelton, Tom Bleasdale (captain), Colin Martin, David Matthews
Front Row (L-R): Chalkie White, Mick Hanney

Leicester winger Tony O'Reilly fends off his opposite winger Donald Davidson in the match between the British Lions and the Junior All Blacks in 1959 – O'Reilly scored 22 tries on the tour

The effect of these changes was "to change Leicester from a club hanging on grimly to memories of the years between the two World Wars to an organisation with a bright future and new traditions to establish."

Chalkie arrived exactly as these changes came into effect. Mike Lubbock began the season wearing 'I' at scrum-half, but the existence of the Extras' 1st XV meant there was a team to play for before Chalkie made his first team debut in a 3-3 draw against Cheltenham at Welford Road on October 19 1957. His first try, in the defeat of Old Blues, the old boys club of Christ's Hospital, Sussex which had once been a genuine first-class club but was now struggling, and would not play Leicester again, came in his fifth match.

Improvement took time to come, with a final playing record of 14 wins, six draws and 19 defeats as poor as anything over the previous decade of mediocrity, but there was a genuine upturn towards the end. Swansea was another club experiencing a fallow period which would end the season with a losing record, but still unbeaten against English opposition before they went down 20-8 at Welford Road in mid-March. The Easter tour then saw three wins for the first time since the war.

Chalkie played in the wins over Bristol and Exeter, but not the victory in between at Plymouth Albion. Deliberately or not, Tigers had got into a pattern of splitting matches evenly across the season between two scrum-halves. The previous year Lubbock had played 21 matches and Freddie Doore 20.

The pattern was maintained over Chalkie's first two seasons. In 1957-58 he played 20 matches to Lubbock's 19, but got the nod against the Barbarians. The following season Chalkie played the first 13 matches, but only 18 in all while Lubbock appeared in 20, including the 9-3 win over the Barbarians.

It was not until 1959-60 that Chalkie made the position unquestionably his, playing 33 of their 40 matches, as well as playing in the Leicester sevens team which played by invitation, and in the Middlesex Sevens in 1959 and 1960. The following season he played 34 matches, although with a straw in the wind in the shape of John Allen's debut against the RAF on January 26 1961. Allen, 13 years younger than Chalkie, was to play 11 matches in a row the following season, but Chalkie remained the main incumbent with 23 appearances.

The dropping of the invitation model did not stop the club continuing to recruit talent from across Britain and Ireland – in 1958-59 fielding Scottish international Ian Swan, England's Phil Horrocks-Taylor, Welsh cap Leighton Jenkins and legendary Irish wing Tony O'Reilly, but never managed to get all four playing together.

One combination that did take the field regularly was Chalkie and Horrocks-Taylor with Brian Ring at centre, father of the stylish Wales international Mark. Brian Ring played 35 times for the club in 1959-60 and 1960-61 – scoring four tries and one drop-goal – and Mark recalled his father saying "what a great player Chalkie was, and how he and Horrocks-Taylor were a very good half-back pair. Dad became very close friends with Graham Willars who used to stay with us when England were playing against Wales in Cardiff and Peter Wheeler used to come down with Graham too after he'd retired. My mum still has all the old Leicester match reports – hundreds of them!"

Phil Horrocks-Taylor during the 1959 British Lions tour to Australia and New Zealand

Gordon Almey watches Llanelli's Welsh trialist Aubrey Gale pounce on Chalkie

Tigers recorded winning records in the last five seasons in which he made substantial contributions. While the Welsh contests remained tough, there was at least one win each season, and they were competitive against big English rivals like Bristol, Northampton and Coventry. Allen inherited the I shirt and made it his until his retirement in 1975 after 457 games, a club record for a back, before becoming Treasurer.

Chalkie left vivid memories with one of his most distinguished contemporaries, England outside-half Phil Horrocks-Taylor. Immortalised in rugby lore by his Irish opposite number, Mick English, who complained that "Horrocks went one way, Taylor the other, and I was left holding the hyphen." He arrived at Welford Road in autumn 1958 after making his England debut the previous January in a 3-3 draw with Wales remembered for opposite number Cliff Morgan defusing a howling wind by keeping play in the shadow of one of Twickenham's massive stands.

Horrocks-Taylor made his debut outside Chalkie in a 14-9 defeat at Coventry and recalls: "When I arrived at Leicester Tigers the established scrum-half was

Chalkie White. I had taken my first job since leaving university with 'Richards of Leicester', an engineering company, having previously played for Halifax RUFC and Cambridge University. Chalkie was a typical scrum-half of that era, he was tough and durable. Scrum-halves did not get the protection from the forwards in those days that they enjoy today. He was not a running scrum-half, he thought about the game and was more tactical, he wasn't captain of the team but he did lead the backs.

"When I joined Leicester, they were renowned for their forward play, Chalkie wanted to play a certain way and I agreed. We did try and throw the ball about and when I got the chance, I tried to move the ball as we had some very good backs. David Senior on the left wing, Mike Gavins at full back and when Tony O'Reilly arrived in October, he played at centre or right wing, we had some real fire power.

"I didn't play for Leicester in the games before Christmas as I played for Yorkshire in the County Championship, while Chalkie also played in the County Championship for Cumberland & Westmorland, he was very proud

Dixie Grammar Schools boys Bob Beason (left) and Geoff Hallam, proudly wearing their England Schoolboy jerseys and caps. Bob, a prop forward, made his Tigers debut in September 1960, went on to play 203 1st XV games for Leicester, and was club President for two seasons (1985-87)

to be a Cumbrian. I remember playing for Yorkshire against Cumberland & Westmorland in a county match at Lidget Green, Bradford. Chalkie was playing scrum-half on the other side, I don't remember the year or the score but I do remember we won, you always remember the wins!

"I was called up as a replacement for the injured Mick English of Ireland on the 1959 Lions Tour of Australia and New Zealand and played in the 3rd Test. At work they weren't happy about me going so I left, and found another job after the tour; it was easy to find a job in those days. I got on very well with Chalkie. In later life, with his strong personality, I wasn't at all surprised when he became a successful coach; he did the same job for a living as a school PE teacher, where he got the ideal grounding."

Horrocks-Taylor was by far Chalkie's most frequent half-back partner, linking up with him for Tigers 61 times. Across his 147 appearances, Chalkie had 16 partners: John Berry (2), Gordon Blackett (5), Arthur Chapman (1), Richard Cooper (5), WA Davidson (2), Mike Freer (39), Mick Hanney (2), Mike Harrison (1), Phil Horrocks-Taylor (61), Colin Littlewood (1), Alan Rees (1), Ken Scotland (2), David Sellicks (1), Brian Small (1), Lyn Tatham (21), Michael Wade (2)

The problems created by the frequent changes in half-back partners were explained by writer Terry McNeil in 1959 after a withdrawal by Blackett, a brilliant school international who played for Tigers while doing his National Service in the Royal Corps of Signals. Acerbically noting that Blackett, who would go on to distinguished service with Gosforth before joining Huddersfield Rugby League Club in 1963, had played only one away match in two seasons with Tigers and was making a habit of late withdrawals, McNeil wrote in *Rugger Review*: "The prime sufferer is scrum-half Chalkie White, who appears to have a fresh partner in every match. White has not been in the best of form lately and this is hardly surprising. To get the best out of a scrum-half, it is essential that he knows his outside-half's game inside out. What has been happening lately is White has been forced to alter his style to suit each new partner. I say it would be far more beneficial to the Tigers in the long run, if they selected the same fly half in every match. I'm sure the team would appreciate such a move."

McNeil was not exaggerating. The Gloucester match was number six in a sequence of eight matches between October and November 1959 in which Chalkie's partner was different to the previous game, the 'J' shirt bouncing back and forth between Blackett, Mike Freer, Lyn Tatham, Horrocks-Taylor and John Berry – Tigers lost five of them. The wins were at home to Cheltenham, who won only once in 13 visits to Welford Road, Nuneaton, who won twice in 55 visits, and away to a Llanelli team which had won only four of its previous 17 matches. It is hardly surprising that continuity of selection became one of the hallmarks of the teams he was to select as coach, particularly in the positions he defined as the team's 'spine' – full back, half-backs, Number 8 and hooker.

8

Playing the Barbarians

Well into the era of competitive rugby, the post-Christmas match against the Barbarians was considered the highlight of the Leicester season. When the club hosted a Rugby World Cup match between the All Blacks and Italy in 1991 on October 13, it was instructive to hear Tigers fans discussing exciting young Italian backs like Paolo Vaccari in terms of the likelihood of their being selected by the Barbarians for the match at Welford Road a couple of months later.

Rugby union's most famous invitation club was founded in 1890, in what not long after became the heartland of rugby league, a birthplace reflecting the city's status within the game at the time. Bradford was the best-supported and, with Blackheath and Newport, the strongest club in British rugby in the decade before the 1895 schism, consistently providing at least two members of the England XV. Cross-city rivals Manningham, the first champions of the rugby league, had a 100% record against Tigers in six meetings

It was a particularly suitable birthplace, since Bradford had already played its part in making rugby tours fashionable. In December 1884, a month after its successful tour of the south, including a 39-3 defeat of Cambridge University, a team from Jesus College, Cambridge, visited Yorkshire where it inflicted defeats on Batley, Huddersfield, Leeds St. John's and Bradford. The extent to which the students celebrated their victory would suggest that the tour had been motivated as much for revenge as the enjoyment and camaraderie. Their captain was William Carpmael, later founder of the Barbarians.

Southern clubs could not afford to tour without a subsidy from their hosts, but a representative touring side allowed southern players to play against leading clubs elsewhere in the country. That players needed to fund themselves would, by definition, make membership relatively exclusive.

Immediately before the launch of the Barbarians, in Easter 1890, Carpmael led the 'Southern Nomads' on a tour, taking in matches against Burton, Moseley, Wakefield and Huddersfield. After beating Wakefield and losing to Huddersfield, they stayed at the Alexander Hotel on Great Horton Road,

Leuchters Restaurant (right) was located on Market Street, Bradford

recorded by historian John Dewhirst as Bradford's premier hotel. On the evening after the Huddersfield game they dined at the equally fashionable Leuchters Restaurant, a product of the city's strong historic links with Germany. The concept of the Barbarians was devised during the dinner course and drinks.

Laurie Hickson and Arthur Perkins of Bradford were among the founder members, and Hickson captained the Barbarians on its inaugural tour later that year. The black and white hooped shirts worn by the Barbarians from 1891 were significant. White was still a premium colour, adopted only by clubs who could afford high laundry bills.

Like their association football counterparts the Corinthians, the Barbarians never confused amateurism with disinterest in money, and they liked turning their fixtures into traditions. Leicester FC was the ideal fixture for the Barbarians because the railway station close to the ground at Welford Road, enabled large gate-paying crowds.

Leicester's first game against the Barbarians was on December 29 1909 which ended in a 9-9 draw. Its starting point was the withdrawal, after 1908, by Fettesian Lorettonians FC – an Edinburgh-based rugby club for former pupils of Fettes College and Loretto School – from their annual Christmas visit to the East Midlands. The Barbarians were invited to take their place in the Welford Road Christmas holiday rugby festival of four games in six days which also included fixtures against Cinderford, Birkenhead Park, and Penarth – which became the Barbarians' Welsh base.

When Carpmael died on December 27 1936, the match played the following day at Welford Road saw both teams wearing black arm bands in his honour – the Barbarians won 20-5. By 1993 the Barbarians had recorded 39 victories, 31 defeats and five drawn matches; the only winning record by a regular visitor to Welford Road other than Newport, Swansea and Cardiff.

The fixture between Leicester Tigers and the Barbarians became the highlight of the Christmas holiday period and the club's season, lasting from 1909 into the post-1995 professional era. It was played for the last time as a regular fixture in March 2006 but returned briefly in November

William Carpmael – founder and first President of the Barbarian FC

Leicester Tigers v Barbarians 1960 – Chalkie executing his famous dive pass watched by teammates (L-R) David Matthews, Colin Martin and Tom Bleasdale

LEICESTER FOOTBALL CLUB

GEN. SEC:—
TELEPHONE NO. GRANBY ~~3359~~ 2781
HOME TEL. NO.
THURNBY ~~020~~ 3359

THE CLUBHOUSE
AYLESTONE ROAD
LEICESTER.

FIRST XV

You have been selected to play
versus Barbarians
at LEICESTER on Monday.
the 28 DEC 1959 19 Kick off 2-30 pm
Train/Bus leaves Station at
Please inform me urgently if you cannot play.
Lunch at Bell Hotel
12 noon

Yours faithfully,
AD Chilton
Gen. Sec.

Leicester v Barbarians, 1959 – Chalkies selection card

POST OFFICE TELEGRAM

No. 44

OFFICE STAMP

BM501 TELEGRAM

Prefix. Time handed in. Office of Origin and Service Instructions. Words.

D 47 6.19 LEICESTER NG 18

OVERNIGHT WHITE 16 LAMBLEY LANE
BURTONJOYCE-NOTTINGHAM =

BARBARIANS GAME DEFINITELY ON LUNCH BELL HOTEL
12 NOON =
LEICESTER FOOTBALL CLUB + + 16 12 NOON +

For free repetition of doubtful words telephone "TELEGRAMS ENQUIRY" or call with this form at office of delivery. Other enquiries should be accompanied by this form, and, if possible, the envelope B or C

(3783) Wt. Y12720—P2574 50m pads 9/50 A.O.St.

Game On! Telegram to Chalkie confirming the Barbarians fixture in December 1961 had not been affected by adverse weather

2014 when the Barbarians beat Leicester 59–26 in their 125th anniversary season.

Chalkie played four times in the fixture, from December 1957 to March 1962, and was on the losing team on each occasion. In those days, a match that was called off for bad weather was cancelled, but the annual Barbarians game was too important, financially, so would be postponed to the spring.

The same was to happen again the following season, when Mike Dymond played scrum-half for Tigers. Chalkie's last match in the usual post-Christmas slot – it was customary for Birkenhead Park to visit on Boxing Day and the Barbarians the day after – was in 1960 when Ray French of St. Helens was among the visitors.

French, a second row who played for England in both rugby codes before becoming the BBC's rugby league commentator, remembers the occasion well: "I was very proud to play my first game for the Barbarians against Leicester Tigers on December 27 1960. The team contained players from many of the great clubs from England, Ireland, Scotland and Wales and there was me representing St. Helens RUFC. If I was asked once I was asked fifty times, are you from St. Helens Rugby League Club. People didn't know that rugby union was played in St. Helens, and they were even more surprised when I told them there was four rugby union clubs in the town.

"I also remember that the Barbarians match was the third game I played in three days. I had played on both Christmas Day and Boxing Day for the English Universities, in games at Llanelli and Bridgend; I travelled to Welford Road on

The spirit of the Barbarians. The original caption for this photograph was 'England's Two Greatest Hookers' – former England hooker John Pullin, the Barbarians touch judge, catches up with Peter Wheeler at Welford Road

Code breaker – Ray French playing at Wembley in the 1966 Challenge Cup Final

the morning of the Barbarians game with my good friend Bev Risman from Loughborough College. My abiding memory of the game was the first time I saw the Leicester winger Tony O'Reilly play; I was impressed with him. He later turned down £10,000 to play rugby league – an absolute fortune in those days. He could turn a man, beat a man, run through or round him – surely one of the best wings in the world at either code in his day.

"Two days after the Barbarians game I played for St. Helens at Moss Lane. Following the game our volunteer barman Peter Twiss, who worked locally in St. Helens, asked if he could speak to me privately. Peter told me there had been a meeting while I'd been playing against Leicester and following my selection for the Barbarians the committee had agreed I would receive a free pint. I immediately asked Peter for a pint of Best Bitter. 'Sorry Ray,' he replied. 'Best Bitter is 1s 2d so you'll have to have Mild!"

Leicester's Ray French, a prop forward, in action with his brother, Roy, at Welford Road (L-R): Brian Hall, Ray French, Bleddyn Jones, Bob Rowell, Nick Joyce, Robin Money, Roy French and John Duggan

Garry Adey in full flight, chased by Barbarian Barry John (left). The Leicester players are (L-R) Graham Willars, John Allen, Peter Wheeler, Roger Grove and Bob Rowell

The Barbarians fixture had far-reaching consequences. As the quality of the Leicester Tigers team improved, so did the Barbarians teams. The annual fixture raised standards and would be regarded by both Chalkie and his players as invaluable when cup rugby was introduced.

Immense efforts were often needed to get the fixture played in inhospitable weather, as illustrated in the letter sent to all Tigers players by Team Secretary, Tudor Thomas, prior to the 1981 Barbarians fixture: "Please make an effort to help with the pitch covering on Sunday morning, 20 December, at 10am, we have new covers this year, so there will be no straw used, the task can be completed in one hour if you turn up to help."

Previously straw had been used to protect the field from frost, as John Alan recalls: "Help was often provided by inmates from Leicester prison. They were tasked to clear the straw when we had to protect the pitch in bad weather; it was a short walk to the ground from the prison on Welford Road."

9

The County Championship – 1960-63

During his time as a Tiger, Chalkie also returned to county rugby. He played for Cumberland & Westmorland, but had to do it the hard way. As an Old Creightonians player, he had – unsuccessfully – played in the county's final trials in 1949, 1951 and 1952. In 1953 he was travelling reserve for all the county games, but never played.

Chalkie made his County Championship debut for Cumberland & Westmorland against a Yorkshire team that included Frank Whitcombe Jnr. (the author's father)

It was not until November 11 1955, when Chalkie played his first county rugby match, as a flanker (or, wing forward as it was known in those days), travelling an 800-mile round trip from Truro School to Kendal RUFC by public transport.

While teaching at Nottingham High School, Chalkie also played for Notts, Lincs & Derby against Warwickshire in the 1958 County Championship. Together with his involvement with Cornwall, this brief link with the three-county East Midlands team enabled him to joke that he had "played for six counties".

It would be 1960 before Chalkie played for Cumberland & Westmorland again, beginning a three-year stint as a regular in the team, journalist Eric Silver, dubbed "the poor relations of the North Division", with staying out of bottom place the limit of their ambitions in a brutally tough regional competition.

The prizes were shared around, with four different teams – Cheshire in 1960, Durham in 1961, Yorkshire in 1962 and Lancashire in 1963 – taking the North Division. These were the years when Warwickshire, usually a thinly-disguised Coventry team, dominated the competition as a whole, but the North provided its main challengers. Cheshire won the title in 1960-61, after Warwickshire were squeezed out at the division stage in a 10-9 play-off defeat to East Midlands, while Yorkshire and Lancashire both reached the final before going down to the perennial champions in 1962-63 and 1963-64 respectively.

Yorkshire's John Kaye records the era vividly: "We are talking about a time when, particularly in the North Division, one had to first achieve county recognition before there was any possibility of further progress towards international representation. The same applied to the South West. Only in the Midlands were the clubs deemed to be stronger than the counties with the likes of Leicester, Northampton, and Coventry, and to a lesser extent Moseley, being recognised as feeders for the international sides. So, the focus in the North was very much on winning the North Division Championship to progress to a semi-final and then, hopefully, to a final and the County Championship. Given the strength of each of the northern counties, this progression was very rare indeed and was to be cherished. If you, as a player, were representing your county there was a hope that somehow you could be a little bit out of the ordinary and an expectation that you might help to bring that elusive championship home."

John Kay's anecdote illustrates what county selection meant in those days: "Mike, my elder brother – who was no mean player in his own right and might have progressed further in the game had contact lens technology been far enough advanced in those days – and I attended the 1953 County

Championship final at Lidgett Green, Bradford between Yorkshire and the East Midlands – won by Yorkshire 11-3. During the game, and I can still recall it as clearly as if I was standing there now, at a line-out on about half-way, Phil Taylor, the Wakefield Number 8, burst through and hooked a bouncing ball with his boot out of the East Midlands' scrum-half's hands. Caught it, then set off at a gallop up the slight slope towards the goal line. With 50 yards to go, and being a back row forward, meant that he didn't quite make the line and score a sensational try but he put Yorkshire into a very strong attacking position. Fast forward a few days and my brother and I were walking along a narrow one-way street in Wakefield when Mike grabbed my arm and said: 'Look who that is over there!' I didn't recognise who it was, so an exasperated Mike said: "It's the GREAT Phil Taylor." Mike was obviously very much in awe of anyone who had achieved county status and above. I'm not sure whether or not, in 1953, Taylor had moved to Northampton, but in 1956 I certainly played with him in my second game for the Wakefield 1st XV at Morley RFC, although by that time he was a guest player. Mike's reaction shows the high regard of county status players.

"There was always an interest, when games were being played against the 'top' clubs, in seeing how many county players they had in their side compared with yours. It was always a gauge as to how difficult a time you were going to have on the field that afternoon. I remember one particular occasion when we were playing away at Hartlepool Rovers, who were one of the strongest Durham County sides at that time, and seeing an * noted in the match programme alongside the names of 11 of their players (two of whom were also British and Irish Lions) and ten of our team. Perhaps our five 'also-rans' were better than their four because we won the game quite comfortably, but the knowledge that we were up against such a quality side would certainly have focused our minds."

Cumberland & Westmorland were never whitewashed, and managed to stay out of last place in Chalkie's final three seasons. There were fine victories over Yorkshire in 1960 and 1961, Durham and Cheshire in 1962, and Cheshire again in 1963, awarded victory when the match was abandoned with Cumberland & Westmorland 19-8 up in the final quarter.

Chalkie's recall, against Durham in 1960, was inauspicious, with his team losing 14-0 at home, but David Frost, early in his long career as *The Guardian*'s voice of rugby, reckoned: "The introduction of White at scrum-half was a wise move by the selectors, for he is the sort of player to make the most of any chances his forwards may provide in the open."

The five county matches were played on consecutive Saturdays in October and November, with a warm-up game against Staffordshire often inserted beforehand as preparation.

Cumberland & Westmorland (14) Yorkshire (11) – Scatcherd Lane (Morley RFC), November 1960
Back Row (L-R): Peter Sutcliffe, Tony Colloby, Mike Howard, Malcolm Corrie, John Graham, John Moffitt, Les Moore, Geoff Edmondson, Wally Leech, Bobby Hogg.
Front Row (L-R): Jeff Edgar, Chalkie White, Bobby Wilson (captain), Alan Tiffen, Frank Burns

Chalkie missed only one match, against Lancashire in 1961, between his recall against Durham in October 1960 and his final appearance against Northumberland almost exactly three years later.

The high point appears to have been in 1962, with two wins and a narrow loss to Lancashire. The win over Cheshire was watched by Eric Silver, who reported: "It was too much, even for the cattle. In a flurry of racing sleet, grasping mud, and well-bred oaths, at Keswick yesterday, Cumberland & Westmorland, the poor relations of the Northern section of the Rugby Union Championship, beat Cheshire by a goal to nil. The cattle in the neighbouring meadow had long broke for cover, the referee's watch gave up the struggle before half-time, the couple of hundred frigid spectators huddled even deeper into the stand and only by the grace of a certain distillery, did your correspondent keep the blood flowing through his fingers and the ink through his ball pen.

"It soon became clear that the odds were heavily on the side which could first exploit an opponent's error in a vulnerable position. In a closely locked match,

Cumberland & Westmorland (17) v Staffordshire (3) – Newport Road (Stafford RUFC), October 1961
Back Row (L-R): Wally Leech, Bobby Hogg, Evan Walters, John Moffitt, Harvey Askins, Geoff Edmondson, Noel Jackson, John Gibson.
Front Row (L-R): John Hope, Jeff Edgar, Alec Davidson, Bobby Wilson (captain), Frank Burns, Alan Tiffen, Chalkie White

Cumberland & Westmorland (9) v Durham (3) – Mint Bridge (Kendal RUFC), October 1962
Back Row (L-R): A.K. Golledge (referee), Geoff Edmondson, Len Barton, Brian Calvin, Doug Murray, John Salisbury, Mike Howard, Nobby Slack, Ken Smart, Wally Leech, E. Clementson (touch judge)
Front Row (L-R): Frank Burns, Jeff Edgar, Joe Southward, Chalkie White (captain), Alan Tiffen, Alec Davidson

Chalkie's club career started and ended with matches against Cheltenham

it was anyone's guess which this would be. As it happened it was Cheshire who slipped, Cumberland & Westmorland pounced and thus the two counties won.

"Tomkins misjudged the angle at which the ball came out after a Cheshire heel near the visitors' line in the fifty-third minute. White swooped gratefully on to the loose ball and crossed for a try converted by Burns. For those connoisseurs who survived the 80 minutes, the memorable, though sparse delicacies, were the line-out duel between Calvin and Rogers, which the former won by a length, by virtue of his cleaner catching and tighter coordination with his hatchet man Johnstone. The calmly sustained control which White exercised over his Cumberland & Westmorland team and the intelligently flighted, if not always successful kicking of Griffiths for Cheshire against the wind. But this was not a day for connoisseurs."

Chalkie was in similar form a week later, as Cumberland & Westmorland gave Lancashire a serious scare, one reporter noting: "Much of the disciplined fire in the Cumberland & Westmorland pack stemmed from the calm competence of their scrum-half and captain H.V. White. He played beautifully to his forwards, using the touchline, starting blindside movements, and leading much of the harassing activity."

Chalkie's final club match, against Cheltenham on November 30 1963, came a few weeks after his final county appearance, against Northumberland on October 26 1963

Team-mate Jeff Edgar recalls him as an inspiring leader: "I certainly enjoyed playing with Chalkie all those years ago when the game was still amateur. I wonder whether the present-day professionals get as much pleasure. He had a commanding voice and, as a captain, his exhortation and instructions to the team were clear and precise. He paid attention to detail and as I was his half-back partner I can remember him arranging a brief get-together so we could get used to each other's requirements, signalling and positioning, as well as tactics."

Cumbrian John Owen MBE, a former President of the Rugby Football Union, remembers him well: "Those were the days when county rugby was at its pinnacle, and progress to the full England senior team was through the county structure. I recall attending a number of coaching sessions with Chalkie when coaching was my main involvement in the game. He was an inspiration to many; not only players but coaches, administrators and indeed supporters of all ages. His ability to communicate with young players was outstanding."

The final county appearance came a few weeks before his last club match for Tigers, on October 26 1963. He was hailed in the match programme as: "A most popular and successful captain of last season`s Cumberland & Westmorland XV and today he gains his 17th cap." His second spell with Cumberland and Westmorland ended as it had begun, getting nilled at home, going down 8-0 to Northumberland.

It was the end of the county-bound road for Chalkie, as Cumberland & Westmorland Rugby Union's Secretary Jimmy Morton explained in a letter to Chalkie, thanking him for his county service: "As we have omitted you from the team to play Yorkshire, the members of the committee have asked me to write and say how much we have appreciated your efforts as captain over the past few seasons. We hope your forceful personality will not be lost to Cumberland & Westmorland and that there will be occasions in the future when you can grace our rugby occasions. I enclose a copy of the XV to play Yorkshire; I hope it meets with your approval!"

10

What Next? – 1963-67

While his playing days were over, Chalkie was hardly idle over the next few years. In family life the most important event was the birth of his and Doris's youngest, Nicholas (Nick).

Their home life was to be warmly evoked in Nick's funeral eulogy for Doris in 2015: "You occasionally swore like a docker which I would guess you picked up in the Navy post-war. And when called on it you'd deny it to the hilt, which was all the more amusing. You brought up three kids who were about as different as they could be. My siblings cast the youngest as the favourite, though you say there was none. Only you and I will know that for sure. You taught us all many things, not least how to spell, though you failed to give me your crossword skills. You held the home together while Dad went to work, and while he travelled and slowly changed his corner of the universe you changed ours by just wanting the best for us and being there for us."

Chalkie bought a Morris Minor and with fellow Nottingham High School teacher Gordon Wood sitting alongside, learnt to drive. He passed his test at the first attempt, despite pulling away from the kerb in third gear.

The car made a big difference to the family's annual summer holidays, a fortnight in the caravan park next to Silloth RUFC in Cumberland. The train and bus journey to Silloth via a stopover with his parents in Carlisle gave way to a car journey which might, in an era when motorways were only just beginning, take up to six hours.

It also gave Chalkie the freedom to continue to travel between the Nottinghamshire family home, in Burton Joyce, and Leicester three times a week. He was elected to the club committee at the first AGM following his retirement from playing, in 1964.

On the field, Tigers were seeing the benefits of the reforms of the later 1950s. The 1963-64 season was their best since the war with 26 wins and 12 defeats, while the Welford Road skyline changed forever in October 1964 with the arrival of floodlights, inaugurated by a match against a Midlands XV.

Peter Tom: "Colin Martin set the standards in place that led to where we are today in my view"

The big moment of this period was the election of back rower David Matthews as captain, who at the age of 28, had thought the honour might have passed him by. Among the first challenges facing him was replacing the man packing down alongside him at Number 8 since Colin Martin had retired at the end of the previous season. There was an almost seamless transition to another new face, the Australian John Quick, who played all but one of their 44 matches.

Far from fading from the season, Martin, now in the tenth year of a visit which in the matter of the classic New Zealand 'overseas experience' was initially planned to have taken two, took on a still more important role, assisting Matthews as *de facto* coach. It was a concept with which the British game remained uncomfortable, feeling it smacked of professionalism.

In 1966 the Lions would succumb to the idea but see little benefit as tour captain Mike Campbell-Lamerton, who as the out-of-his-class leader of an outgunned party facing one of the most formidable of all All Blacks teams, should have welcomed all the help he could get, chose instead to marginalise former Tiger John Robins. That Robins travelled as 'assistant manager' typified the euphemisms applied to disguise the job and a distrust which only began to fade once the examples set in Wales by the organisation created by Ray Williams, the national teams coached by Clive Rowlands and the Lions, inspired in New Zealand by 1971's 'assistant manager' Carwyn James became evident. Martin, a product of the New Zealand system which had long accepted coaching at club and provincial level – although not, oddly for All Black touring teams, leaving players accustomed to such guidance reliant on their captains – had no such hang-ups.

As he told David Hands in *The Tigers Tale*: "New Zealander Colin Martin had brought the club success in the 1960s, organising them into a fearsome forward unit which was particularly well served in the back row. The backs though were never forgotten, with wings like David Senior, Graham Pulfrey and David Bird regularly collecting tries. In my view it faced up to the times. Captains were men with family and business responsibilities, and needed support, competition was increasing year by year and certainly no longer could 15 brilliant individuals defeat a well-organised team. In addition, I had always held the view that players liked to play the game well and a coach/captain combination could more readily achieve that objective, with one important rider – the captain is ultimately in charge, the coach has a supportive role."

Leicester prop forward Roger Grove

While the 1964-65 season had seen a drift back into mediocrity, with 20 wins and 19 defeats, the next two under Matthews and Martin were among the best in the club's history to that point. The 30 wins in 1965-66 were the most since 1922, and followed by a club record 33 in 1966-67. There was still a tendency, however, to fall short against the very best opposition, but the Barbarians were beaten in both years – in 1965-66 thanks to a hat-trick of tries by Quick – and the list of those beaten the in 1966-67 included Newport, Bristol, Gloucester, Llanelli, Aberavon and a double over Northampton.

Roger Grove arrived in 1966 after 145 games at prop for Bristol, more than 30 games for Somerset in the County Championship and a final England trial. He would play two more final trials while with Leicester, and became captain from 1971-72

Grove remembers: "My earliest memories of Leicester are when Colin Martin was a player. At that time, I was at Bristol, and Colin was performing in the Tigers back row. Those were cases of Bristol backs against Tigers forwards. Tactically, Bristol went for a lighter and more mobile pack and the players were given the licence to innovate and play off-the-cuff. Bristol worked hard just to contend with the likes of the Leicester heavies Martin, Matthews and Willars. Colin Martin was always prominent, both physically and verbally, as he was clearly 'the leader of the pack'.

"On moving to the East Midlands in 1966, I was invited to join Leicester by Kevin Andrews, when David Matthews was captain, and accompanied in the back row by Graham Willars and John Quick, a Number 8 from Randwick in Australia. These three were by far the most effective back row that I had the pleasure of playing alongside, and probably a legacy which sprung from the influence from the Colin Martin years in Leicester.

Rival captains René Bonnefont of CASG (Club Athlétique des Sports Généraux, Paris) and Bob Rowell exchange mementoes at Welford Road, February 1977. Rowell was the last Leicester player to be capped by England (1965) before Chalkie began coaching the club.

"I quickly settled into different training and playing methods. Colin Martin was still influential on the training field and, being a New Zealander, he was very keen upon hard slog in training. He knew the forward game inside out and was most of his focus, while the backs worked independently as was the system at that time with most clubs. I can clearly remember the endless lapping around the pitch in the semi-darkness, whereas at Bristol, lapping was before training, and training sessions were all about devising and practising plays and new systems – the exciting stuff. Becoming a Tigers forward was like stepping back into the Middle Ages, when working towards the opposition's line was winning the line-out and kicking forward to the next line-out and so on, but by the time Chalkie took charge Colin had already left the club."

Grove's move from Bristol to Leicester typified the era in being driven by reasons outside rugby. In the pre-professional era, club loyalty was strong and players would rarely change clubs, occasionally for greater rugby opportunities or changing locality for reasons of employment. Good, recognised, players would remain with their smaller local clubs and win international caps in spite of their strong club loyalty.

As a committee man, Chalkie was a spectator of all of this, albeit an active and informed one from his seat in the box at Welford Road, but his likely future direction was evident in his membership, from 1963, of the RFU's first Advisory Panel on coaching.

11

The Early Coaching Years – 1967-71

Chalkie initially served as a member of Leicester's committee from 1964-67, until taking responsibility 'for playing standards and style' in 1967 and he retained a strictly limited conception of the role. He explained this during an interview published in *Rugby World* in a 1979 article entitled 'Committee man who Coaches' – by which time he was recognised as one of the most successful coaches in the game. The title might have seemed like yet another of those euphemisms surrounding the early days of coaching, but this committee role was part of Chalkie's evolution towards his eventual role with Tigers, not an immediate takeover. As so often in his career, it was a matter of being the right man in place at the right time.

"I regard myself at Leicester as a committee man who coaches," he commented. "I don't think you can separate the two. I think the coach who regards himself as coach of the club and nothing else is on very isolated ground; you've got to be part of the set-up. And the committee-work at Leicester is where it starts; it is where you gain the respect of the non-players; you've got to have respect from both sides, the players and the non-players. And I have been here ever since.

"David Matthews was having a three-year stint as Skipper and was running short of ideas towards the middle of his third term [in 1967, so] I used to pop into the dressing-room at that stage. Colin Martin had laid the foundations of a coaching pattern *à la* New Zealand some years before, when I was playing there, and I started helping David out. It became a very easy thing once you are in; players look around for a whipping boy, they look around for someone to blow the whistle at the right time, to put the lights off when they stop - and it starts from there. There was no attempt on my part to move in and coach as such. It developed from helping the team, which, in fact, is all a coach does. He helps the players in the team he is connected with and when he becomes a club coach, he is there to help the players in the club.

"It wasn't quite a drift, [into the coaching role] but there was no deliberate march into it. It was knowing the players, and, of course, this can sometimes

Leicester scrum-half John Allen

present a problem for people who take up coaching – both the players they've played with and the players who have come into the side after them. When I began coaching there were players there who had taken my place. I didn't retire; I was overtaken by the younger men coming in. John Allen, who is now Treasurer of the club, took over my place and played a jolly sight better than I did at that stage. So one found a role for oneself at the club, and this mutual respect develops and you make lots of mistakes.

"Kevin Andrews, a fellow committee-man, for whom I have a great respect, was a skipper in the early days. He laughed at some of the ideas I tried in those days; but there is no laughing now. We still make mistakes, but it is accepted that these mistakes may be stepping stones to something else."

Many years later, writing to Ged, Chalkie added: "A hurried note with the article from *Rugby World*. It is part of a chat that lasted a long time ... as you can guess. He's left out some bits that I would have liked in – for example, the tremendous support I have had from my wife and family etc, etc – things that are taken for granted so often. Next time maybe I can square the record."

As an accomplished rugby player Chalkie White was renowned for being tough and durable, tactically savvy, and he thought and prepared for the game far more than most. Combined with a teacher's mindset, his rugby playing experiences had prepared him for this moment. Occasions to obtain the latest coaching information were rare. In early 1967 Brian Lochore's All Blacks visited Welford Road, which was too good an opportunity to miss for Chalkie.

Ged remembers: "I think it's likely that Dad first met Charles Saxton (and probably Fred Allen too) in 1967 when New Zealand were touring the UK and played the Midlands, London & Home Counties at Welford Road. He'd have gone to the game aiming to meet the New Zealand coaches for an exchange of ideas and thoughts on how the game should be played and coached. I can remember standing at the end of the tunnel with Fred Cox (the groundsman) when Bedford's Danny Hearn was carried past me on a stretcher and I followed them into the changing room. I was ushered out, went back to the end of the tunnel and carried on watching the game.

"The New Zealand coaches would have been a huge influence on Dad. His saying, 'Pressure, Patience and Ploys' is a perfect example of Dad using other coaches' ideas for the benefit of his own players. He probably adapted Saxton's saying of using 'Position, Possession and Pace' to create his own, and now reading Dad's copy of Fred Allen's book *On Rugby* [published in 1970], I see a number of phrases, sayings and ideas in the book that would be familiar to a lot of players who played in teams that Dad coached."

One of those new ideas concerned Garry Adey, who joined Leicester in early 1967. A committed Leicestershire man from Loughborough who joined the Tigers and quickly had an impact at Number 8 through his uncompromising style of play. Along with Peter Wheeler, who arrived later, a hard edge was introduced along with a higher percentage of good ball, much to the satisfaction of the backs, and of course Chalkie.

At training one evening, Chalkie suggested that Garry, who had won under-15 county caps as a prop, should consider switching from back row

Rodger Arneil, David Matthews, Eric Bann, Roger Grove, and scrum-half John Allen

to front row. Garry was not enamoured with the suggestion but reluctantly agreed. After several buffetings Garry walked away saying, "Chalkie, I'm staying at Number 8 even if it's in the Extras or the Swifts – no more."

Local youngsters like Adey were far more typical arrivals at Tigers than established internationals from elsewhere. A rare exception was Rodger Arneil, already a Scottish cap and British Lion who joined in 1969. Grove recalls: "His height and general presence, particularly at line-outs, made him a great asset to ball-winning. Due to work and other demands and international duties there were numerous gaps in his continuity and attendance." He played 25 games in two seasons before moving to Northampton, which involved far less travelling for work.

Arneil was capped 22 times by Scotland between 1968 and 1972, and recalls: "I played my first game for Leicester at home against Wilmslow in November 1969, and scored a try in a game we unfortunately lost. I had originally lived in Galashiels in the Scottish Borders and had a job with Coats Patents, a company specialising in yarn manufacturing, based in Paisley. I was learning to be a management trainee, when I was transferred to their office in Leicester and joined Tigers. I stayed in a farmer's house in Tur Langton with Tom and Nancy Watts, where I was made very welcome. I have fond memories of Jerry Day, Tudor Thomas and of course Chalkie White, I also played in a very good back row with Garry Adey and Graham Willars. I'd toured with the British Lions to South Africa in 1968 and flew out to New Zealand with the Lions in 1971 as a replacement for Ireland's Mike Hipwell."

Roger Grove added: "Coaching was done through the more prominent and experienced players, normally teachers or the like. Full back Peter Colston, filled the player-coach role at Bristol when I played there, and this system quickly placed our methods far ahead of our opposition, tactically, and with the appropriate fitness levels. He pioneered a forward throwing at the line-out; previously wingers always used to do the job, but with Bristol's wingers struggling, I had a go, and it went from there. Leicester, like many other clubs were in lag and on reflection it was hardly surprising."

So, he recalls the arrival of Chalkie in 1967 as "a breath of fresh air", with the new coach well ahead of the game as practised at the time: "Anyone could bully a group of players around the pitch especially when they were tired and unable to answer back, but Chalkie was analytical and he posed the question to the players which made them think. He integrated the forwards with the backs rather than only practising group skills. I remember the first time I heard one of his sayings, which I liked, 'act quickly and keep it simple'. Like any radical changes of method, the players were cautious initially, perhaps because the role of coach had not been defined fully by the RFU at this point. As a facilitator, his general knowledge of the game was sufficient to recognise a problem and in doing so was prepared to communicate and enable a player to address and hopefully solve their own problems.

"In the early days, Chalkie had to step cautiously as older established players found the discipline of training quite difficult to take. Gradually, as Chalkie established himself players began to realise the advantage of organisation in all aspects of the game. The bulk of the players responded to the challenges his methods presented, while some players found difficulty in these methods, mainly the older personnel; I guess time would settle these differences, whatever their thoughts eventually more clubs appointed coaches."

It was also, Grove recalls, a pretty primally tough world: "In the '60s all successful clubs needed enforcers; it was their job to protect the skilful players in the team, and to dish it out when the occasion demanded. Mainly because referees had to exercise control single handily, touch judges were usually provided by the clubs therefore their opinion upon most issues was invalid, especially in Wales, consequently a lot of violent incidents took place behind the referee's back. Dave Watt provided the service for Bristol. He had a short fuse and operating from the second row could pose a risk for the front row forwards at scrum time when he 'sent one through'. Equally, Peter Tom seemed to have a calming influence upon potential aggressors within the opposition ranks; he certainly was an asset in enabling the game to proceed without too much hindrance."

Chalkie's encouragement of running rugby earned Grove's gratitude from the first minute of the first match of the 1967-68 season at Bedford: "Tigers received the kick off, and our forwards secured the ball. Mike Harrison, at centre, then broke the defending line and was tackled under the Bedford posts. Mike held on, releasing the ball to me, for a two-paces touchdown, all from the kick-off, in just 30 seconds! It was confirmed after the game was over that, for a short moment in time, I was the highest try scorer in the land, quite unusual for a front row forward. Thank you, Mike."

A 24-8 win in what was usually a tough local derby was a pretty good start, and Tigers won their first seven matches of the 1967-68 season, including a win over Harlequins at Twickenham. Nor was the end of this run, a 6-6 draw at home to Coventry, regarded as any sort of failure. While it was the third draw in a row with Coventry at Welford Road, they were the dominant club in English rugby and Tigers had not beaten them since 1959.

Grove remembers: "At this time Leicester rarely won against the Welsh teams at home and hadn't won away from Welford Road, in Wales, for years. Competition was always keen amongst the four main clubs within the Midlands. During the 1960s Coventry were always difficult to beat home or away, whereas, ourselves, Northampton and Moseley usually shared the honours. Coventry developed a most effective front five; their style of play took them collectively into the England team. They had a very successful set of backs, who couldn't fail with the amount of ball that was secured by their pack."

Nor, in spite of that fine start, were Chalkie's early years the overnight, instant success his later achievements and reputation might have suggested. As he himself remembered, there was something of a falling off as the 1967-68 season progressed, bringing him into more active involvement.

Rex Thorpe, a Tigers watcher for more than half a century, recalled: "It was not all plain sailing in the early days; change was not what some players wanted. There was a meeting between Chalkie and the players to discuss the changes to their training regime, and after much discussion Chalkie White asked the players, 'Do you want me to coach you or carry on the way you are'. The majority wanted him to carry on."

Tigers remained good, rather than great, over the next few years, winning 27 games to 12 losses in 1968-69, 26 to 15 in 1969-70, and 23 to 20 in 1970-71. The Barbarians won all four festive period matches over this period, but there were some notable achievements within those results.

The 15-6 defeat of Coventry at Welford Road on March 19 1969, was a huge moment for the club, as Grove recalls: "Breaking the Coventry stranglehold over Leicester was probably Chalkie's first big achievement. Between 1959 and 1969 Leicester had not beaten Coventry once. Breaking the Coventry stranglehold ... was a reasonable statement, although it would be fair to point out that their degree of intimidation kept them well ahead of the field, it was not until the opposition were prepared to match their aggression that the results became more balanced."

Peter Wheeler joined Leicester Tigers from Old Brockleians RFC in November 1969

Players who were to have a significant impact on the club were starting to arrive, according to Grove: "Bleddyn Jones arrived from south Wales and soon established himself in the first team. John Elliot, from Nottingham, and ex-Loughborough Colleges occupied the hooking spot during the late '60s then Peter Wheeler arrived from the London area about the same time as Dave Pickering, a Scot, both very capable players with high potential. Peter was quick to display his potential and soon established himself in the top spot. He was part of the new generation in the club and contributed greatly to the successes to come at the Tigers.

"In 1970 Dave Shaw arrived, he was at Loughborough Colleges before joining Leicester, when Tigers were short of second row players. Peter Tom and Kevin Andrews were winding up; Eric Bann was installing himself, therefore Dave Shaw was able to fill the emerging gap. Dave was a serious student of the game and contributed well. He was a master at Worksop College when playing for Leicester, but unfortunately left to join Headingley at the beginning of 1972 season, later becoming the RFU's Director of Academies. Doug Norman, the Tigers' President 'recruited' Nick Joyce in 1968, after a Leicestershire Schools tour, in three seasons he played for the Swifts aged 16, the Extras aged 17, and the 1st XV against Fylde aged 18 in 1971."

Nick Joyce joined Leicester, aged 16, in 1968

Grove recalls that Chalkie's coaching made a big difference to recruitment, with local players keen to join Leicester: "I remember Dave Forfar coming to training. Dave was the Lewis Moody of the late '60s. Not a creative player but nothing would get past him; my memory of him was scrambling on the ground fighting for the ball. Ball-playing opposition backs must have despaired with Forfar, as he never bought dummies, and more often than not finished up with man and ball. He was extremely popular both on and off the field, very dry and very funny."

While the 1969-70 season brought a chastening 35-0 Christmas thumping by the Barbarians, its last few weeks saw a home win over Newport and the first defeat of Coventry at Coundon Road since March 1954. The following year was less successful, with a run of eight wins in the last ten matches needed to avert the Tigers' first losing record since 1957-58.

It was a record which, in modern, professional, competitive rugby might have led to a sacking. Tigers committee, aware of the effectiveness of much of the work Chalkie was putting in and also of the extent to which coaching was making ground as an accepted part of the game, instead chose to reinforce his role.

Grove, who was appointed captain at the same time, recalls: "At the end of 1971 season I was approached by the committee as my name had been put forward for the captaincy. The main issue was 'how did I get on with Chalkie', as the club intended to pass more responsibility towards him. I was quite agreeable with his methods although I was aware not everyone agreed with the way he worked. After every match, Chalkie and I had a quick casual meeting to talk over immediate thoughts and would back that up with a phone call on Sunday evening.

"Along with captains and secretaries from the Extras and Swifts we would pick the teams for the following weekend. These meetings took place before Tuesday training, which limited the available time as Chalkie and I needed to get on with training. I was living and working near Peterborough, a 65-mile drive, they were always busy evenings.

"Chalkie was present throughout the introduction and promotion of coaching, and it appeared that the RFU became aware that most clubs with any foresight were formalising their own brand of coaching. During the summer of 1971, Chalkie and I were invited to attend a weekend course for coaches and captains at Lilleshall Hall in Shropshire. Most senior clubs were invited and sessions were staffed by the Union's 'top badges'. The main message was 'to go forth and teach or coach'. Judging by those in attendance, the captains spoke for themselves, the RFU were taking the first steps at organising a coaching set-up. There were also recently retired players who in later years went on to occupy important spots on the coaching ladder. The door was now open to enable players to learn the game properly which enabled young lads who had never played rugby before to dip their toe in the water. It was after the RFU course that we arranged the first-ever Leicester Tigers pre-season training weekend at Cromer.

"All serious clubs trained twice each week. Quite regularly we would play mid-week, so we could be playing three games in eight days. Obviously, these matches were against colleges, forces teams and authorities, therefore training would be reduced otherwise family contact would be minimal. The Barbarians game at Christmas was a massive event, therefore attendance for training in December went sky high. The whole day was a massive happening for the players and their families. The fixture certainly put the Tigers apart from the rest!"

12

The Competitive Era Arrives – 1971-72

The 1970-71 season also brought, along the corridors of power at Twickenham, discussions and decisions which would transform English club rugby and provide the framework for Chalkie's greatest achievements as a coach.

It was particularly momentous for RFU committee members, since it acknowledged for the first time that the County Championship, played by the county unions and which formed their personal powerbases, might not be ideally suited to its role as the English game's pre-eminent competition and route for progression by ambitious players towards international recognition.

It was part of a process of modernisation which the game's rulers, committed ideologically to amateurism, feared would ultimately lead to professionalism and, whatever one thinks of their priorities, it is hard to deny that they were ultimately proved right.

Tired of their exclusion from power structures and an endless diet of friendly matches, the leading clubs became more assertive, in 1968 staging a series of meetings chaired by Ronnie Boon of London Welsh. Their proposal for a 25-member national league was rejected out of hand by the RFU as 'against the interests of amateurism'. The clubs responded by forming their first representative body, the Association of Gate-Taking Clubs, which continued to press for the introduction of some competitive rugby.

In 1970 the RFU set up a sub-committee chaired by Micky Steele-Bodger, in spite of his magnificently old school name and appearance, a progressive member of the hierarchy, later among the leading figures in enabling the 'free gangway' for amateur players between the two rugby codes, assisted by former England wing John Smith and Bob Weighill, a committee man who became Secretary of the RFU in 1974.

In October 1970, with most RFU attention focussed on their centenary season, they recommended the creation of an 'RFU Knock-Out Competition'. After consultation it was agreed at the December Executive Committee to recommend a start the following season, 1971-72. The proposal was for a

Former England international Micky Steele-Bodger, who won nine caps in 1947-48

competition based on the FA Cup with regional preliminary rounds contested by junior clubs, leading up to national rounds for which 32 nominated clubs would pre-qualify.

Old values did not go entirely by the board. It was proposed that the winners should receive a plaque rather than a cup, that the final would not necessarily be at Twickenham and that 'there should be no mention of leagues' in connection of the new competition. Steele-Bodger, who became chair of the sub-committee responsible for the competition, noted that they needed a fairer season of qualification for the later rounds than nomination by committees, and that this should only last for the first season.

Traditionalist media were clearly unimpressed. This striking break with previous practices went unmentioned in Uel Titley and Ross McWhirter's *Centenary History of the Rugby Football Union*, which instead found space to comment on the menu at the Centenary Dinner, while the first season was also scarcely more noticed in what proved (perhaps uncoincidentally) to be the final edition of the *Playfair Rugby Football Annual*.

There was no separate section for it in a publication which dedicated space to the Universities (*both of them…*), the Hospitals Cup, the Armed Forces, the Barbarians and the Middlesex Sevens, and no report of the final. There was a photograph of the winning Gloucester team, but their triumph merited two short paragraphs in the 'Season in the West' section, much less than the space devoted to Gloucestershire's first County Championship win since 1937.

Gloucester Captain Mike Nicholls is presented with the inaugural RFU Knockout Cup following the 1972 final at Twickenham

Not that anyone in Gloucester will have been too concerned. Their prop Robin Cowling, later to join Tigers, recalls: "I won the first of four RFU Knockout Cups while with Gloucester in 1972. It was the inaugural year of the competition, and there was a real excitement in the city. Moseley had England lock Nigel Horton sent off after only three minutes and they ended the game with only 12 men after two of their players went off injured. It's fair to say we dished out some punishment that day and lived up to our reputation as being the 'Leeds United of rugby'. We went out to do a job and we did it. Needless to say, the Press didn't like us for it. No-one in Gloucester cared about that, though, and our local MP Sally Oppenheim-Barnes took us on a tour of the Houses of Parliament to celebrate."

The *Playfair*'s Midlands correspondent Geoffrey Green gave most emphasis to complaints about scheduling from club fixture secretaries but did acknowledge the run to the final by Moseley, attributed to the appointment of former captain John White as coach. Moseley had become the first English club to 1,000 points, with full back Sam Doble contributing an all-time record 581, and won more matches than ever before in their history. Green argued, in a passage suggesting that Tigers had given little publicity to Chalkie's role: "Leicester set out some years ago to show off the advantages of a team coach, and have suffered through not keeping it up. Moseley had seen the light, it only remains for Coventry to do the same, if they delay much longer, they will miss the boat altogether."

The Tigers' cup debut had been inauspicious, with the first of what proved to be a series of away draws sending them to Beeston to play Notts (who were not to become Nottingham until 1974). Although not far down the road, Notts had been only an intermittent presence on Tigers fixture lists, but their recent improvement had been reflected in the scheduling of a visit to Welford Road later that season. They showed quite how deserved that elevation was by defeating Tigers 10-3, with Chalkie and his defeated squad taking particular notice of the 19-year-old full back instrumental in their defeat – William Henry Hare (nicknamed 'Dusty' as a two-day-old baby by his father, due to him looking as if he'd been 'born in a barn'), a young farmer who was already a first-class cricketer with Nottinghamshire. Revenge was to be taken with a 40-9 hammering at Welford Road with John Duggan, Peter Wheeler and Bob Barker all crossing twice, but the disappointing pattern of Tigers' early years in the cup had been set.

Other than the cup it was not a bad season for Tigers. The losing run against the Barbarians ended with a 20-14 victory and there were wins over cup winners Gloucester, Bristol and, perhaps most cherished of all, a double over Newport. The Gwent club were perhaps not the force of old, but had inflicted so many hammerings in the past that these wins, particularly the 25-11 win at Rodney Parade, meant a great deal to the club.

Dual-code international winger Keith Fielding, who was also capped by GB RL, playing in a special game to mark the RFU's Centenary, when England & Wales faced Scotland & Ireland at Twickenham 1970. He also achieved success in the popular BBC programme Superstars (1977-82).

Tigers also beat Moseley 11-9, with tries by Garry Adey and Graham Willars, when they met at Welford Road on November 27 and looked to have scored over them significantly earlier in the season, but that triumph proved short-lived.

England winger Keith Fielding got married and moved from Birmingham to Leicestershire at the beginning of the season, taking up a teaching post at Alderman Newton's Grammar School, having met Deputy Head Tudor Thomas while on teaching practice at New Parks Boys School. In an era when Leicester had few current international players, it was a considerable coup when Thomas persuaded Keith to switch allegiance from Moseley to Leicester, on the understanding that he started in the Extras.

The England winger played two weeks in the Extras, scoring a hat-trick, before being given his debut away to Harlequins at Twickenham on September 25 1971, where Tigers won 20-17.

"Following the game," recalled Keith. "I went for a steak meal with full back Robin Money and Tudor Thomas – I think we did a runner and left Tudor to pay the bill! The next week I found myself in the second team in favour of returning-from-injury John Duggan. After a discussion with selection committee members about the selection protocol that was put to me and I agreed to, I was disappointed and got in touch with Moseley who told me I was welcome to return as long as I started in the thirds which I did in mid-week, the following Saturday I played in Moseley's 1st XV and the following week in the England final trial!"

Club captain Roger Grove's recollection of Fielding's brief stay differs from that of the England winger, but is not necessarily incompatible with it. What both versions show is Chalkie's rejection of the old 'invitation' model for Tigers, with stars allowed to come and go as they wished. There could be no special cases in a team context, with everyone contributing fully to the cause.

"At the start of my captaincy, Keith Fielding left Moseley and made himself available for Leicester," recalled Grove. "He came with a huge reputation of try scoring with both club and England. Collective training was becoming an essential to any ambitious club and, early season, Chalkie and I decided that training attendance would be a factor in team selection. Most of the players accepted the logic of this. An immediate problem emerged when Keith announced that he would not train due to the distance he lived away from Leicester. Sadly, we had to part company, and Keith returned to Moseley."

A more durable relationship was formed with centre Brian Hall, who would become not only a valued player, but a close family friend. He remembers: "I was a late convert to rugby. At Mundella Grammar School I played football and took up rugby only when a new Welsh PE master arrived. I met Chalkie through playing in the County Championship with Notts, Lincs and Derby, where he was the coach, at the time I was playing in the centre for Notts RFC. He told me I should come to Leicester, and I did at the start of the 1971-72 seasons. I had a job with a Leicester company at the time so the move made sense.

Brian Hall – 1st XV captain in 1977-78

"Chalkie asked me to pick him up for training which I did and I carried on for the next 12 years. I didn't ask him why, but I drove fast and Chalkie didn't. The cynics used to say it was because I wanted to be in the side, but there is also no truth in the rumour that when Paul Dodge got in to the 1st XV I tried to convince Chalkie he would make a better winger than a centre during the journey!"

1971 also brought a significant windfall for Chalkie and his siblings when their father won £69,000 on the football pools, equivalent in purchasing power to around £870,000 in 2025. Annie was able to give up her job at the sweet factory and the couple moved to a bungalow in Green Lane, Carlisle. Albert's death from a stroke in 1973 meant that a considerable sum had to be paid in death duties, but at the time of the win he had settled £5,000 on each of his three children, almost certainly more than a year's pay for Chalkie at Nottingham High School.

When their next-door neighbour in Lambley Lane, Burton Joyce, died, also in 1973, Doris and he used their extra cash to buy his house and knock the two together into a much larger dwelling.

"When Dad was knocking the two houses together," recalled Stella. "Over a period of weeks, he had stripped out the copper hot water tank, various electrical cables and lead from the roof of the 'new' house. All this was loaded on to the back of the Land Rover he had borrowed from the school. On a very hot day in summer 1973, Dad and I drove to a scrap dealer's yard near

Chalkie and Doris at Lambley Lane

Robin Cowling (centre) brought a wealth of experience when he joined Leicester: (L-R) Peter Wheeler, Nick Joyce, Cowling, Steve Johnson

Nottingham and off-loaded everything. Because they made a mistake, all the metal was weighed as copper which was more valuable than lead, so we walked away with a load of cash (much more than we should have had). Dad drove out of the yard 'burning rubber' and laughing gleefully!!

"Another aspect of the task of knocking two houses together," added Stella. "Was the element of 'unpaid' labour, with Dad doing as much of the work as possible due to working to a budget, which meant Ged, me and, on occasion Nick, provided unpaid labour for months. From the start, this included learning how to: clean off used bricks; correctly calculate the mix and load up a mixer to make concrete; build a concrete drive in sections; make shuttering for the concrete we were laying; strip wallpaper, and take down lath and plaster ceilings. All done to the exacting near-professional standards set by Dad."

13

Lyons and Tigers – Leicester's Youth Team

Important as the arrival of competitive rugby was to prove, the landmark event of the 1971-72 season, perhaps one of the biggest and best decisions in the long history of the club, was the formation of the Leicester Tigers Youth team after a meeting in March 1972.

The initial idea for a youth team came with the emergence of an exceptional group of players who had represented Leicestershire U15 at schoolboy level during the 1971-72 season. Keith Smith, Stuart Dexter, Jonathan Flint and Steve Kenney had all also played in the England U15 final trial, with only Kenney winning selection for the final squad. He also captained the team in their first game.

Destined for a long career as Tigers scrum-half, Kenney recalls: "Dave Lyons was in charge of that successful schools team and he just said, 'This is too good an opportunity to miss – we have got to get these lads into the Leicester Tigers'."

Lyons, an archetypal figure of the post-war English game, was a PE teacher from Cardiff who taught at Roundhill High School and had played six games at centre for Tigers in the 1966-67 season, scoring in the 25-10 defeat of Bristol at Welford Road just before Christmas.

Recalling the emergence of the youth strategy, Lyons commented: "The roots of Leicester Tigers Youth were embedded in the Leicestershire Schools U15 Group. In the 1967-68 season I coached with Steve Betts, then the following season I was in charge of the U15 Group with Doug Cox as assistant when regional competition in Leicestershire (North, Central, South and West) began for the U14 level which obviated the need for U15 trials. The beginning of all-day squad coaching on Sundays at Roundhill and Thurmaston Schools, in 1969-70 and 1970-71 contributed to the unbeaten U15 season, including a famous win over Yorkshire Schools, which led directly to the establishment of Tigers Youth by myself and Jerry Day – a great man who did so much for Leicester rugby."

The vital meeting was held at the Leicester clubhouse, with the club represented by Jerry Day, Eric Lacey and Harry Sibson: "My request of being

Dave Lyons congratulates Roundhill School's Leicestershire U15 players (L-R) Keith Smith, Stuart Dexter and Steve Kenney

in sole charge of the Youth team was accepted, with Micky Deathe as my assistant," recalled Lyons. "The first fixtures were arranged at the end of the 1971-72 season against Nottingham and then Derbyshire, both at U16 level. Both games resulted in big wins. This led to Joe Pickup being appointed by the club as Match Secretary of the Tigers Junior Rugby Sub-Committee, to formulate the first full season's fixtures for 1972-73."

The objectives of the sub-committee were three-fold: to organise as many fixtures as possible outside Leicestershire, but not more than 20 miles away; to charge £1 subscription with full membership rights; and the youth team was to train separately and should not be used to fill gaps in the three senior sides.

The inaugural match was held on April 15 1972, against Nottingham Cubs, with a debut victory of 78-9. It was the beginning of a process which contributed to Leicester's greatest successes. The team that day was: Marcus Hellyer; Richard Lett, Mark Wyatt, Stuart Dexter, Keith Smith; Jonathan Flint, Steve Kenney (captain); Philip Hemsill, Mick Briggs, Cezary Siwek, John Fraser, Richard Hull, Joseph Krych, Andrew 'Angus' Collington, Paul Nennett.

Boosted by the addition of several older (U19) players, particularly forwards who had played at higher county age groups and at local senior level, the youth team's first full season, 1972-73, was "felt to be a promising start" according to the Leicester Tigers committee minutes.

Commenting on that inaugural season, when fixtures were arranged against teams from Wales and the North of England including the rugby union clubs in Wigan and Widnes, Dave Lyons said: "The match between Aberaman Youth and Leicester Youth grew out of the Leicestershire U15 team. Matches with Cynon Valley Schools, based in Aberdare, had been arranged some years earlier by myself and sports teachers in the Cynon Valley. I wrote and prepared the programme at Roundhill High School and arranged for hosting of players and staff in Syston and district. Joe Pickup (ex-Chairman of Leicestershire RU) had been appointed Fixture Secretary of the new Leicester Youth and I worked closely with Joe in the inaugural year setting up a fixture list.

"I had a relationship with some Cardiff schools, whereby teachers and players of the visiting team would stay for a couple of days at the homes of their opposite numbers. I did this at Roundhill from 1967 to 1974, and on one occasion we put up almost 100 people – three rugby teams and three soccer teams – from a Cardiff school. Arthur Thomas, the school's PE teacher was a friend of mine who had played for Wales' amateur soccer team when he was only 18 years old. Those visits were mostly twice a year, one home, and one away."

Any youth system needs good products to prove its worth, and Lyons vividly remembers his first sighting of a young Tiger who would help transform the fortunes of the team: "In about March 1969, one of the lads at Roundhill High School, called Mick Selby, himself a very good soccer player, and in the same year as Steve Kenney, told me of a very good footballer at Syston Junior School. I showed an interest and remember young Selby saying, 'but you'll never get him to play rugby – he loves soccer too much!' Within days I made sure I went to Syston Juniors to view the new prospect, and Steve Kenney came with me."

Kenney, who was hauled out of his year two humanities class to accompany Lyons, also remembers the occasion well: "We drove to my old junior school, St. Peter and St. Paul's, to watch an 11-year-old, Paul Dodge, playing football for the school. As we stood on the touchline, Dave asked me, 'what do you think of the goalkeeper'. 'He's not bad, and he's not let any goals in,' I replied. 'That lad will play for England at whatever sport he decides to play. Do you know his mum and dad?' I didn't, but my parents did, and the rest is history as they say.

"His instinctive 'ball sense', movement and spatial awareness convinced me," continued Lyons. "Consequently, when the new school year started at

"When the youth team began, a star amongst stars appeared," commented Chalkie about Paul Dodge, who would later captain his club and country

Roundhill, in September 1969, I made sure that Paul Dodge was at the first practice for the Hawks, the U13 rugby team – the U14s being the Ravens. I made sure 'Dodgy' was in the squad for the season's opening match for the U13s although he was at U12 level. This was simply to get him playing rugby as opposed to soccer, because his age group had not played rugby before. It would take me two to three months to get them to the level required to play 15-a-side competitively. It worked! 'Dodgy' was hooked.

"I think Dodgy played for the Swifts in the same season that he played for the Midland Counties (East) v Australia at Welford Road. In the opening minutes he split the Australian defence before delivering a perfect pass for the wingman to run in the opening try. From Leicester Tigers 3rd XV to that level in a few months, it must have been the half-time team-talks in the Swifts or maybe it was something Fred Cox, the groundsman, put in the oranges!"

However, Kenney's account describes Lyons as much more than a talent-spotter. As a coach he set standards that prepared his young charges for the step up into the adult game: "Dave was the driving force and he set very high standards, telling us at school that the tools of our trade were our kit and boots. We had to have ironed shirts and shorts and clean boots, I remember one game when he didn't let Paul Dodge play because although his boots were clean, the soles of his boots were dirty. He wanted players who were very fit and very prepared, and to have different ways of playing, but the responsibility was put back on to the players on the pitch to work it out themselves. He taught us to be pros, so when I later had Chalkie White as my coach I'd already had a very good grounding."

While not actively involved, Chalkie's overall role at the club and an inherent interest in the processes of coaching meant that he took a strong interest in the youth team, where possible watching their training sessions and matches. From long experience of both, Kenney recognised the similarities between his two teacher-coaches: "He was very much along the Chalkie White lines in terms of giving you all the tools but you had to take them out on to the pitch and use them. Even at school, as 11-year-olds, Dave Lyons would get us together in a room and talk to the team and to the individuals, and you had to have a notebook to take it all down. It was done to help your understanding of what worked. Chalkie would also do that, pointing at little incidents in a game, talking you through and asking why you made certain decisions and you had to have an answer. You learned that way rather than just forgetting it, and Dave was the same."

Scrum-half Steve Kenney in his debut season playing against the Barbarians in December

At one Sunday morning session Steve Kenney was asked to do some work with the U15 scrum-half, Marcus Rose. After the session Dave asked what he thought of him, to which Kenney replied, 'I think he's a very good rugby player but not at scrum-half'. Dave agreed and switched him to full back.

Due to his rugby commitments at Loughborough Grammar School Rose didn't play for the Tigers Youth team, however the club kept an eye on him, and Rose made his debut for Leicester at full back against Bristol in 1975, and went on to gain ten caps for England.

It was not all plain sailing, however, as Lyons explains: "By the end of March into

April, Leicester refused my request to rid themselves of the 3rd XV which I considered to be an impediment to the development of professional standards at the club. There was a particular and impending example of that for the start of the next season. The only player from the youth squad, at the end of that highly successful first season, who would not qualify, by age, for the team that coming season was an outstanding young flanker called Stuart Clow. Stuart was clearly of 1st XV quality and should not, by any measure, be forced to play at 3rd XV level simply because it suited the club's unwritten, but often spoken, policy.

Marcus Rose playing for the Midlands

"Also, there would be unaccountable and long-lasting damage done to the relationship with local clubs, which, through the success of the youth team, not only in results but by promoting and strengthening those relationships, had been waxing strong. Sadly, the club, via diktat of the committee, refused my written argument for change and resorted to the *status quo*. I felt, through my commitment to Stuart Clow and his future development as a rugby player, and to all those who would follow him, that I could not accept that they would be required to move automatically from a highly organised, professional outfit to a largely makeshift bunch of over-aged enthusiasts and willing amateurs. So, sadly, I resigned and perhaps even more sadly, Micky Deathe chose to join me.

"I know that the existence of the Swifts at the time presented an impenetrable barrier to having beneficial relations with the local clubs in Leicestershire, whereby they would willingly send their best young players to the Tigers to benefit the players, Leicester FC, the clubs themselves and the whole of Leicestershire rugby. Don't forget that only a few years earlier the Tigers had been an 'invitation only' club and did not see local rugby as relevant. Consequently, my developmental concepts were, apparently, totally outside the club's understanding, hence the parting of the ways."

Future Leicester captain Ian Smith joined the youth team for the 1974-75 season. As a pupil of Wyggeston Grammar School for Boys, where he'd been nicknamed 'Dosser' by his back-row teammate Vinnie O'Hagan due to his playing position rather than for a propensity to fall asleep in lessons, Smith

Leicestershire Colts 1974-75
Back Row (L-R): John Wilkins, Neil Hall, Paul Dodge, Paul Stone, Vendis Afflick, Steve Mitchell, Mark Ball
Seated (L-R): Mick Newton, Steve Collins, Keith Smith, Angus Collington (captain), Stuart Dexter, Dave Putnam
Front Row (L-R): Steve Kenney, Mick Lee

had a first class grounding in rugby from two former Leicester Tigers captains: introduced to rugby by full back Robin Money, then strongly influenced by Head of Sport, Mike Harrison (also a product of Wyggeston Grammar School for Boys and Loughborough Colleges). Leicester-born Harrison made his debut for the club in 1962 and played 210 games for the 1st XV as well as five England final trials.

"Mike was very much a Leicester Tigers man," recalled former Leicester captain Roger Grove. "He played from the 1960s and has given of himself during every decade until now both as a player and an administrator. There are many who considered that he should have been selected for England. His knowledge of the game was enormous and he taught many notable names who later appeared for Tigers. In later years, Mike and I travelled the globe in pursuit of rugby and we hold a strong bond which still exists to this day."

Initially coached by Dave Lyons and then by his successor ex-Tigers player Rex Skelton. 'Dosser' Smith says: "Rex was a good coach and looked after us socially – he always bought the lads a drink. My teammates included future 1st XV players Steve Redfern and Vendis Afflick. At 16 I played in the Swifts with the French brothers Ray and Roy, then my first game in the Extras, when Dave Forfar got injured, at 18, and by 1978 I managed to get a place on the bench for that year's John Player Cup final against Gloucester at Twickenham."

Steve Redfern made his 1st XV debut in October 1976

The likely impact of young players who had come up through this route could be foreseen, as Kenney recalls: "We hadn't been used to losing games in the schools or youth teams, and obviously the young guys come in and you want to make a name for yourself. I remember a training session when I was in the 1st XV when Stuart Redfern, Chris Tressler and Wayne Richardson were scrummaging against us and took one against the head. It showed their spirit. They weren't giving way just because those guys were internationals.

"I knew that when they came up, they'd do well, and wouldn't be happy to sit in the 2nd XV. We all wanted a piece of that. It was a team that was there to win. The youth team graduates became a core part of a team which went from strength to strength under Chalkie, and provided the success upon which every subsequent generation has been built."

The blueprint for the future of the Tigers had been set, and over the years the products of the youth team went on to put the Tigers at the forefront of English rugby.

14

Building the Foundations – 1972-76

It would, though, be a while before Lyons' tiger cubs reached the 1st XV. The 1972-73 season saw the try revalued to four points, leading Chalkie and new captain Graham Willars to set a target of matching the 1,000 points that Moseley and Coventry had achieved in the final season of the three-point try, and 30 wins. They fell just short on both counts, scoring 988 – which, including 148 tries, would have been a club record even without the arrival of the four-pointer – and winning 29 of their 46 games. The 683 points conceded were also a record, and would have been even without the revaluation.

The Barbarians were beaten again, as were Gloucester, Newport and Llanelli at Welford Road. The club also enjoyed their first cup run of any note, even if they came close to embarrassment in the preliminary round, scraping past Nuneaton – regular opponents who rarely troubled Tigers, although they had beaten them in 1968 – by 23-22. Another squeaker took them past another familiar foe, Bedford, 21-17 in the first round at Goldington Road, then Hinckley were beaten 16-4 in round two. However, with ambition beginning to flower, a 7-0 defeat to Sale in the quarter-final at Brooklands ended the cup run.

Tigers could at least plead ill-luck of the draw. After seven cup ties over three years they had yet to play at Welford Road, and their vulnerability on the road was shown spectacularly by a 45-6 humiliation at Coventry, that season's cup-winners, and a 42-0 stomping at Bath.

A notable arrival that season was England outside-half Alan Old, but injuries limited him to five matches, four of them at centre with Bleddyn Jones now firmly established at outside-half. Abrasively intelligent and always prepared to call out stupidity, however eminent – Alan Old has recalled his no-holds-barred disagreements with selectors as a regular feature of England training sessions – already had five caps when he arrived from hometown club Middlesbrough. Dave Shaw, a teacher at Worksop College who played 57 matches in the second row for Tigers between 1970 and 1973, was instrumental

Alan Old – "Chalkie was a good friend and the best coach I ever experienced"

in getting him a job at the school and steered him, with assists from Horrocks-Taylor and Mike Gavins, towards his club

"I first became involved with Chalkie when I joined Leicester in August 1972," said Old. "Until then all my rugby had been for Middlesbrough where at that time the coaching was organised and mainly delivered by the captain. From day one I was impressed with Chalkie's organisation, passion and understanding of the game at team, unit and individual level. Two situations which I experienced with Chalkie demonstrate why he was so well liked and popular with his players.

"In one of my first games for Leicester, against Saracens, we spent ten minutes playing to Chalkie's instructions of feeding the ball quickly to the wing, then through our excellent back row keeping possession we would swing the ball out to the other wing. Whilst we had made some good progress and gained position we hadn't cracked the defence. As I had played against the opposition full back a couple of times, I said to Brian Hall – one of our centres –that with the next piece of possession I would drop the ball on the full back's head. I duly did this and, under pressure from Brian, the full back dropped it and one of the Leicester players picked up and scored the opening try. By mixing up the tactics we then enjoyed a comfortable victory.

"However, after the game Chalkie took me aside and said, 'You changed my tactics'. To which I replied, 'but I'm on the field and you are off it.' To which he responded, 'Good answer, we are going to get along well!', and we did. Although, because of injury, I spent only two seasons at Leicester, it was a privilege to be coached by Chalkie. I was with Leicester when I won further caps for England and I then went on the 1974 Lions tour."

Another notable addition late in his first season was Welsh flanker Paul Ringer, who joined in March 1973 and rapidly became the Leicester enforcer, as former teammate Robin Money explained: "Paul Ringer played open side and was a fearless tackler – he would put his head anywhere. As the team ran onto the field we would have a final word together before kick-off, but 'Ringo' was already in amongst the opposition players looking at numbers on jerseys till he found the outside-half and would always say that he should watch out all afternoon because he would be after him. On an Easter tour, against a northern club, he promised the opposition's fly half that if he did manage to catch the ball, he would get him all the same."

Paul Ringer playing for Monmouthshire against the All Blacks in 1978. He made 56 appearances for Leicester Tigers while studying at Clifton Teacher Training College in Nottingham

Paul also had what he called his 'sports' car, which was a clapped out Morris Minor 1000 with a golf club, tennis racket and a football in the back window, which was the only link the car had to sport. He would always arrive early because his car had no reverse gear and he needed to secure a parking place he could exit in a forward direction.

Ringer was destined for either, according to perspective, notoriety or martyrdom for being sent off in the ferociously-contested England v Wales match at Twickenham in 1980. As Old recalled: "It was very interesting playing with Paul as he was totally committed to protecting his fly half and other backs. When he was sent off at Twickenham for 'offences' against both Dusty Hare and John Horton, if he had actually managed to remove them from the pitch, then I would have been the replacement. I did ask him if I would have received the same treatment from him – he just grinned and said that he would have to think about it! It was great to have him on your side."

Anecdotes of his being warned for 'trying too hard' while at Tigers probably owe more to Welsh stereotypes about English club rugby, but he has recorded that former teammate Peter Wheeler, who was among the players who tried hard to raise his spirits as they socialised in the evening after his sending-off.

Ringer became a regular the following season, another marked by mixed fortunes. The 24 wins included one at Stradey Park, little more than a year after the All Blacks had fallen there. In the cup, there was an early exit at Northampton and the Barbarians won 16-7 only five days after one of the better results of the year, an 18-12 win at Old Deer Park over London Welsh, whose appearance on the fixture list, like that of Gosforth, showed recognition of upwardly mobile clubs.

Garry Adey (ball-in-hand) was Chalkie's most selected player with 376 appearances. A tough and uncompromising forward, described by Ian Smith as "The hardest man I ever played alongside." Also in shot are (L-R) Bob Rowell, Eric Bann, Chris Baynes and John Dawson

If the Barbarians were the fixed highlight of the season, overseas touring teams – arriving more frequently in the 1970s – were seen as the great thrill of the pre-competitive era, bringing both novelty and a touch of the exotic to Welford Road.

First to arrive that season were Fiji. Touring the British Isles and Canada, the Fijians had earlier opened the centenary season of Swansea RFC but spoilt the celebrations at St. Helen's by beating their hosts 31-0. Swansea's season improved somewhat by winning the Welsh Merit Table.

It was only a fortnight since England had narrowly beaten Fiji 13-12 in the opening match of the five-game tour of Fiji and New Zealand, which had denied Old's services to Tigers, and would shortly be transformed from fiasco to triumph by a 16-10 defeat of the All Blacks in Auckland – the first victory in New Zealand by any of the 'home' unions – which still looks among the more extraordinary results in the game's history.

As noted in the match programme: "There is, no doubt, this is one of the great occasions in the history of Leicester rugby, and we give an extremely warm welcome to tonight's glamorous visitors. Probably very few sides have captured the imagination of the rugby loving public to the same extent as the Fijians, not only for their uninhibited love of running with the ball on every possible occasion, but also for their sheer skill and exuberance when doing so.

"When they first came to Britain in 1964, they almost caused a dramatic sensation, by holding a representative Welsh side to 28-22. Even the ranks of Tuscany could scarce forbear to cheer at the Arms Park that day. Praise indeed! Since that time, they have taken on a more disciplined type of rugby, but nothing can subdue their un-orthodoxy in open play. What is truly astonishing is they can produce a team of such calibre out of a population smaller than that of our own city."

Leicester full back Robin Money remembers: "I joined Leicester in 1968 where I came under the coaching influence of Chalkie White who was way ahead of his time as a thinker on the game and as a coach. We played Fiji at Welford Road in September 1973, the previous Saturday they had beaten a strong Swansea side 31-0. The night before the match I had a dream that late in the game, in a packed stadium, we were leading by one score when a 17st Fiji winger came hurtling toward me with the try line close by, which woke me up with a start.

"The next night, at the match and by a strange coincidence, we were leading by a score and a very large quick Fijian winger was heading my way ball-in-hand. This time it was real and I couldn't wake up. Fortunately, for me, the touchline was close by. I think I shut my eyes, got between his legs and he fell over me into touch. We won the game 22-17 and many pints were drunk in celebration."

"There is no doubt in my mind that Chalkie should have been the England coach," Money continued. "He certainly had a real positive effect on me as a player."

Three weeks later Tigers defeated the Sydney club Randwick, famed for the attacking style adopted in the 1920s under the influence of Wallabies centre Cyril Towers.

Peter Wheeler kicked two goals against Randwick

The two victories were long-remembered highlights, but were arguably a mixed blessing. Defeats at Coventry, Northampton, and a cup exit at Franklin's Gardens followed in the next few weeks. By early December, *Leicester Mercury* writer Paul Neal was reflecting: "At this time of year, one is accustomed to talking about a Leicester Tigers side animated by the prospect of the approaching Barbarians match and preparing itself for the occasion with a series of convincing wins. This picture is rather different this season.

"Although the Barbarians match tends to look after itself, in the sense that the players always raise their game, one can only feel that the apparent apathy about proceedings at present must have a harmful effect on performances. One of the difficulties, I'm sure, is that the club had two important games very early in the season against Fiji and Randwick. So the natural pattern, with the Barbarians game being the goal to work for, has been disrupted. The high point reached with the magnificent win against Fiji in only the fourth game of the season, and the second triumph over Randwick only a few weeks later has produced an inevitable backlash, which is part of the present problem.

"There are other factors too, in a number of positions the lack of competition has meant that some players have been sure of their places which is never a good thing. A corollary to this has been the frequent sketchy attendance at training, a situation that is bound to be reflected in the sort of unconvincing displays that have occurred more frequently in recent weeks than one would have liked. The matter of training is always a touchy issue. The very nature of this amateur game eschews compulsory attendance. Yet fitness and team work are so vital at the level Tigers play their rugby. Players do not relish the abrasive, close quarter exchanges, so inseparable from what is essentially a fierce contact game.

"Coventry invariably know they are a winner when they start to play a hard, aggressive type of game. It's no good saying the Counden Road bogey is to blame, for there are other examples of tough, torrid forward clashes that have gone against Tigers this season. Take Gloucester for instance, a team incidentally that usually beats Coventry or to a lesser extent Moseley, both have profited from out doing Tigers this season. It is a weakness in Leicester's game which many consider to be absolutely fundamental. There is a lot of truth in the old adage – win the forward battle and you win the game

"Part of the legacy that Tigers have inherited by switching the emphasis to total rugby is that no one in the mould of John Quick or Pete Tom have appeared. Say what you want about running rugby, but it's the side that dominates possession that calls the tune. Gloucester need not have bothered about bringing a back division when they played here; the forwards and goal kicker Peter Butler won the day.

"As I have mentioned, December 27 won't be too great a problem. Traditionally, the Barbarians game is a Christmas entertainment with plenty of running and passing. However, clubs these days are judged by their performances, against the teams that constitute the main core of top British rugby, in this respect Tigers face two very important games before the Barbarians."

As it happened, Tigers beat both Bristol and London Welsh before falling to the Barbarians, but the hint of concern was not misplaced. The following two seasons are covered in David Hands' club history under the title 'Back to the Depths'. There was an important new arrival at the start of 1974-75, in Gloucester prop Robin Cowling, who had moved to Market Harborough to take up a post as a farm manager. He had played 216 games for Gloucester, winning the first RFU Cup knock-out final in 1971-72, appearing for Western Counties against the All Blacks in 1972-73 and four consecutive County Championship finals.

"It was Peter Wheeler who persuaded me to come to Leicester," explained Cowling. "He had just got into the England set-up as understudy to John Pullin, and it was a toss-up between Leicester and Northampton as to which club I joined. Peter was one of the first captains who saw recruitment as part of their job, and he had put the effort in so it was Leicester Tigers I joined. I always liked the Leicester boys; it was a fixture we all looked forward to at Gloucester. I also got on very well with Graham Willars, we always had good nights out.

"Not many clubs had coaches at this time; Chalkie was the first coach to get rid of oranges at half-time. Bedford was always the first game of the season and he started by weighing us before and after the game to show our weight loss. Half-time oranges were replaced by a green liquid which helped with our rehydration."

Leicester Tigers – winners of the Midlands Sevens, 1974: (L–R): Bleddyn Jones, Graham Willars, Robin Money, Peter Wheeler, Mike Marshall, Brian Hall and John Reeve

Bedford were beaten 19-12 but, properly hydrated or not, Tigers had their first losing record, if only by a margin of 20 losses to 19, since 1957-58. Only 72 tries were scored in 40 matches, the Barbarians waltzed to a 43-4 win and, under the somewhat convoluted rules used in the early years of the tournament, Tigers did not even qualify for the Knockout Cup.

Cowling performed well enough to be an England reserve the following season, in an age before tactical replacements were permitted, kept in the shadows by the formidable Fran Cotton, but 1975-76 was not much better, with 23 wins to 21 defeats including a 20-11 loss to the Barbarians. It threatened at one point to be considerably worse with eight consecutive defeats – and if it was no shame to be beaten by Swansea or Gloucester, serious clubs no longer expected to have any difficulties with Oxford or Cambridge Universities.

The losing run was ended by the latest thing in exotic southern hemisphere visitors. Sydney club Eastern Suburbs were on a seven-match tour of England and Wales to celebrate their 75th anniversary. John Blondin, who captained the team after tour skipper Jimmy King had dislocated his shoulder, remembers:

The Barbarians' Mike Gibson grabs John Duggan's jersey, watched by Phil Bennett and Fijian international Pio 'Bosco' Tikoisuva, in the 1975 fixture

"The day before this game our Prime Minister, Gough Whitlam, was sacked by the Governor General which probably took our game off the front pages. Our goal kicker, Ross Field, had one or two kicks charged down when he went to adjust the ball. We could not do this in Australia however maybe local rules, which he was unaware of, worked in Leicester's favour. I do, however, have fond memories of Leicester having coached a former Scottish international Craig Joiner and also ex-Wallaby John Welborn, both of whom played for the club."

After 16 seasons and 457 appearances for Leicester Tigers, scrum-half John Allen, ended his playing career by scoring a try in a win against Bath on September 13 1975 and, much to the delight of the long time incumbent Stan Thorpe who commented "I've been waiting for this point!", promptly assumed the position of Treasurer on January 1 1976.

Grim rugby normality reasserted itself the following week, however, when Tigers lost 10-7 against Liverpool FC in the cup, now sponsored by cigarette manufacturers John Player. There was a home draw at last when the qualifiers were played, late in the season, for the following season's tournament. Tigers entertained Westleigh, a club from the Leicester suburbs, usually regarded as more feeder than rival, at Welford Road, and took no chances with selection, but they needed all the help they could get, scraping through 19-15. It was back on the road for the next round, to Kettering, where a 14-6 victory secured involvement in the 1976-77 tournament.

It seems unlikely that a modern coach would have survived two such modest seasons. The stands at Welford Road mixed echoing emptiness with a fair amount of grumbling. Thankfully, though, the relief expedition was on its way, perfectly timed and trained for the arrival of a new competitive dimension with the introduction, in 1976-77, of the Midlands Merit Table, a staging point in the game's gradual, reluctant progress towards accepting leagues.

It did appear, however, that Leicester's fortunes were about to turn, as Steve Kenney explained: "The 1975-76 season was the first year that first graduates from the youth team came into the senior squad, and although it wasn't a massive improvement on the previous season, the 1st XV did win more games than they lost. The attitude had changed, though, as the youngsters were not used to losing, but Chalkie now had the basis of the type of team he wanted. Leicester Tigers were now benefiting from some of the best local talent Leicestershire had to offer."

Examples of that new breed of Tiger included Jez Krych who made his debut, against Blackheath, on December 14 1974, and Angus Collington came on as a replacement against Moseley on March 19 1975. In addition, during the 1975-76

John Allen – who swapped his playing boots for book-keeping at Leicester Tigers

Former youth team player Angus Collington made his 1st XV debut against Moseley

season, debuts were handed to Steve Kenney, Jonathan Flint, Paul Dodge, Andy Beevers, Alastair Grocock and Marcus Rose.

"In 1974, as a 16-year-old, I played for both the Swifts and the Extras," explained Paul Dodge. "One of my early games for the Extras was during September against Coventry's 2nd XV at Welford Road. The Coventry back line was Bill Gittings at scrum-half, Dick Cowman at outside-half, Geoff Evans and Peter Preece in the centre, David Duckham on one wing and Peter Rossborough at full back. All were England internationals who'd started the season late and so were getting up to speed in the seconds. It was like chasing shadows that day and needless to say we lost, but it was one of the first big games I played in and I learned from these experiences when I made my 1st XV debut for Leicester in 1975 against Bedford."

Nor did Tigers give up on talent from other sources. Terry Burwell, destined for a highly influential career at the RFU, had already experienced the coaching of another of the great innovators, Jim Greenwood, at Loughborough University before arriving in 1975.

"I joined Leicester Tigers in 1975," commented Burwell. "After playing with Brian Hall for East Midlands v Middlesex. We both lived in Northampton at the time and, whilst I didn't drive, Brian certainly did and so long rugby discussions ensued up and down the A50. Brian had made similar journeys with Chalkie from Nottingham and it was from that we both became huge advocates of the 'coaching' and 'life' philosophy that Chalkie instilled in us.

"I was a full back at Loughborough College and again at Northampton, but my arrival coincided with Dusty Hare joining from Nottingham, so Chalkie suggested I play in the centre for the Swifts and then the Extras. I was fortunate at Loughborough to be coached by Jim Greenwood, one of the great coaches of the time and then equally fortunate to be under the tutelage of Chalkie, who was to become such a great coach and player influencer. Training on the Rec was unforgiving, the bank at the end of sessions was a lung-buster and leg-breaker but alongside this we developed skills and game management and a sense of togetherness that were Chalkie's *forte*. Everyone was engaged, no '1st XV and others', a club and coach committed to building a team of all levels and abilities.

"I spent hours post-training in the downstairs bar and again at the front of the bus, listening and learning, not just about rugby, as Chalkie invariably had a view and a perspective on everything. His mantra became my mantra; 'you're responsible for the ball through the next pair of hands and be sure that whatever you do, on or off the field, you leave your teammates, family and colleagues in a better place than when you started'.

"I remember watching the great Australian Schoolboys team – who were to become the 1984 Wallaby Grand Slam team – with him when they trained at Tigers, and it was obvious how his mind never stopped learning or thinking about the next stage of game development. First and foremost, he taught me honesty in appraising how I played, giving me the skill of self-analysis long before video and GPS, which ensured I could picture my game and those around us.

"He said, without arrogance, 'lots of people can tell you how well you played – I'm here to help you play better'. So much of what he did in team building was ahead of his time: pre-season at West Norfolk RUFC, shuttles on the sand dunes, sleeping in the changing rooms with Dave Forfar hiding all the sleeping bags. Then another year we went to Hoylake RFC on the Wirral, and a comment on an early Sunday morning run, as we ran along the beach to Royal Liverpool Golf Club and the Dee estuary, stuck in my memory. We stopped and Chalkie gathered us round then pointed across the river to Wales and quietly said 'the enemy lives over there', followed by a walk in silence back for breakfast."

"I've spoken to many Tigers teammates over the years and all agree that 'H.V.' influenced our lives beyond the grass rectangle – shaping our values and friendships ... quite simply he was coach, friend, mentor and in some ways father figure, but you also had to know when to stay clear as he could bite as well as feed, but always for the best." Terry Burwell

Policeman Steve Johnson had been on Leicester's radar for some time before he finally joined in 1976, as he explains: "My introduction to playing for the Tigers was somewhat delayed. When I left school, I played my junior rugby at the Vipers and for the Police Cadets. At the age of 19, when I became a constable, time off for anything other than police rugby became virtually impossible so I restricted my playing for the police and had to say goodbye to the Vipers.

"I was 21 years old when I was first asked whether I would join the Tigers. At that time, I had a young daughter, a mortgage, and I was a young police officer restricted by shift work to be readily available to play when requested. Money was very tight so that was another major consideration, as not only was the membership fee to play going to be an issue but I needed to work overtime on Saturdays where possible to bolster my wages. I managed to progress in my police career and got promoted to sergeant in the Criminal Investigation Department [CID] where not only was my pay improved but working hours were more flexible, allowing me to work split shifts and swap duties to accommodate my playing rugby. I was already playing for the county ahead of my Leicester Tigers colleagues.

"Nick Joyce was already at the club and other police officers had played for the Tigers so with little encouragement I was now able to throw my hat in the ring and join the Tigers in 1976. I was 26 and the move saw me coming to the notice of British Police rugby where I played in an almost all international team for seven years and subsequently England B.

"Chalkie White and the team made me very welcome. I do, however, recall my first, and nearly last, training session at Bradgate Park, and my surprise at how a small-in-stature-man could have such a loud voice and x-ray vision to spot people hiding behind trees trying to avoid the next torturous shuttle run. It was relentless. Eventually we got to Old John where we were to run back to the car park and finish. Off we went and I soon started walking, but on arrival at the car park it was pitch black and everyone had gone. I felt like death and questioned my sanity as to whether I would ever go again. I did, and the rest was history.

"The training was hell on Mondays. Chalkie had a saying that 'fatigue made fools of us all' which has always stuck with me and is as true today as ever. Chalkie was a visionary.

"Injuries were always problematic in that they impacted work and you were heavily reliant on goodwill from employers when you needed time off. There was no access to medical treatment for players. On a number of occasions, I presented at work with stitches or with an arm or leg in plaster when I was in the CID but was able to continue working. One cup final comes to mind, against Gloucester, where in an off-the-ball incident a Gloucester player and colleague in the British Police team punched me in the face knocking out my front teeth. I just spat them out and carried on. It would never happen in today's game thank goodness. What really annoyed me was that I couldn't drink after the game so went home early on the supporters' coach and it cost me over £1,000 in dental work. That's how it was then so thank goodness we've moved on."

This influx of talent was reflected in 1976-77 with 26 wins to 13 defeats and was much more the sort of playing record the Welford Road faithful were accustomed to. Bedford were beaten 34-13 in the first Midlands Merit Table fixture and second place reflected a real improvement on previous seasons, even if defeats by Coventry and table-toppers Moseley – who also knocked Tigers out of the John Player Cup as road trips returned and Wakefield were beaten in a twice-postponed first round tie – reflected their place in the regional pecking order. Northampton were beaten home and away, Swansea and London Welsh at Welford Road and a visit to Paris saw CASG, Club Athlétique des Sports Généraux, defeated 28-4.

On December 27 1976, Leicester Tigers beat the Barbarians 12 – 8 with a team that included three former youth team players Paul Dodge, Steve Kenney and Jez Krych.

Leicester Tigers (12) v Barbarians (8) – December 1976
Back Row (L-R): Chalkie White, Steve Johnson, John Duggan, Garry Adey, Brian Hall, Dave Forfar, Nick Joyce, Jim Kempin, Bob Barker, Robin Cowling, Peter Wheeler, Paul Dodge
Front Row (L-R): Dusty Hare, Larry Parkes, Bleddyn Jones, Bob Rowell (captain), Steve Kenney, Jez Krych

Cowling's breakthrough into the England team came a couple of weeks later and he went on to win eight caps, battling heroically through one game against France with a dislocated shoulder which cost him a Cup Final appearance against his old club, Gloucester and their Cup conqueror of 1971.

Off the field, a new member of staff was recruited, as explained by John Allen: "In the late 1970s, Leicester Tigers employed, on a part-time basis, three people; a bar manager, a lady to help with administration and a cleaner. This became four when Derek Limmage was hired, originally as a 'handyman'. It was Jerry Day who saw Derek's potential as a groundsman when he kept telling people to keep off the pitch! Derek learned his trade from Fred Cox before he retired."

The good times were returning, and this time with tangible prizes to be had for achievement.

15

Argy-Bargy – Los Pumas 1976

In 1976 the Argentina rugby team toured Wales and England for the first time, playing six matches in September and October. Five of the six matches were played in Wales, including a fixture against a Wales XV. Argentina won their first three matches before playing their only game outside Wales, against the combined Midlands and North of England team, widely termed as 'North & Midlands', at Welford Road.

Fixtures of this sort meant that tourists were still seen outside the major cities. Argentina was not yet seen as a major Test nation – Wales refused to issue caps for their match – but were a rising force. As coach of the Midland Counties (East) team who had been the only English region to beat the Australians a year earlier, Chalkie was the obvious choice to coach a team led by legendary Lancashire and England prop Fran Cotton. The game would have far-reaching consequences for both Chalkie and the Leicester club.

Chalkie – coached the Midlands and North of England to victory over an England XV in 1975

"Nottingham High School master Chalkie White won't be short of personal ambition when his North & Midlands team play Argentina at Leicester on Saturday, in the Pumas' only English game on the current tour," wrote Mike Matthews in the *Evening Post*. "For some judges consider that White, coach of Leicester Tigers, could be one of the men to take England out of the international wilderness. If the North & Midlands, coached for the match by White, can tame the Pumas, White will have achieved a rare hat-trick that can only strengthen his claims for a top England job.

"He coached the Midland Counties (East) side that was the only English regional side to beat the Australians last season, and also guided the Midlands and North of England to victory against England, both on his own club's home ground. White was at Cardiff Arms Park on Saturday to see the Pumas defeat Cardiff, for their second successive Welsh victory. Although the final margin of the tourists' victory was narrow enough, White was not deceived, 'At one stage it looked as if they would score 40 points, I am not underestimating them'. Neither I suspect will the North & Midlands players, many of whom know they can go a long way towards an England place with a good display against the tourists. Nottingham full back Dusty Hare is looking better than ever. His defence has improved and wingers are finding him a much more difficult player to get round."

This was only the second occasion the combined teams of the Midlands and North divisions had played together, as team captain, Fran Cotton, explained: "At that time I was working as a PE and maths teacher at Leigh College. Chalkie phoned and asked me to be captain and he was the first coach I had in my career to discuss selection with. We had a good rapport and we spoke weekly leading up to the game. The background to the Argentina game was they had toured Wales and stuffed the teams they had played, utilising their monster pack – the bloke I played against was the biggest prop I'd seen. We picked a strong team to play a structured game to beat the Pumas, the back line we selected of Steve Smith, John Horton, Tony Bond, Paul Dodge, John Carleton, Mike Slemen and Dusty Hare was the same as started for England when we won the Grand Slam in 1980."

So impressive in Wales, the Pumas were brought back to earth at Welford Road, going down to Chalkie's regional combination 24-9. Hare kicked 17 points and helped create the only try for Mike Slemen, while John Horton kicked tactically according to Chalkie's instructions and landed a drop goal. The Pumas, frustrated by their opponents' stifling tactics, were confined to two penalties from Becca Varela and another from Sansot.

Writing in the *Evening Post*, Mike Matthews reported: "England's rugby establishment, as well as a vocal section of the crowd, were less than delirious after watching the North & Midlands end the Argentinians' run of wins. White's strategy was based on similar lines to that which

"It was a disgrace what happened to Chalkie" – Fran Cotton, Midlands and North of England captain

defeated the Australians last season and it worked again. The Pumas, winners of all their three Welsh games, were well and truly tamed and several of the combined side must have enhanced their England prospects.

"Dusty Hare is playing the best rugby of his career and even his critics are being won over by his increasing maturity, strength and improved defence. The Nottingham full back dominated the scoring, he kicked well, five penalties, one from the half way line and a conversion, he provided the decisive build-up for the game's only try by winger Mike Slemen who looked pretty sharp throughout.

"Horton added a drop goal but his emphasis on tactical kicking denied his backs the chance of showing their attacking qualities. The crowd soon let the fly half know what they thought of him and it was not flattering. Personally, I still rate him the best prospect England has, quick on his feet and with a useful side step very much in the Welsh mould and that can't be bad! The North & Midlands forwards scrummaged superbly, props Colin White and Fran Cotton giving hooker Peter Wheeler all the support he could wish for. The Argentinians, physically impressive, were let down at key moments by their handling and could score only through penalties by Beccar Varela (two) and Sansot, yet they were good enough to ensure, as White put it, that 'we couldn't afford any grand gestures'."

This might have been thought a significant triumph, propelling both coach and players towards the England team, but the outcome would be very different, for Chalkie at least. The most powerful figure in English rugby was Dickie Jeeps, who had moved on from a remarkable playing career in which he played a record 13 Lions Tests as a back, into administration. The caricature of senior RFU figures is often unfair, but one does not rise to the presidency without considerable abilities, and Jeeps was among the most formidable figures to hold the office. His year in office would catch the eye of government, and in 1978 he was appointed Chairman of the Sports Council. He was a man of strong opinions, and not someone to cross.

Ian Todd, a smart and well-informed rugby journalist, reported Jeeps' reaction in his column in the *Sun* article headlined 'On the Blind Side': "Dickie Jeeps is smarting from the first serious setback to his Presidential campaign to put pride back in to English rugby. He got no pleasure at all when the North & Midlands became the first side to beat the Pumas of Argentina. Jeeps was appalled by the negative tactics and he is furious with Chalkie White the Leicester coach who ordered them. For White, a coach with a crack record against touring teams, the end justified the means. He saw the Pumas beat Cardiff and concluded it would be suicide to take them on in a running game. But for Jeeps, the victory over the Pumas wasn't just drab and dreary, 'it was a slap in the face' said the RFU President who opened his year in office with a personal plea for open attacking rugby. Jeeps, a brilliant scrum-half in three championship winning sides, has a vision that the path to glory should be blazed playing the Harlequins way."

Reflecting on the furore, Fran Cotton commented: "It's easy to criticise and say this is this and that is that, but unfortunately Dickie Jeeps the RFU President, didn't understand the quality of the opposition we played against. A week later it took a 40-yard Phil Bennett injury time kick for Wales to win the game 20-19 against Argentina at Cardiff. When coaching was in its infancy, Chalkie was one of the first coaches in England of real quality, turning out a strong Leicester team year after year, an original thinker, he did a lot that others didn't. I respected his communication with me and how he used the knowledge of the players for selection. He was almost too honest for his own good. People don't always want to hear the truth and sadly Chalkie never got a look in for England."

RFU President Dickie Jeeps

Chalkie was unrepentant, telling reporters: "That was the only way to play and win. There was no way we could take on their big centres in a winning game. Cardiff tried and failed, and with two promising but inexperienced midfield boys in Paul Dodge and Tony Bond so would we."

Yet while Chalkie may have damaged his chances of ultimately coaching England, there were immense benefits closer to home. Dusty Hare was still with Nottingham and had won a single cap in 1974, but his experience around the Argentina match triggered the move which launched one of the greatest of all Tigers careers.

"I was introduced to Chalkie White when I was at Magnus Grammar school," recounts Hare. "When I left school in 1969, I went to play rugby for Newark as a 17-year-old, and I was at this time a professional cricketer for Nottinghamshire. Chalkie was often referred to locally as rugby union's Brian Clough! During my one season at Newark I was selected to play for Notts, Lincs and Derby in the County Championship, coached by Chalkie White. We played against Leicestershire, and I remember it being a foggy day. Bleddyn played fly half and I dropped two goals, it was refereed by Larry Lamb of the RAF.

"Without Chalkie White I could well have been a one cap wonder; I owe him everything I've achieved in rugby and a lot more." Dusty Hare

"I had joined Nottingham RFC and stayed there because I was playing cricket for Nottinghamshire. Chalkie took an interest in me, as he did many other young players. He used to call me to chat about rugby and he became a mentor to me – it wasn't just me, he helped many rugby players – and he asked me if I wanted to join Leicester Tigers.

"I was capped by England in 1974 at a time when my cricket career was going nowhere, I was thinking about joining Leicester in the summer but never made the move despite the fact my gut feeling told me to do so. When I was selected for the North & Midlands team to play Argentina, I knew I had to go because this was the standard I wanted to play week in, week out. After the game I left Nottingham straight away. In those days you had to write a letter to the Leicester Tiger's committee to ask if you could join the club – Leicester wrote back accepting. I had to also write a resignation letter to the Nottingham committee.

"My first game for Leicester was away to Northampton in the Extras side and I scored all the points in a 24-21 victory. From then on I never once put on a Leicester shirt and finished on the losing side against Northampton in my 394 games. My 1st XV debut was mid-week against Oxford University at Welford Road, we won 46-8, and I scored 22 points. I then played against Swansea away where we won again. It was a busy start to my Leicester career. During my time at Leicester I was never dropped. I came close a few times but wasn't dropped.

"Chalkie had a huge influence over me. When I was growing up, he was always talking to me about rugby and how I could improve. He became like a second (rugby) father. He had a brilliant mind, and the attention to detail in the feedback he gave after I'd played a game made me realise I had to start thinking about my game a lot more. Chalkie lived in Burton Joyce, but was a reluctant driver on match days, if Brian Hall couldn't pick him up, I did, he didn't talk about current affairs in the car there was only one subject, rugby."

16

The First Final – 1977-78

Dusty Hare, having made the short switch from Nottingham was already making the full back shirt his own, but recruitment never stopped for Chalkie, and Nick Jackson joined Leicester, making his debut against Harlequins at Welford Road on March 4 1978.

"I went to Nottingham High School, from 1966 to 1976, from age eight to 18," recalls Jackson. "Chalkie worked in the senior school as a PE teacher, house tutor, occasional maths teacher and of course rugby coach. So, from age 11, I had PE lessons led by Chalkie, and he also assisted age-group rugby lessons, through to the sixth form where he was more heavily involved with

Leicester Tigers 1977-78
Back Row (L-R): Harry Sibson (Team Sec.), Jerry Day (Hon. Sec.), John Allen (Hon. Treas.), Larry Parkes, John Duggan, Steve Redfern, Angus Collington, Steve Johnson, Arthur Hazlerigg, Garry Adey, Ray Needham, Ian Smith, Chalkie White (coach), Ken Kinder (President)
Front Row (L-R): Dusty Hare, Jim Kempin, John White, Tim Barnwell, Nick Jackson, Brian Hall (captain), Bob Barker, Nick Joyce, Steve Kenney, Paul Dodge

Steve Smith watches Nick Jackson contest a line-out with Sale's Ian McKie

the 1st and 2nd XVs, along with the other PE teacher, Geri Thomas.

"Chalkie was always very keen to include and develop all the boys in the class, not just the 'sporty' kids. He was also, as we know, a disciplinarian, if you ever forgot your PE kit, or swimming trunks, you were directed towards the lost property box to find anything that vaguely fitted so you could take part. Swimming could always be done in your underwear!!

"I captained the school 1st XV in my last year at school under the coaching of Chalkie and Geri, and gained selection for the county (Notts) U19s, and from there to the three counties [Notts, Lincs & Derbyshire] U19s. On my last day at school in July 1976, I went to the gym to say farewell to Chalkie and Geri, and it was then when Chalkie invited me to come down to the Tigers. Prior to that conversation I had not considered my senior rugby options, but as always, Chalkie was very positive, always encouraging people to try to be the best version of themselves.

"I had to re-sit my A levels, so joining the Tigers was put off for 12 months, but I kept in contact with Chalkie. Over the following years as my rugby career developed I spent a lot of time travelling with Chalkie to Leicester as we both lived in Nottingham, and many happy hours were spent chatting, mainly about rugby but also many other subjects. Chalkie most definitely was the biggest influence on my life outside of my family."

Malcolm Foulkes-Arnold also joined Tigers at the same time. A student doing a seven-year architecture course at Leicester Polytechnic, initially studies limited his appearances to the Swifts and the Extras. The former Harlequins second row had to earn his stripes the hard way: "I realised I had to apply myself and get much fitter, I wanted to win and be part of it all, but I had to be patient. The biggest turning point in my career was when I broke my nose after five minutes in a brutal game against Swansea in early 1981. I stayed on the field and dug in with the rest of the lads. Later, when Nick Jackson was sent off against Bath, I took my opportunity and played more first team games. The tour to Zimbabwe was significant in my development where we were in an all-but professional environment; the way we ate and trained and prepared for the games. As a group we got very close and it made a big impression on me."

This was the season when Tigers at last punched their weight in the new competitive world, when playing progress was reflected in growing crowds. Where some games at the start of the decade were played in front of crowds of less than 1,000, packed houses were now much more common. The steady upgrading of Welford Road continued with the unveiling of a new scoreboard supplied by Adey Steel, a Loughborough-based business run by Arthur Adey, Garry's father.

Tim Barnwell is tackled by Northampton's Chris MacInnes at a snowy Welford Road in 1979

Chalkie's car journeys across the East Midlands became still more focussed on Tigers' fortunes, with his chauffeur Brian Hall becoming club captain.

Another new recruit, Tim Barnwell, a wing, joined from Coventry: "I was playing for Coventry with the likes of Peter Rossbourgh, David Duckham, and Geoff Evans, scoring an interception try in the 1974 RFU Knockout Cup final win against London Scottish. However, I wasn't very happy there and in summer 1977 I was invited to tour with the Anti-Assassins, a sort of mini-Barbarians team. On that tour were Nick Joyce and Garry Adey. They persuaded me to join Leicester, not a great deal of money changed hands for my signature, in fact John Allen only paid my travelling expenses to the Leicestershire border!"

It was also the season in which Arthur Hazlerigg, who had played five times in 1976-77, became a regular in succession to Bob Rowell. Arthur's distinctive background was to make him the butt of the press box with Martin Johnson's humour – he was born and lived in a stately home, scion of a family which had been raised to the baronetcy in 1622 and the peerage in 1945. He was just to miss becoming a member of the House of Lords, succeeding his father in 2002 as 3rd Baron and 15th Baronet; three years after hereditary peers had been pruned back by the Blair government. Family history pointed more towards cricket, since his father had captained Leicestershire, but Arthur was a tough, hardworking second row who was a regular for the next four seasons.

"Arthur became a great character in the Leicester team," recalls Steve Johnson. "He is the only player I've seen who took the field with a pressed, monogrammed white handkerchief in his pocket. He could be seen in a game wiping mud from his face or blowing his nose it was a sight to behold."

Arthur Hazlerigg closes in on Moseley scrum-half Chris Gifford

It was still a season of mixed fortunes. There were wins over Swansea and Bristol, but the Barbarians triumphed 12-6 in front of a crowd of 19,000. The Tigers were also, for once, out of the running in the Midlands Merit Table, dropping to fifth after an end-of-season loss at Rugby.

This was a match that Chalkie missed, under circumstances showing how far the lives of top-level rugby coaches have changed since. Where his modern equivalents are full-timers who can call on coteries of equally professional assistants, Chalkie was held up by his day job at Nottingham High School, where the death of groundsman Maurice Wood had thrown extra duties on all PE staff. As he wrote to his son Ged, "I had to stay behind for a while helping to tidy things away."

Nor was the Rugby fixture one of those inconsequential meetings with less exalted local rivals that continued to dot the schedules of even the strongest clubs until the coming of leagues. Chalkie wrote to Ged: "I wanted to go as we haven't won at Rugby for 17 years yet we never fail to score less than 25 points when we play them at Leicester. A genuine bogey side."

Chalkie had played in that last 31-3 win at Rugby in 1960. The 17-13 defeat in his absence in 1978 was the seventh and last in a sequence that included three consecutive draws between 1967 and 1974. It was also the Tigers' last visit to Webb Ellis Road until Rugby Lions' brief rise to top levels in the early days of the national leagues. The bogey was finally laid to rest in April 1993, when a Tigers team including 11 players who would clinch the club's first post-Chalkie cup victory defeated their already-relegated hosts 28-5, the try-scorers including both Underwood brothers.

However, Dusty Hare's 304 points were a new club record, and fortunes changed decisively for the better in what was now called the John Player Cup, with a series of home fixtures. Hartlepool Rovers were beaten 9-3 in the first round. Rosslyn Park in round two might not look much of a challenge to modern eyes, but were a serious threat in this era with Andy Ripley at Number 8, and had reached the final in 1975 and 1976. Tigers also went into the match short of match-practice after a frozen February in which four consecutive cancellations had followed a 0-0 draw with the Royal Navy at the start of the month, but Rosslyn Park were seen off 25-16 in what David Hands recalled as a 'brilliant display'. The quarter- and semi-finals both brought familiar visitors to Welford Road.

Northampton were defeated 20-11 in the quarter-final, at the cost of losing skipper Hall, who cracked two ribs. That ruled him out of the semi-final three weeks later against traditional rivals Coventry. Tigers, though, went in with the reassurance of having beaten Coventry in their previous two meetings and made it three with Hall's deputy, Bill Reichwald, dropping a goal, as did Hare, as part of his 14-point tally in Leicester's 25-16 win, with veteran Bleddyn Jones and rising star Paul Dodge crossing for tries.

Hall was back for the final, but Cowling was not so fortunate. He had appeared only five times in a season ended by a heroic performance for England in Paris.

"I'd spent the best part of 40 minutes playing with a dislocated shoulder at the Parcs des Princes in 1978," remembers Cowling." By then six replacements were allowed but crazily you were only allowed to use two – by doctor's agreement. As Andy Maxwell and Peter Dixon had already gone off, we'd have been down to 14 men if I'd left the pitch too. Fellow prop Mike Burton said, 'You can't go off, you're one of us', so I put my hand in my pocket and carried on. It probably wasn't the wisest thing I've ever done."

Wing John Duggan reminisced that before the final, "There was a real buzz in the city, and particularly from all the rugby fans." At the same time this was an era in which only England matches could fill Twickenham, and the cup final was still some way from establishing itself as a day to parallel its football and rugby league counterparts.

Duggan recalls the massive effort made to persuade as many Tigers fans as possible to make the trek to West London: "What we needed was to fill as many coaches and buses as possible, and in order to reduce the overall cost to fans, and hopefully encourage more to attend, some of us players worked on getting sponsors for the coaches to cover the transport costs. Myself and Peter Wheeler were particularly active on this front. Peter with his corporate connections in the city centre insurance businesses and legal practices, worked on that market.

"In 1978 I'd been appointed as a PE and science teacher at Lancaster Boy's School in Leicester, whose Welsh Headmaster, Sidney Ifano 'Van' Hopkins, was also the BBC Radio Leicester rugby commentator. The school had a catchment area in the affluent Stoneygate and Knighton district of the city, and had plenty of parents who were rugby fans and ran businesses. I persuaded a number of them to sponsor coaches for the cup final.

"I also walked up and down the Queens Road shopping area which was on my doorstep, and found a very receptive group of businesses who would sponsor a coach. This involved cold calling at these shops and persuading them to help in the task of getting as many fans to Twickenham as possible. Some of the shops were owned by parents from my school, who were willing to contribute and who also helped me to persuade their neighbouring shops to contribute. In all, I managed to cover the costs of about 12 coaches and we ended up with a huge convoy of coaches and buses from Leicester, full of Tigers fans, contributing to the attendance of over 24,000, which was the biggest there had been to that point. A great effort by players had contributed to this Tigers Army making their way to Twickers!"

The team's own journey down, and in particular their overnight stay on the way, is recalled by Ian Smith: "The squad travelled south the night before the game to stay at the Runnymede Hotel in Windsor. Some of the players decided that they would accompany their evening meal with glasses of red wine, and as the wine was delivered to the tables, Chalkie said, 'If the night before a game you normally drink red wine, carry on.' The momentary silence that followed his words was quickly followed by the red wine being removed. Subsequent cup finals saw the squad travelling south the day of the game rather than the night before. A tradition I experienced as player and continued with as the Tigers coach."

Ian 'Dosser' Smith – future Leicester captain and coach who was awarded life-membership in 2017

It was, Duggan remembers: "Great to see the army of red, white and green urging us on." They were, though to be disappointed in the tough contest reported by Gloucester's daily paper, *The Citizen*:

John Duggan is assisted off the Twickenham pitch to have a head wound stitched – he later returned to the field of play

"Favourites Gloucester and lively Leicester were locked in closely fought combat in this afternoon's John Player Cup final at Twickenham. The Cherry and Whites led by 6pts to nil at half-time, through a Richard Mogg try superbly converted by Peter Butler. The excitement had reached fever pitch when Peter Butler kicked off, and the referee ordered a set scrum between the Tigers' 25 and the 10-yard line. Steve Mills took the first heel against the head and Paul Howell kicked high up to the line, where the ball was marked and the danger cleared. John Simonett won the first line-out, tapping down to Mike Burton, and the first ruck was under way. Gloucester's scrummaging power stood out in the early stages and they drove beyond the 25 where Dusty Hare gave Leicester temporary relief with a clearance kick following a line-out. Three Leicester forwards needed attention in the first six minutes Another Hare clearance, this time a penalty, followed more power scrummaging by Gloucester."

"The Cherry and Whites then moved the ball smoothly from a line-out, only for Butler to be halted by a tremendous John Duggan tackle. Both players were hurt in the incident, and Duggan went off holding his head. Butler was able to resume after treatment. Hare opened the goal kicking duel with two long range penalties, the second of which passed dangerously close to the near upright. Duggan, his head heavily bandaged, returned after 15 minutes and flanker Steve Johnson resumed his normal place in the pack. Leicester showed their scoring potential with a smart move on the right involving Duggan, and Garry Adey tried to force his way through from a scrum 30 yards out. Burton was caught as he attempted to break from a maul soon afterwards, and a Leicester boot hacked into touch inside Gloucester territory. Johnson became the fifth Leicester player to need medical attention, but he did not have to leave the field. Gloucester's first penalty chance came after 21 minutes with Butler only just failing with a huge kick from two yards inside his own half. Howell harassed his opposite number, Steve Kenney, following

Gloucester try scorer Richard Mogg playing for England B

a scrum and Hare did well to take a poor pass and find touch. Twickenham erupted as the Cherry and Whites opened the scoring in the 36th minute with a great try. Tremendous forward pressure, in which Burton and Gordon Sargent were prominent, started it off. Then the offensive switched to the left where Williams made ground, sent Boyle on a crunching run and finally Richard Mogg eluded at least two tackles before crashing over in the corner. Butler added the conversion points with a magnificent kick from the touch-line. Gloucester continued to exert pressure as half-time approached, and Richard Jardine attempted a drop goal but the ball failed to gain height.

"The second half got under way with Hare kicking the ball dead, and then the Tigers' full back had a penalty chance from 45 yards when Gloucester were caught offside at the scrum. However, the ball faded and passed outside the far upright. Leicester's backs then indulged in a series of dazzling passes, but they failed to gain much ground and Brian Hall finally kicked away possession. Hare made no mistake with his fourth penalty shot at goal from more than 30 yards, to cut the Tigers' arrears to three points. Gloucester's first effective second half onslaught came from their pack, with skipper John Watkins and Simonett attempting to dive over. Leicester did well to keep them out, and eventually hare gained 60 yards with a magnificent clearance. He repeated the good work when his line came under pressure again. Gloucester ran the ball from a short penalty inside their own half, and Boyle appeared in the line to send Clewes away. The right wing was eventually bundled into touch. But Leicester began to look much more dangerous, and fought back with some determined work by their pack before having to retreat temporarily in the face of the Butler boot.

"Suddenly the Cherry and Whites were under great pressure with Mogg scrambling the ball into touch only five yards out. After a couple of partial clearances, Butler got the ball away to the 10-yard line. It seemed anybody's match now, and there was everything to play for. Hare missed a wide angled penalty. A soccer-style fight broke out among youths at one end of ground and spilled over onto the pitch. Match halted temporarily; resumed. Whistle went with Mike Burton attempting relieving touch kick and Gloucester had won their second final. Thousands of supporters invaded pitch to congratulate Gloucester."

That report will have been compiled under the fearsome deadline pressures – demanding instant reaction but offering minimal scope for reflection – of the Saturday sports editions which in the late 1970s were still on the streets of almost every significant English or Welsh community within an hour, or even less, of the matches finishing.

The following Monday, April 17, *The Citizen's* reporter was given a chance to offer a more considered opinion of the action: "The 24,000 crowd which saw Gloucester defeat Leicester 6 pts to 3 in Saturday's John Player Cup final at Twickenham, was a record for the competition and for an English club match. And 12,000 were Gloucester supporters, who literally took over rugby's head-quarters for the afternoon. It needed Gloucester, the country's best supported club, to really get the six-year-old competition off the ground. There was never any question that the record of 11,500 for the Bristol v Coventry final in 1973 would be smashed."

Gloucester coach Mike Nicholls, who captained the 1972 cup-winning team, said afterwards: "It was all too close for comfort. Our half-time margin was not really sufficient and when Leicester came back with a penalty, I was really worried. If Bob Clews had managed to score, we would have sewn it up, but we had to sweat it out to the end. I felt we controlled the forward exchanges better than Leicester, who looked dangerous from broken situations. There was no time when they worried us from set play."

Skipper John Watkins added: "The game was played in a good spirit throughout, but full credit to Leicester. A lot of sides would have cracked under the pressure. The defences were magnificent. I cannot remember a single bad tackle. Every time you got the ball there was someone on you. I am a little disappointed that we could not score more, but that is to Leicester's credit."

Watkins thanked the thousands of Gloucester fans, not only for their support at the final but in the four previous rounds. Of his match-saving tackle, Richard Moggs said: "I just managed to get across and knock him into touch." He was thrilled at having scored Gloucester's winning try because "we needed the points, as we knew they would come back in the second half."

David Hands, rugby reporter of the *Leicester Mercury*, said, "We were just not allowed to play the running game that we wanted to. It always looked like a Gloucester win because of the amount of territorial advantage they had."

Framed addresses signed by the Gloucester team were presented to Mike Nicholls and John Watkins. "We wanted to show our appreciation after all they have done for the side," said a player, and after a champagne celebration,

GLOUCESTER	Referee: R. C. QUITTENTON (London/Sussex Referees' Society)	LEICESTER
Touch Judge: R. F. Johnson (London Society of Referees)	KICK-OFF 3.30 p.m. International	Touch Judge: G. Feest (Eastern Counties/Suffolk and N. Essex Referees' Society)
Red and white jerseys		Green, red and white hooped jerseys
15. P. E. BUTLER	FULL-BACKS	O. W. H. HARE
	THREE-QUARTERS	
14. R. J. CLEWES	RIGHT WING	N. M. J. DUGGAN
13. B. J. VINE	CENTRE	M. P. W. DODGE
12. R. JARDINE	CENTRE	L. B. P. HALL (Captain)
11. R. R. MOGG	LEFT WING	K. R. G. BARKER
	HALF-BACKS	
10. C. G. WILLIAMS	STAND-OFF	J. B. JONES
9. P. R. HOWELL	SCRUM-HALF	I. S. KENNEY
	FORWARDS	
1. G. A. F. SARGENT	PROP	A. R. E. NEEDHAM
2. S. G. F. MILLS	HOOKER	B. P. J. WHEELER
3. M. A. BURTON	PROP	C. S. P. REDFERN
4. S. B. BOYLE	LOCK	D. N. J. JOYCE
5. J. H. FIDLER	LOCK	E. A. G. HAZLERIGG
6. J. A. WATKINS (Captain)	FLANKER	F. S. R. JOHNSON
8. J. F. SIMONETT	No. 8	G. G. J. ADEY
7. V. J. WOOLEY	FLANKER	H. D. J. FORFAR
Replacements: 16 R. Etheridge, 17 D. Pointon, 18 P. Kingston, 19 M. Curran, 20 F. Reed, 21 E. Pinkney.		Replacements: R. S. Money, W. M. Reichwald, T. A. Walley, J. R. White, A. P. Collington, I. R. Smith. The first replacement will wear the letter P, the second replacement the letter Q.

DRAWN MATCHES. In the Final, if at the end of 40 minutes' play each way, the scores be equal, the tries be equal and the goals from tries be equal, there shall be an immediate period of replay between the same sides without replacements of seven minutes each way, with a one-minute interval. If no result is then achieved the match shall be adjudged a draw.

12 13

Gloucester (6) v Leicester (3) – John Player Cup Final, 1978

players and officers left the Twickenham dressing room wearing victory ties inscribed 'GRFC – John Player Cup Winners, 1978'. "It was all done in secrecy," said Secretary Terry Tandy. "If we had lost, the ties would have been burned." Brenda Bennett, wife of committee member Jim Bennett, obtained the transfers and Debenhams supplied the ties. Gloucester expect their profit from the competition to be about £6,000. They receive £2,000 for appearing in the final and the club's commission from ticket sales is £1,000."

Tigers' disappointment was summed up by Steve Kenney, who said, post-match: "We wanted to win for the blokes who won't have another chance." Jones, who was to retire the following season after a club record for an outside-half of 333 games, Duggan and Barker were not to get another shot, but for the remainder of the men defeated at Twickenham, the cup remained a matter of unfinished business.

17

Winning the Cup – 1978-79

Club Secretary Jerry Day would argue at the end of the season that 1978-79 could be seen as "one of the most successful in the history of Leicester Football Club," and had no doubt that, "The foundation of our success this season was realised in the dressing room at Twickenham after the Leicester v Gloucester John Player Cup final in 1978. The players were bitterly disappointed and they realised only too well that their performances had been a great disappointment, not only to themselves but also to the loyal members and supporters of the club. Amends would have to be made. During the 1978-79 pre-season training, there was a feeling throughout the club that the players were going to achieve something rather different this season. Participation in the 1978 final motivated players and generated an enthusiasm for and a dedication to rugby football. Attendances at training improved, a register of attendance at training was kept, weight checks were taken during training sessions as well as before and after matches."

Jerry Day – Leicester FC Secretary (1966-82)

Chalkie White had a new lieutenant on the field when Peter Wheeler succeeded Brian Hall to start his second stint as captain. He also looked at strengthening the team. Nigel Gillingham (RFU President 2023-24) came from Surrey and had played for Richmond FC as a teenager, but once the England U23 lock had been despatched to Nottingham High School for his third year teaching practice while studying at Loughborough, his future in club rugby was pre-destined.

"I first met Chalkie during my second year at Loughborough," recalled Gillingham. "When there were regular training sessions, taken by Chalkie, for players in the England and England U23 squads. In the third year at Loughborough, you spent a whole term (either the autumn or winter terms) in a school on teaching practice. Mine was in the winter term of 1976, and I was allocated to Nottingham High School. Why I was allocated there, I do not know. The PE Department was run by Chalkie, head of PE, and Geri Thomas, master in charge of games. Nick Jackson was head boy at the school at the time and also later became a Leicester Tigers player.

"The day consisted of leaving Loughborough at about 7am, before breakfast was available in the refectory, catch the bus to Nottingham city centre, then walk to the school in time for a 9am start. The morning consisted of me taking PE lessons in the gym, swimming pool and playground, and mathematics lessons in a classroom. Then, after a school lunch, every afternoon I made my way to the school playing fields about two miles away to help with a year-

Under the Welford Road lights, Nigel Gillingham contests a line-out for the Midlands Counties (East) against Australia in 1975

group's games, which typically of an independent high school of the time consisted of rugby, cross country and I think some hockey, although I do not remember being involved in the latter. Those games sessions finished about 4pm. So, I then got a bus back into Nottingham city centre, to catch the bus to Loughborough to arrive, if on time, five minutes before the refectory closed. I remember, that term, spending a fortune on take-aways, because often the only meal that I had was the school lunch and the day was physically tough. The evenings were spent writing up reviews of the lessons taken that day and doing lesson preparations for the following day.

"During the early part of the term, those lessons were observed by the teacher who would normally be taking that class to offer the benefit of their experience. Then throughout the term you had four PE lessons (not the games' sessions) and four maths lessons assessed by tutors from Loughborough. Those assessments dictated your ultimate grade; satisfactory for me, nowhere near the outstanding that some others in the year received. I have to say, Chalkie was not the best in providing advice on gymnastics, swimming and the like, but his rugby sessions on the games field in the afternoon with the pupils were brilliant, as you might expect.

"While at that time I was going to be a PE teacher and, therefore, not sure where I would play my club rugby, when in the autumn of 1977, again at an England U23 session at RAF Stafford, I was persuaded to join the RAF and name the club I would want to play for so that postings could be arranged accordingly, I had no doubt that it should be Leicester with Chalkie. So, after Initial Officer Training and my Physical Education Officer's course in summer of 1977 and winter of 1978, I joined Tigers for the 1978-79 season."

A still more significant capture was made from Moseley, with outside-half Les Cusworth, already on the verge of England honours, arriving with impeccable timing to replace Bleddyn Jones. His vividly detailed recollections of Chalkie are informed, not only as one of his most important players, but their common ground as teachers and coaches:

"When I lived and taught in Walsall in 1978," explained Cusworth. "I was playing for Moseley Rugby Club and the North Midlands county team. We actually won the County Championship for the first and only time in that year, and Chalkie came along to one of the games. He told me if I ever fancied coming to Leicester I would be most welcome. At Moseley I was battling with Martin Cooper, who was at that time the current England international fly half, while Leicester had just lost in the John Player Cup final in May 1978 to Gloucester, so the chance to join them was just too good to miss.

"It was October 1978 when I finally made the decision to accept Chalkie's invitation. I was advised to call Tudor Thomas, who was at that time the Tigers'

1st XV Secretary, who sternly and promptly advised that there were travelling expenses of four pence a mile but only up to the Leicestershire county border near Hinckley and no further! I received £3.76 a trip and John Allen checked every session I attended.

"Tudor became one of my dearest friends at the Tigers. In 1978 the M69 had not been fully completed and I was living in Walsall, so the journey to Leicester from Walsall was partly via the A47 via Hinckley and Earl Shilton. It was quite a trek to training that first occasion which took me an hour and 45 minutes. When I arrived on that dark, wet damp Monday evening, I was obviously a little anxious and about ten minutes into the training session Chalkie sent all the backs away for handling exercises but told me I had to stay with the forwards. I immediately thought this was a bit strange. He set up a practice in between the five-yard line and the touchline and told me I had to tackle, one by one, the two packs of forwards in front of me, from a rolling start. No holds barred, the forwards came at me like savaged dogs – they thought it was Christmas. I scragged one of the 16, while the other 15 forwards all gained great delight by running around, through or over me in order to score. Not one tried a sidestep or change of pace! After the session I was aching and sore and didn't get home until 12.30am. My first thought was that's it back to Moseley with my tail between my legs!

Les Cusworth began his career with Wakefield RFC before joining Leicester in 1978

"Next morning in the school staff room, I was thinking 'what kind of a coach is this guy Chalkie White?' He had humiliated me in the training session the night before in Welford Road, then at 8.30am, before class registration, there was a phone call. It was Chalkie White, who told me, 'You've shown us your weaknesses, now we'll concentrate on what you're good at'. Just as I started to wonder 'what the hell am I doing at Leicester?', he said, 'You're playing against Swansea on Saturday'.

"At that time, Bleddyn Jones, who had played well over 300 games for the Tigers, was the current fly half. After training, when the teams were announced and he had been told he was not selected, Bleddyn came over to congratulate me on my selection. He told me he knew I was travelling a long way and that if at any time I needed a bed, I was most welcome to stay with him and his wife Sue. So, for three Mondays in November I stayed with them. We forged a very special lifelong friendship, and I am godfather to Helen, Bleddyn's daughter, and his wife Sue is godmother to my eldest daughter, Hannah. Bleddyn hardly played another game for Leicester, but we stayed in regular, at times weekly, contact for over 40 years until he sadly passed away. His selflessness, warmth and generosity were incredible, indeed he was an incredible human being and such a dear, special friend.

"One of Chalkie White's major assets as a coach were his versatility and creativity. The only training facility available at that time was the 'Rec', today called The Nelson Mandela Park. The lighting and illumination of the field were very basic, using the street lights and some telegraph poles with lighting attached, that ran along the side of the pitch and you could only just about see the pitch markings. The playing surface wasn't the best either, and was covered in dog mess, litter and broken glass – you name it, it was there. Being a public park, we encountered people walking dogs, kids larking about on their bikes, boys having impromptu football kick-abouts and even a full-scale cricket match, all while we were having pre-season training. This was the training ground for one of the best teams in England! We had to carry the tackle bags and shields across the road from the home team dressing room, the Extras had to carry the two sets of posts and crossbars for their matches, which the players erected themselves before matches and took down afterwards. The last player to leave the training ground turned the lights off in the fuse box at the corner of the Rec where the Welford Road traffic lights are – at the time of writing the box is still there today. Any other coach would have walked away from this; we were not allowed to train on the main pitch on Mondays or Thursdays and only allowed a light 20-minute session on Thursday night's team run, so as not to damage the pitch for Saturday's game. Jerry Day, the club's excellent Secretary, and Head Groundsman Derek Limmage would personally guard the stadium pitch on Monday and Thursday evenings to protect the hallowed turf. They both had great pride in the magnificent state of the playing surface which allowed us to play the expansive style of play that Chalkie insisted upon. The forwards were regularly banished, with the scrum machine, to the car park, and all other scrum sessions were held at the Rec. Chalkie used all this to our strengths, making us realize that we had to be so grateful for the pleasure of striding out on Welford Road on a Saturday afternoon.

"Chalkie White was a very hard man, but you knew exactly where you stood with him. He would say: 'Why kick the ball when you can run it, if running can give you more advantage, ball in hand you can always control the game.' Crucially, he taught the midfield the importance of getting over the gain line. He coached us for hours and hours, from a line-out with full opposition, with off-the-top ball then a flat pass from Steve Kenney or Nick Youngs. In just two passes I had Paul Dodge running at the 10's inside shoulder – he was the first coach to teach me this. Sometimes Robin Cowling and Steve Redfern would try to get involved, but he would rush over and say, 'Don't give it to the props.' He wanted speed and quick ball with continuity, change of angle and deception, and lots of variety with an attacking philosophy.

"When we played Wasps in a John Player Cup semi-final tie in Sudbury, they had been on a great run of results with a team packed with internationals. We beat them convincingly by over 40 points, scoring tries from all angles and positions, including one from a counter attack by Dusty Hare from our own try line. I remember my dear friend Tony Hopkins, a lifelong Tigers' member and committee man, saying that was the best Tigers display he had ever seen. That kind of coaching methodology, instilled in us by Mr. H.V. White, was 40 years ahead of its time.

"On one occasion, when he wanted to refine the backs' handling skills to increase our dexterity and use our fingers more in the catch-and-pass technique, he brought tennis balls and two dozen eggs to a practice session. The forwards were given the tennis balls and we were handed the eggs. He made us place an egg on the back of our hands then let it roll off and catch it without breaking the shell: 'See how long you can go without smashing the eggs,' he said. We had some great ball handlers, like Clive, Paul and Dusty and lasted about 15 minutes. The forwards meanwhile lost the tennis balls! Only joking fellas!

"In the early 1980s, just before kick-off in a match against the RAF, he told me, 'You are not allowed to kick the ball tonight,' and with a smile he added, 'or you'll be in the Extras on Saturday.' So I asked him what I should do if I was on my own line. 'Run it,' he replied, 'the best bit of ball you get might be under your posts in the second minute of the game. Use it, why kick it away?' That was his vision and thinking. Never stand still and always be one step ahead. He was a key factor in laying the foundations for the Tigers of today. He wasn't a romantic, and would be a disciplinarian when he had to be, but he gave every player the skills and confidence to express themselves. He made Ian Smith into a modern openside flanker with the ability to link the backs with the forwards in a dynamic way designed to create continuity and cohesive attacking ball. He also prepared a very fit agile team with a dynamic set of forwards and creative athletic backs. A coach like Carwyn James of Wales – well ahead of his time.

"Chalkie would also insist that all of his players developed their skills to the limit. Practise, practise and practise again, that was his mantra. Paul Dodge and Dusty Hare used to come to training half an hour early to practise kicking the ball from-hand, and he told me to do the same and learn from them.

Peter Wheeler, Chris Tressler, Mark Duffelen and the other hookers would do the same for throwing into the line-out. He also made Steve Kenney, Nick Youngs, Mick Merriman and all the other scrum-halves do 200 passes a night, firstly off their left and then off their right hand, and some with no back lift. At that time in England there very few coaching with that attention to detail. It was like an academy set-up way before academies were even thought of. He once told me, 'If any player hasn't touched the ball at least 100 times in my session, it hasn't been a good practice.' I think he must have forgotten his early comments about the props not to touch the ball!

"A few weeks before the Barbarians game, the players used to help Derek Limmage and the volunteers cover the main pitch with straw to protect the field from frost. Later, a plastic cover was purchased which the players used to help lay out into position. At that time, Alan Foster was a 2nd XV coach who worked as a PE instructor at HM Prison Glen Parva, a young offenders institution, and organised training there in order to take pressure off the pitches at the main stadium and the Rec.

"Chalkie liked small-sided games for skills sessions and he also liked 12 v 12 sessions – always with forwards against backs – in a form of touch-rugby league. In those skills sessions he was always encouraging me to attack the isolated forwards. On one occasion I sold a dummy to Robin Cowling, and scored a try. Five minutes later I found myself in the same situation and thought, 'no problem he's toast.' However, before I could sell him another dummy, he stiff-arm tackled me and gave me a bloody nose and a split lip. I looked at Chalkie, who had a wry smile on his face, and before I said a word, he blasted out, 'You deserve it, you've got to learn to look after yourself. If you can't take it, don't give it.' Some weeks later when we were playing Bristol, one of their forwards, John Doubleday, kept hitting me late. 'I've had enough of this,' I thought, so the next time I threw a wild swipe at him, thinking 'that will teach him.' Unfortunately, John never flinched and I ended up with a dislocated thumb!! My father went mad with me and said, 'If you can't do it properly don't do it at all!'

"Chalkie also incorporated small-sided games such as a rugby league-type American football, where you could pass in any direction, forwards, backwards or simply run or kick the ball in order to develop our skill set. At Glen Parva we used to play basketball, volleyball –sometimes while in a sitting and crawling position – as well as five-a-side football and many other skills-based games with cones and markers. We didn't realise it at the time, but everything we did was designed to increase our spatial awareness, improve our scanning techniques and developing our off-the-ball abilities. Relying on his extensive range of contacts, he also analysed the opposition and planned ahead for each game even when, at that time, there were almost no video recordings of club games. Yet he knew all about the teams we played against, their strengths and weakness, and planned accordingly to beat them. This was way before people had even heard of analysis and team evaluation. His pioneering approach and gifted coaching skills were a key part of Leicester's rugby development, but he was also well aware that we had to be the fittest team in order to prevail and that strength and fitness were the keys to success. Hence the pre-season training at a suitable beach on the east coast, and organising five mile runs to Leicester Forest East in rush hour as well as sprinting shuttles up and down the legendary shale 'bank' at Welford Road. The forwards always took the left side of the bank, while the backs were told to use the right. I think Peter Wheeler had worked out that the left side was ten meters shorter and had less of an incline than the right. To this day, I'm sure the Redfern brothers, Granite and Pebble, still believe they had beaten all the backs on these punishing uphill races.

"On many occasions during matches, Chalkie would stand on the shale bank and shout instructions, with a bellowing voice. He was always on the lookout for ways to make the player and the team perform better. We would always have one ear pricked up for the next gem of information coming our

Colin Martin and Chalkie defending the 'bank' at Welford Road

way! After the matches he would pepper you with questions and expected an immediate response, such as: 'In the second minute you had the ball on our 22 with a three-on-one overlap, so why did you kick it?' At that stage of my development, I couldn't even remember what I had done in the 72nd minute, let alone in the 2nd! He continually strived to be one step ahead of the opposition.

"He was always improvising, like when, for stamina development, we had to run up and down the steps of the main stand, while for our speed work, we used the tunnel underneath the Crumbie Stand, as our running track. It was not unusual to do 100 full-length sprints and shuttle runs in the training session, his voice booming down the tunnel: 'Whilst you're doing this, other teams will already be in the bar.' I can't remember a training session being cancelled, nor can I remember Chalkie White being absent. In an era when the club had the most basic facilities, the standard of fitness achieved at Leicester Tigers was unrivalled.

"My dad was a coal miner and used to travel down to watch the Tigers. Later in life, when he was struggling with his health, my brother Roy, Uncle Terry and my dad used to drive from Wakefield to watch nearly all the Tigers matches both home and away. Chalkie would always, as he did with many people, find the time after matches to say 'hello' – he had a way of making everyone feel welcome. I would still say I've never seen a better coach, and I don't know of anyone who could hold a candle to him. What a legacy he has left with so many people in so many different ways."

Les Cusworth's arrival at Welford Road brought Bleddyn Jones career at Leicester to an end, prompting Bleddyn to write the following letter to Chalkie White: "I would like to thank you personally for your contribution as a coach to my ability as a rugby player. My mind goes back to 1969 when I came to Leicester, a sapling in the ideologies of the game. The fact that I've been able to develop my skills at the highest level with such a wonderful club owes a great deal to you over the past nine years. Finally, I would like to thank you for your contribution to me as a man. Your values on life, your honesty and integrity have left a deep impression on me. I will obviously miss the playing side for a while, but I will always remember a

Bleddyn Jones – Chalkie's second most selected player with 333 appearances for Leicester

quote of an ex-international, 'The friends you meet and the friends you keep is what makes rugby such a great game'. Thank you for being a good friend of mine."

Although his playing days were now over, Bleddyn Jones maintained his association with the Tigers by succeeding fellow Welshman, Sidney Ifano 'Van' Hopkins as the BBC Leicester matchday commentator in 1987. The two Welsh speakers were knowledgeable, articulate and passionate broadcasters who became the highly respected and much loved voices of Leicester rugby for five decades.

Fine player though Jones had been, demonstrated by Leicester supporters voting him the all-time finest Tigers fly half in a 2008 Legends XV poll, the mercurial Cusworth added a fresh dimension to Leicester's play. Only a narrow defeat at Coventry prevented them from winning the Midlands Merit Table. Tigers finished second in a manner illustrating the still slightly offhand attitude of clubs to the table. Their match at Nottingham on November 28 was cancelled because of frost. It was far from a foregone conclusion that Tigers would have won – as Nottingham enjoyed a fine year and came third – but even though five months of the season remained, the match was not rescheduled and Tigers were unable to secure the victory that would have tied them with Coventry on seven wins out of eight.

In other matches, revenge was taken over Gloucester with a 9-7 victory at Kingsholm, Northampton were thumped 32-6 at Welford Road, while tries by Steve Johnson and Garry Adey saw off the Barbarians 18-6. The Nottingham match, however, was the first of nine cancelled because of frost.

Other clubs, Jerry Day noted, had dropped their training schedules during the freeze. Chalkie, simply produced an amended programme: "Players travelled to Nottingham for a strenuous indoor programme, and in Leicester they ran through snow and on ice-free pathways whenever and wherever they could be found. No excuses were accepted for not training and the players accepted this readily. The attitude had to be right if they wanted to be successful. The rest of Chalkie's thinking was crystal clear. He barked the importance of quality possession, handling, fitness and organisation. The static maul had to disappear, players were forbidden to get cut off, space had to be used and possession retained at all costs. In keeping with the man himself, Chalkie demanded honesty, not only from the players, but also from everyone connected with the club."

Their luck of the draw continued to hold in the early rounds of the cup where Northampton received another pounding, by 29-3, and Broughton Park were beaten 30-7, but the run of consecutive home ties was ended by the quarter-final draw, which sent them to Goldington Road. Bedford had beaten a slightly under-strength Tigers line-up minus both regular goal-kickers, Hare and Dodge, 10-8 only a few months before but were unable to repeat the trick as Hare scored 18 points, including a try, in their 22-12 win.

The semi-final draw looked pretty tough. Wasps were in the early stages of the process that would change them from an amiable suburban operation famed for the sheer number of teams they ran, into one of the dominant forces of the English game in the coming decades. Their 36-14 defeat of Tigers at Sudbury in November had been against a team missing ten regulars, but as Day pointed out, Tigers had developed sufficient depth that other big names had been unable to beat apparently depleted line-ups.

Wasps had approached their first semi-final with high hopes, but were put to the sword by a performance which was among the best in Leicester history, certainly up to that time. In their most important and arguably most demanding match of the season to that point, Tigers recorded their biggest win, an eight-try 43-7 hammering.

Martin Johnson, a young *Mercury* journalist who was beginning to get noticed for his waspish wit, deployed on occasion at the expense of sub-standard performances, could hardly contain his admiration, reporting: "There are occasional moments in sport which intoxicate the senses ... Tigers handed out such a beating to Wasps that those members of John Player Cup final opponents Moseley who watched it on the box yesterday must have staggered from their armchairs with an inferiority complex matched only by a tramp at a palace garden party.

"The score line suggests that either Wasps were bad or the occasion – their first ever semi-final – proved too much for them. In fact, they were simply unlucky enough to run up against what must have been one of the finest club performances for many years. Everyone knew that Wasps would be in trouble if Leicester's backs saw too much of the ball and, thanks to overwhelming superiority up front, they were rarely without it ... Tigers were so quick to the breakdown and Kenney's service so precise, that Les Cusworth was handed the perfect stage for his precocious talents. He's not going on England's summer tour, which leaves the selectors with enough egg on their faces to make a large omelette."

Another writer reckoned Tigers' display simply, "the most compelling performance I have seen for an English club for years." Skipper Wheeler was quoted as being determined to make up for the defeat in the previous season's final, while Day interpreted centre Terry Burwell's view that Tigers could not lose as meaning that "the players could not live with the possibility of disappointing their supporters yet again."

No less determined was Duggan, who had been injured in the quarter-final against Northampton. His place had gone to youth team product Mick Newton, who scored twice in the hammering of Wasps. Duggan returned the following weekend, Easter, for the visits of Neath and Maesteg. Tigers won

Leicester winger Mick Newton started his playing career at Melton Mowbray RFC

both, but Duggan broke his collar bone in the Maesteg match.

"I have no doubt that John would have played had he not got injured, and rightly so," noted Newton. "Chalkie had no choice but to then pick me. It was the icing on the cake so far as my rugby career went, plus I won a few shillings at pontoon on the bus down there!"

It looked for long periods as if the Leicester majority in an 18,000 crowd were to suffer a second consecutive disappointment, as Moseley took control with a try from wing Laird and a drop-goal from outside-half and captain Martin Cooper, to lead 9-3 at the break. Full back Akenhead extended their advantage to nine points shortly after half-time, but Hare, rated Man of the Match by watching Welsh immortal Bleddyn Williams, added two penalties to his early drop-goal to bring Tigers back to 12-9, and Steve Kenney went over on the blind side with three minutes to go, Hare adding the conversion for a 15-12 victory.

Williams reckoned that, "If Leicester had had more pace on the wings, they would have clinched the match long before the end," arguing that they had failed to make the most of opportunities created by Hare's incursions into the line.

David Hands thought it, "A final unmatched for excitement if not for technical excellence," as Tigers clawed their way back into it. Both he and Williams noted that Moseley were disrupted by injuries to Corless and Nutt, but Hands argued, "It was a win for character as much as anything else. From the technical point of view, Moseley had been better in several departments, but Leicester, with the disappointment of 12 months previously nagging at them, would not allow victory to slip away this time. They had also picked up the important All Black habit of being a full 80-minute side."

Jerry Day was delighted, commenting that "The John Player Cup was destined for Welford Road and Chalkie White actually smiled," and on this apparently unprecedented note, Tigers headed off to a civic reception, their defence of the trophy already in mind.

Daily Mirror journalist Chris Lander had, before the match, reported Wheeler's determination to "win it for Chalkie", in part in recognition of his

Leicester Tigers celebrating their first John Player Cup success
(L-R): Ken Kinder (President), Peter Wheeler, Robin Cowling, Tudor Thomas, Chalkie White, Paul Dodge, Nick Joyce, Jerry Day (Secretary)

22 years of service, but also because he had recently been passed over as England's next coach. While an intermittent presence in England squads for much of the 1970s, Dusty Hare saw enough on the occasions when he was called up to have a sense of how training developed over that time.

According to Hare: "When I first became involved with England, coaching in the backs was restricted to run-throughs of various set moves. John Elders was in charge then and there was nothing like the organisation there is now. Then John Burgess took over in 1975, and suddenly we were training on Sundays and showing a more serious approach to the England team, but although I was in the squad, I never played under him. He was like the next Lancastrian Dick Greenwood, in the matter of chest pounding, and trying to install in us the pride of playing for England. Yet, despite success in South Africa [1972] and New Zealand [1973], England had a terrible first half of the seventies with whitewashes in 1972 and 1976, and of the 20 Five Nation matches in that period, England won only four.

"With Tony Neary and Fran Cotton following John Pullin as captain, England had experienced leaders. Yet, somewhere it all went wrong. The

"The RFU were blind to the fact that Chalkie White was the best coach in English rugby" – Dusty Hare

biggest problem was that the selectors tended to make decisions straight away, just when players had got a settled side. It was all change at the slightest set back, and experienced, quality players were thrust aside in the search for the perfect formula. Peter Colston took over when Burgess decided he had had enough after the tour to Australia in 1975. My only caps under him were at third choice in Paris 1978 and against the All Blacks later the same year."

Chalkie's record with Tigers and Midlands, including his victories over Australia in 1975 and Argentina, meant that he was one of three candidates short-listed, along with England Schools coach Mike Davis and Lancashire's Des Seabrook, when Colston stepped down after three years in March 1979.

Mike Davis won 16 caps, at lock, for England (1963-70) and later developed a shrewd eye for identifying talent as a coach

Budge Rogers – England's Chairman of Selectors

Lander reckoned that "White's record made him the obvious man," but it was Davis who got the job, a decision that Lander reported had "everyone at Leicester incensed" and determined to embarrass the committee box at Twickenham with their performance in the final. Davis had taken England Schools to a Grand Slam and was to do the same with the senior side in his first season. Considering how long he had been away from first class rugby and that he had no senior coaching experience, he learned very quickly.

Despite having the advantage of being a former international player with 16 caps, Davis was as surprised as anyone else when he was offered the job: "I was coaching the England Schools 19 Group side at the time. I had been asked to coach the South West team and was then watched by Derek Morgan. Later I got a phone call from RFU Secretary Bob Weighill, who asked me if I was interested in the job with the England senior side. When I was told later that I had been given the job I was again surprised as I had only coached school boys at this stage.

"Budge Rogers was Chairman of Selectors at the time. In addition to Budge and myself, the committee included Derek Morgan, John Finlan, Mike Weston and John Young. The Chairman of Selectors was appointed by the RFU, the selectors were then appointed by Budge. Regarding the coaching job, there were three candidates, myself, Des Seabrook of Lancashire and Chalkie White of Leicester Tigers. Naturally, Bill Beaumont and the northern lads wanted Des to have the job, while the Leicester Tigers players were behind Chalkie, and quite right as well.

"If Chalkie or Des had been given the job both would have done a first-class job, in a role where there was no blueprint or guidelines. For the England team, selection was everything, and Budge Rogers was meticulous. We would go over and over different positions until we got it right, but I rated myself a good selector rather than a good coach. Typical of Chalkie, he wrote me a lovely letter congratulating me on my appointment and offering his support."

18

Keeping the Cup – 1979-80

In keeping with their policy of never standing still and continuing to evolve in search of further strengths, there was fresh close-season recruitment with Kevin Williams and Clive Woodward both following the footsteps from Loughborough of Nigel Gillingham. They had seen their former teammate become a cup winner in his first season, and would be tempted with the prospects of a planned international tour to be followed by Tigers' centenary season in 1980-81.

"I joined Tigers in 1979," recalled Williams, "after four successful and enjoyable years in university playing for the Loughborough Students team – mainly under coach Jim Greenwood who developed an expansive type of 'total rugby' that allowed us to compete against some of the best English club sides of the time such as Gloucester and Leicester. Tigers had beaten Moseley in the John Player Cup the season before and Leicester was the most obvious choice for me at the time – especially to have a better chance for higher representative honours, than it was to go back to Wales, or move to London Welsh. However, having played against Tigers on a couple of occasions as a student, and experienced their style of play, the decision was not that straightforward.

Kevin Williams made the short journey from Loughborough to Leicester

"After some interesting discussions with my student teammate, Clive Woodward, who was also in the same position as myself and also looking at options post-university, we came to the conclusion that it would be worth popping along to pre-season training to see what the then newly crowned English champions could offer. Although we were warmly welcomed to the club by players and coaching staff alike, we experienced some painful 'non-contact' training sessions as the current incumbents made certain that we knew there would be stiff competition for us to break into the first team ranks!

"The coaching style of Chalkie White, whilst not the same as our previous coach, worked well for us as he also challenged the players to think about the game – both on the field and in the clubhouse afterwards. He challenged all players to improve and we very quickly learned that praise had to be earned. His famous saying was 'Let the press tell you how good you are – I will tell you how to get better.' We both felt absolutely at home with the competitive, but friendly family atmosphere and decided to stay – in my case for the rest of my playing career!"

Woodward went straight into the 1st XV for the opening day at Bedford, despite the assumption of many Tigers fans that the cup-winning team would get first shot, and scored in a 34-12 romp that saw Hare take a big step towards another record season with 26 points including two tries. Ten of the first 11 matches were won before a Swansea team on their way to a first unofficial Welsh title since the First World War won 27-12 at Welford Road, with five Merit Table wins including a 42-4 thumping of Northampton setting Tigers well on their way to winning the competition for the first time.

Clive Woodward formed a formidable centre partnership with Paul Dodge at Leicester

Woodward, an astute thinker destined for his own dazzling career in coaching, was taking notice of Chalkie, "who brought out the best in us". In his memoirs Woodward compared Chalkie to his other mentors, Earl Kirton and Jim Greenwood:

"Like Greenwood and Kirton, Chalkie also believed that your first bit of ball might be your best bit of ball, so you'd better make the most of it – it was the one common message coming from these three great coaches. He too encouraged us to be creative with the ball and to use everyone on the pitch effectively, an approach to rugby that would have been very hard for me to give up after Loughborough.

"And where other coaches in the top clubs were known to scream and yell,

Chalkie always treated us with respect. At training he was clearly conscious that we'd been at work all day and made every session fun and enjoyable. I'd sometimes drive three or four hours from tough sales meetings just to get to a session. Chalkie's style was to have the groundsman there with big hot mugs of tea for everyone on arrival. He really believed in the importance of little things, something most coaches overlooked completely. We could talk to Chalkie ... and he'd actually listen. He might not have agreed with our views, but no one was left out of the equation if they had something to say ... His secrets to success were simple and so blindingly obvious."

The Leicester squad was further strengthened in December when Mike Poulson also joined Tigers from Loughborough University: "How I joined Tigers was pretty simple really. Apart from a bit of union at school I only played rugby league growing up – originally at Wakefield Trinity then for Castleford juniors up to A-team level, it was a brilliant set-up there with greats like Malcolm Reilly and Dennis Hartley coaching. After graduating I did a post-grad year at Loughborough, where Clive Woodward was captain. After Loughborough I was working for Rank Xerox in Leicester and tried to commute and play rugby union for my hometown club Wakefield, but the travelling was too much. I was already good mates with Clive and I knew Les Cusworth, who was in the same year as my sister at school, so I moved to Tigers. I played my first game for the Swifts at Lutterworth and made my first team debut at home against Headingley."

The Barbarians game was lost 9-8 in a quagmire, but this was to be just about the only setback of a season which, from early on, had Secretary Day predicting a third consecutive trek to Twickenham. Thirty-three wins equalled the club record, but that might not have counted for very much in the eyes of Tigers fans had they not included yet another of the cup runs to which they were becoming accustomed.

The opening round brought Orrell, upwardly-mobile beneficiaries of the new competitive era which gave them the chance to upset teams who would not previously have given them the fixture – on one famous occasion leading a Harlequins captain to report being "ambushed in a lay-by just off the M6" to Welford Road for only the second time in their history. They were not disgraced, going down only 16-7 as Smith crossed once, Cusworth dropped two goals and Hare kicked two penalties.

Next up was a challenging trip to Moseley for a repeat of the previous season's final and, just as pertinently, of their only Merit Table loss that season. However, as Hands recalled "there was seldom much doubt of the outcome this time" with Dodge outstanding in a 17-7 win in which Cusworth once more landed a drop goal.

Cusworth did it again, adding a drop goal, in a 22-0 quarter-final victory over London Scottish which failed to enthuse the critics. One journalist reckoned

Scottish were "dreadfully unambitious" and Tigers "almost over anxious to live up to their attractive image" in a tie which saw 34 penalties awarded. Hare landed three of them, converted Smith's try and after only three and a half years with the club took himself to within single figures of Bob Barker's all-time club record of 1,117 points. Hare took the record a fortnight later at Sale in the same game as John Duggan equalled Barker's modern tries mark of 158.

Hare added a further 12 points the following week at Harlequins, defying the winds which spoilt the John Player semi-final as Tigers won 16-9, Dodge scoring the only try. Their 12th win in a row, it earned them another trip to the same part of West London on April 19.

Bob Barker a consistent points scorer throughout his 320-game career for Leicester

They arrived strangely out of sorts. While they had won at Neath, never a simple proposition, their victorious run had juddered to a halt with losses at Pontypool and Bristol. The win at Neath also had its costs as Duggan, still tied with Barker on 158 tries, picked up an injury and for the second year running was ruled out of the final.

As Prop Steve Redfern, who was playing his third final, recalled: "Each year the number of travelling supporters who made the journey from Leicester became bigger and bigger to such an extent that it became like playing a home game at Welford Road."

Irish, in their first final, played a tight, disrupting game and had the satisfaction of scoring the only try through back row Smythe. They also maintained their record of keeping their line intact in cup games, but to no avail. As David Hands recalled, "There was none of the excitement of the previous year, largely because it was always obvious Leicester would win." Pressure and field position earned them a succession of scores through two outstanding kickers – Cusworth adding two more drops while Hare claimed 15 points from four penalties and a drop, in a comfortable 21-9 win.

While hopes of a record number of wins and reaching 1,000 points were thwarted by limp displays in the remaining matches against Rosslyn Park

Leicester Tigers scrum-half Steve Kenney finds a gap in the London Irish defence

Chalkie visiting Leicester's three Lions on tour in South Africa in 1980 – Clive Woodward, Peter Wheeler and Paul Dodge

Lions centre Paul Dodge surges past Colin Beck (left) during the match against the Junior Springboks at the Wanderers Stadium, Johannesburg. A replacement for the injured Welsh centre David Richards, Dodge played in the final two Tests on the 1980 tour of South Africa

and Moseley, Tigers still went into their centenary season in the best possible shape. But there was much to come before the home celebrations started as three Tigers toured South Africa with the British Lions – Woodward and Wheeler as original selections and Dodge as a replacement.

When all three were chosen for the Third Test, Chalkie, saying "If I live for another 100 years it will never happen again," dug into his savings to pay for the trip to Port Elizabeth. There was no happy ending – the Lions lost 12-10 and Woodward was blamed for the decisive try – but the surprise visit by their club coach was well-appreciated.

"We didn't know Chalkie was coming to see us play in South Africa," said Dodge, "and it was great to see him. It made it an even more special occasion."

Nor was that the end of a memorable summer for Chalkie and the Tigers, as they set off on their centenary tour of Australia and Fiji.

19

The Centenary Tour: Australia & Fiji – 1980

The tour was the idea of the club's Secretary Jerry Day, who envisaged playing against teams in all the major rugby playing nations, representatives of whom had all played at Leicester. Because of restrictions on time that players and officials could devote to the tour, it was eventually decided to reduce the countries to be visited and to play teams with whom Tigers had recent associations.

An important part of the plan was to return the 1973 visit of the Fijians, who had attracted the largest crowd for a club game at Leicester for a match long remembered by those who played or watched. Sydney clubs Randwick and Eastern Suburbs had both visited Leicester in the previous four years, and a further link with Randwick was John Quick who played Number 8 in the late 1960s, scoring Tigers' first hat-trick against the Barbarians. The game against Queensland was a reciprocal arrangement, with the home game at Leicester in October during their tour of the UK.

The tour was envisaged as a forerunner for further such ventures, yet anyone envisaging it as a holiday was advised by the indefatigable John Allen, who added the task of providing a tour report to his other endeavours, and to stay out of ear shot of Chalkie, who was quoted at some length: "There are various kinds of tours. From the Lions tours where players are involved in games two matches higher than our Five Nations Championship, to the social tour – ours is somewhere above half way. We have set ourselves a tall order, particularly with the first half of the tour, which involves three, matches in Australia. We'll be up against some very good players and, I don't want to be disrespectful, but some of our lads who are not internationals will be stretched, but I still want to win all six – I'm only satisfied with the best. Our first match in Australia against Queensland will be a tough one.

"They were the provincial champions last season and although they lost the title in Sydney this year, they will be hard to beat. For me, though, the big one, the show piece, will be our match against Randwick. It will be the Australian club champions against the English club champions. It will be

Leicester Tigers Tour Squad – Australia & Fiji, 1980
Back Row (L-R): Ian Smith, Steve Redfern, Angus Collington, Steve Johnson, Nick Jackson, Nigel Gillingham, Nick Joyce, Garry Adey, Dave Forfar, Chalkie White (coach)
Middle Row (L-R): John Duggan, Dusty Hare, Paul Dodge, Mark Duffelen, Peter Wheeler (tour captain), Kevin Williams, Terry Burwell, Tim Barnwell, Ray Needham, Paul Stone
Front Row (L-R): Brian Hall, Andy Key, Les Cusworth, Mike Merrimen, John White, Steve Kenney, Larry Parkes

interesting particularly because of Australia's recent success against the All Blacks and this is the one I would very much like to exhibit our skills and start out on a fine game."

Tigers' one worry was that Wheeler had injured his neck on the last day of the Lions tour, had not trained since his return and was under orders to rest for two weeks: "That's a blow to us; the Australians and Fijians are half way through their season and should be at their peak, so to lose a player of Peter's experience for more than two games will be a blow to us. There is a danger that by starting the season in August some of our players will be sick of the sight of a rugby ball by December or January, but it's up to me and the wise old heads of the club to look out for this and prevent it from happening."

In Wheeler's likely absence it was agreed an experienced hooker was needed as cover. John White, who had been the alternative to Wheeler for much of the 1970s before losing that role to Mark Duffelen, was added to the party which left Birmingham airport at 9am on July 31 *en route* to Amsterdam, where White joined them.

There was an eventful overnight stop in Vancouver, reported in *The Telegraph*, which became national news: "The Leicester Tigers players waiting in the queue for their flight to Brisbane when a married couple standing nearby started arguing violently, at first the players tried to ignore the incident thinking it was just a domestic argument that had got a little out of hand, but the woman then started to physically attack her husband apparently in an attempt to prevent him from taking their children out of the country. She lunged at him a couple of times with a large carving knife and stabbed him once under the arm. As the scuffle broke away Dave Forfar got around her and caught her in a bear hug while Number 8 Garry Adey whisked the children out of harm's way, and second row Nick Joyce and centre Brian Hall wrestled the knife away from the women. The whole family were taken away by Canadian security guards."

Continuing via Honolulu and Sydney, the tour party arrived in Brisbane on August 2 at 11.00am. Any doubts the Tigers had about the seriousness of the Queensland match were dispelled within minutes of their arrival, when the state team announced they intended to field the same team that had beaten the All Blacks a month ago on the same ground and just returned victorious from a three-match tour of New Zealand.

"This is going to be the toughest match on tour for the Tigers," noted Allen, "and it is terribly unfortunate they have to play within three days of their arrival after a 12,000-mile journey, in temperature around 75 degrees, and without injured skipper Peter Wheeler, but this is the sort of challenge that sets the adrenalin running of coach Chalkie White and his Leicester team. That Queenslanders lay great stress on this match is shown by the fact that the TV cameras will be there and a video recording will be shown throughout the state in the evening. Queensland has 12 Test players, past and current, in their line-up, including Australian fly half Paul MacLean. With the firm dry conditions, the game is expected to be fast and open on this well-appointed Ballymore Ground with its 75ft high goal posts, its newly extended grandstand and its grassy banks for standing spectators"

On Monday August 4, at a floodlit Queensland Cricket Club, the Leicester party attended a dinner in their honour, where several, met past Australian Test Cricketers, Ray Lindwall, Bill Brown, and "Slasher" McKay.

"I captained Leicester in the game against Queensland in Brisbane," explained Nick Joyce. "Steve Johnson had been promised the captaincy which he undertook for the rest of the tour, but before the Queensland game 'Johno' told me he was right behind me and would give me his support in any way he could."

"A cloudy day cut temperatures to a more reasonable 65 degrees," noted John Allen in his tour report. "After the opening minutes when Leicester ran well with the ball, Queensland counter attacked and left wing Brendan Moon nearly created a try. From a maul 30 metres out from their line, Leicester were penalised and Paul Maclean put Queensland into a 3-0 lead in the seventh

"Leicester – Champion rugby club in England: Garry Adey, Tim Barnwell and Steve Johnson spell out the message with their Tigers jerseys from their Brisbane hotel" – The Courier Mail

minute. Leicester were running everything they could, with flankers Smith and Johnson very fast on the loose ball, and for ten minutes Leicester were well in Queensland's 22.

"Leicester were driven back by a long-range penalty, 15 metres into their own half, and a fine break by full back Gould put right wing Peter Grigg away, but he was well tackled by John Duggan who had come across. From the line-out, an untidy tap back gave Queensland a simple try in the 20th minute.

"Queensland looked quite quick in the backs, but Leicester's cover defence was well organised. In the 27th minute, however, left wing Brendan Moon, holder of 11 Test caps, put Queensland further ahead when he took a long pass, handed off John Duggan and raced round for a fine try which Maclean converted to make it 13-0. Leicester worked their way into the Queensland 22, and from a maul near the line Adey charged over for a try which Hare converted. Two minutes later Hall went off with an injured arm, and was replaced by Burwell.

"There was a rather indecisive opening ten-minute period in the second half which saw a

Queensland's Wallaby winger Brendan Moon

lot of inaccurate kicking by both sides. A Leicester forward was spoken to by the referee in the 60th minute, and Maclean increased Queensland's lead to 16-6 with a penalty goal. Queensland had numerous chances with left winger Moon, looking particularly sharp, but it was full back Gould who eventually broke Leicester's defence in the 77th minute with a fine try which Maclean converted.

"Steve Johnson made a great dash for the line in one of Leicester's rare visits into the Queensland 22, but Smith was held up just short. Queensland were penalised, and from a tap penalty by Kenney, Adey crashed over for his second try which Hare converted, and the final whistle went."

The Tigers team were reported to be annoyed with themselves for not playing as well as they might have done, but local opinion was impressed by a club team taking on the might of a state. The tourists then moved on to a two-day break at Surfers Paradise on Queensland's Gold Coast, losing no time in getting down to the extensive white, sun-baked beaches and into the warm, clear water of the South Pacific. This was no holiday, of course, and they were soon back to the realities of a training session, with Chalkie putting them through their paces from 9am onwards.

Next up in Sydney were Eastern Suburbs, keen to avenge their 22-15 defeat the Tigers inflicted on them in 1975. Among ten changes, giving everyone a run-out in the first two matches, was full back Andy Key.

Speaking about the tour, Andy Key reminisced: "The Leicester Tigers centenary tour was a dream come true for me, and for my fellow tourists

Leicester flanker 'Dosser' Smith puts his shoulder to the wheel in training

Mick Merriman and Mark Duffelen as we were the youngest in the tour party and had been teammates in the Tigers youth team. My own circumstances had changed somewhat in the months leading up to the tour when my girlfriend of three years, Jo, discovered she was pregnant and we made the decision to 'tie the knot', that June. We were both delighted when, two weeks before the tour, our daughter Nadine was born on July 18, and with the full support of both families, I received their blessing to go and enjoy the trip of a life-time."

Andy Key emulated his dad Maurice, to also play full back for Leicester

The match against the Eastern Suburbs was played on Sunday August 10 and saw a solid victory for the Tigers, as noted by John Allen: "This win over Eastern Suburbs, Sydney, was very heartening indeed, especially with so many young and inexperienced players in the side, and it has kept morale high in the party which is already in excellent spirits.

"Among the spectators were ex-Tigers players Pete Clements, John Tipper, Roy Webber from Belgrave RFC, and John Quick – quite a Leicester reunion. Families pic-nicked in the club grounds and there was a general party air, but any resemblance to Twickenham ended abruptly at that point. The playing surface was largely devoid of grass, and one corner of the pitch was totally bone hard. In the latter half of winter here, the temperature was in the high 60s and the locals were complaining of the cold.

"Les Cusworth opened the scoring with a penalty goal in the third minute, and with the forwards getting a good share of the ball, especially from the loose, the back division was given plenty of scope for running. Mick Merriman snapped away busily at his forwards' heels and harried his opposite number in to errors, whilst at other times he handed out a good service to his fly half or had a nibble or two of his own to give a very tidy all-round performance.

"There had been several forays into the opposition 22 before the first try came in the 26th minute, when a move including excellent handling by Johnson, Parkes, Stone and Burwell put Williams over for an excellent try which Cusworth converted before kicking his second penalty goal to give Tigers a 12-0 lead at half-time.

"The second half opened with a fine run by Andy Key to put Barnwell away. He cut inside, fed Gillingham who was stopped, injured an ankle and was taken off to be replaced by Joyce. Eastern Suburbs got a penalty goal, kicked by ex-Wasps full back Geoff Richards in the 50th minute, but five minutes later Andy Key rounded off a fine move and crowned off a fine individual performance with a try which Cusworth converted to make the score 15-3 in Tigers' favour.

"Clouds of dust rose as the forwards set up rucks and mauls with Forfar, Johnson, Jackson, and Collington prominent in the loose, and Needham, Joyce, Duffelin and Stone doing valiant work in support. It was no surprise when, after an interception by Needham, a move developed for Barnwell to score after a jinking run from the 22. Cusworth converted in the 75th minute

"Tigers relaxed somewhat as the game ran into injury time and Suburbs nearly scored, but Leicester's defence, aided by some poor handling by the home side, held out quite comfortably."

Next was the match with Randwick, a clash of England's champions with New South Wales's leading club, which captured local imagination. Randwick showed how seriously they were taking it by flying the Ella brothers – Mark, Glen and Gary – who had made their name on the Australian Schools tour of 1977-78, and whose presence usually doubled the gate, back from the NSW tour of New Zealand.

"The game against Randwick was billed as the world club championship final," recalls Ian Smith: "Prior to the game the press posted a photograph of us holding up our famous lettered shirts spelling the word 'Champions'. Before the Randwick game, Chalkie White pointed out to me that the Randwick fly

'Champions' (L-R): Ian Smith, Paul Dodge, Brian Hall, Les Cusworth, Tim Barnwell, Angus Collington, Mike Meriman, Kevin Williams, Paul Stone

half, Mark Ella, was a very special player and nobody tackles him. This gave me a huge incentive to pressurise him and make my tackles, which I did."

Played on Wednesday August 13, Steve Johnson led a much-changed Leicester team due to injuries to Gillingham and Hall, while Duggan was a late withdrawal. Paul Stone kept his place at prop for his second match.

"A vintage performance by the Leicester forwards, and almost flawless play by the Leicester backs, and Dusty Hare's superb kicking gave Leicester a convincing victory over Randwick, 31-19," wrote John Allen in his tour report.

"Just before the game started, blue skies with temperatures in the high 70s gave way to dark cloud drifting in over the palm-fringed Coogee Bay to lower the temperature considerably more to Leicester's liking, and for a short period there was even rain as well.

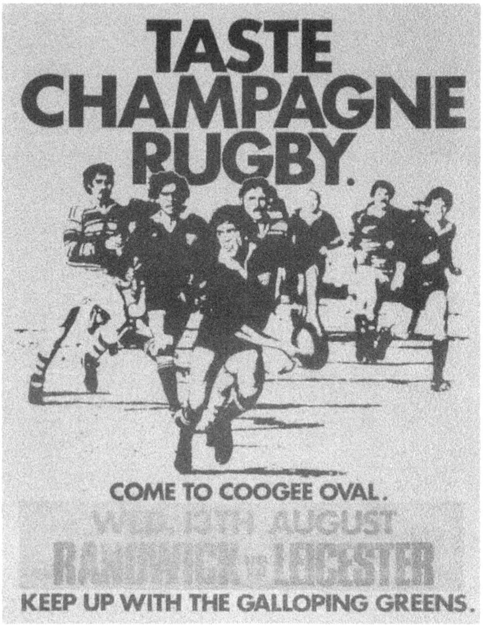

Leicester v Randwick at Coogee Oval

"Although Leicester held the upper hand territorially and had taken a 3-0 lead through a penalty from Dusty Hare in the eighth minute, Randwick scored 13 points in a short space of time through two excellent tries by their wingers running out of defence, and a penalty goal by their ace goal-kicker Ramsey to add to a conversion. This ten-point lead was quite against the run of play, but it had the home crowd bubbling with excitement at the thought of putting the 'Champion Club' in its place.

"In the 30th minute, Cusworth, who was having a great game, switched play from right to left, Redfern robbed the Randwick forwards and fed Dusty Hare who made a magnificent run from the halfway line to put Smith over for a try which Hare then converted, and to aid Leicester's morale he then kicked two penalty goals, one from 55 metres, to give Leicester a 15-13 lead.

"This was a lead they never lost from then on, because the forwards who had threatened to take the game by the scruff of the neck began to dominate the Randwick pack in no uncertain fashion, and on a couple of occasions in set scrums they shoved the Randwick eight for 15 metres. The whole team pulled out every trick in the book and ran the Randwick defence ragged. Hare kicked another penalty followed by a drop goal. John White scored a try from a tap

Despite Mark Ella's tackle, watched by teammate Tim Barnwell (K), Leicester Tigers forward Ian Smith scores a memorable try against Randwick

down at a line-out five metres out and Cusworth rounded off the scoring with a neat drop goal from 25 metres.

"The Leicester side had taught the New South Wales champions a sharp lesson in the art of forward play and Leicester held their heads high as indeed they deserve to do so – a fact which the Randwick supporters were quick to appreciate as they cheered the Tigers resoundingly off the field."

Both Ian Smith and Steve Kenney remember the way in which Chalkie's ability to respond to match situations, even against an adversary of Bob Dwyer's quality, was vital to this victory.

For Smith, "The first half saw the Randwick team dominating. Chalkie sent on a message to encourage us to 'maul' more, which we did. Dusty made a break and fed me the ball. I was delighted to score the try which led to Tigers being declared unofficial world club champions. Oh, and as I scored the try, Mark Ella's attempted tackle could not stop me. The delight in the

Tigers' changing room was amazing, a memory that will stay with all who were fortunate to be a part of it."

While Kenney recalled: "Bob Dwyer was running Randwick at the time. For the first ten minutes of the game, they played us to bits. So, we changed from playing a wide game to a forward game. After the match Bob Dwyer said, 'we saw the ball for ten minutes and then not for the next 70.' To beat a full strength Randwick on their own track must go down as one of the Tigers' great victories. At the after-match reception, we were honoured by the presence of Nick Shehadie and John Howard, President and Treasurer respectively of the Australian Rugby Union. On our last evening in Australia, Chalkie White was invited to speak to the Randwick players. I'm sure they found it interesting and instructive."

Leaving Australia for Fiji, Tigers could reflect that they had been a credit to themselves, Leicester, England and rugby football, but it hadn't all been about rugby. There were equally vivid memories of trips on the Brisbane River, to the Koala Bear Park, a boat cruise around Sydney Harbour, a visit to the Opera House, a warm welcome from the local people, and the inevitable but pleasurable after-match celebrations – with the presentations of ties, plaques, pennants, and books – a civic reception at Randwick, and finally a completely free day before heading to Fiji. The 5am alarm call and four-and-a-half hour flight to Nadi Airport on Friday August 15 left the team little time to prepare for Leicester's first game in Fiji the following day – also to be John Duggan's final appearance for the club.

John Allen's tour report described Leicester's first match in Fiji when the Tigers faced Lautoka: "On a well grassed, though hard, pitch with a background of tropical trees, hibiscus flowers in profusion and picturesque hills all bathed in sunshine from a cloudless sky, Leicester beat Lautoka,12-6, with Dusty Hare kicking two drop goals from tap penalties and converting a try from Ian Smith. For the home side, centre-three-quarter Vesivesi Bose scored a try which full back Rabitu converted.

"In the end, the victory was a tribute to Leicester's physical and mental endurance. If anything, they physically out-lasted the home side in heat approaching 90 degrees. Particularly in the second half, they had to put up with up with what was, to put it kindly, rather inexpert refereeing. Admittedly, the referee appeared to know more about the laws of the game than the home players, but the head-high tackles and off-side play that often went unpunished were a test of patience. Leicester players stood up well to all of it and never lost their discipline, which was a great plus mark in their favour.

"The game never really got going. The home side had little organisation, but in true Fijian fashion they ran everywhere and got in Leicester's way. Leicester's forwards' attempts to pull in the opposition pack were thwarted

John Duggan, a regular try scorer for Leicester Tigers (1970-80), played his last match against Lautoka in Fiji

by repeated and blatant off side play which went largely unpunished. When a tackle was made the game was often stopped, so consequently it proceeded in fits and starts. The local sides approach was rather wild, arms flailing everywhere, and they were not averse to the odd trip-up or two whenever an opponent went by, but they had a great deal of natural ability and ball handling skill. It was not a great spectacle by any stretch of the imagination, but a useful win which has established Leicester in Fijian eyes, a defeat would have been disastrous."

"It was so hot in Fiji, you were just glad to be in the shade and out of the sun," recalled Ray Needham, and after the match the players travelled 12 miles back to their hotel for a shower. The non-holiday theme continued when those who hadn't played were dropped off three miles away and told to jog back to the Gateway Hotel where, that evening, a reception was held around the swimming pool, followed by a concert of traditional Fijian singing.

John Allen reported that: "The 130-mile coach ride from Lautoka on the east coast, across to Suva on the west was a wonderful experience. For the first 40 miles we travelled on good roads, past hundreds of acres of sugar cane fields which in turn gave way to rolling hills and a new forestation programme designed to give some diversity to the local economy. Then we rode along dirt roads for the next 50 miles, for most of the way skirting the shores of the Pacific Ocean with its indigo blue waters breaking on coral reefs half-a-mile out to sea

"Then we came upon a scene of devastation over many miles. Devastation caused last Easter when 90 inches of rain fell in four days, bringing down huge slices of hills, ripping out chunks of road and washing away houses, animals and crops. Hundreds of dead trees still lie in heaps on the waterlogged ground as the homeless still live in tents while their houses are being re built. It was a salutary lesson that amidst all this beauty, ugliness of a kind is never far away.

"Back to the rugby football, for tomorrow's game against the Fijian Combined Services, multiple injuries and the sharing out of games amongst the players caused the selectors a few minor headaches. None of the injuries are serious, but they're just taking a bit of time to heal. The Combined

Services are reported to be a little more physically mature than last Saturday's opponents, but with the match being played at 5pm, and with the weather a little cooler on this side of the island, Tigers are looking for their fourth successive win in this match. Meanwhile, for those of you at home, who have been rather envious of all the sunshine we are enjoying, let me tell that it has been raining nearly all day here."

Played at the Fiji National Stadium in Suva on Wednesday August 20, Leicester Tigers won the fifth match of their tour, defeating Combined Services, 8-4, as reported by John Allen: "Leicester, making one late change from their selected side when prop forward Paul Stone had to withdraw because of a cold with his place taken by Steve Redfern, kicked off with the wind and rain at their backs on a firm pitch which, after two days of rain, was slippery and covered in pools of water.

"For the first ten minutes, Leicester dominated the play and it was no surprise when they took a 4-0 lead, when in the fifth minute Tim Barnwell jinked over from 15 metres for a try after Cusworth had made a delightful break on the short side after the Leicester pack had put in a tremendous shove that sent the opposing eight backwards at a trot. Cusworth did some fine tactical kicking; ably assisted by the Leicester pack which was giving him excellent possession. Both sides, were however, finding handling a bit difficult at this stage.

"Gradually the Combined Services began to get more into the game, and in the 21st minute a magical bit of passing put Sela in for a try to level the scores. He would have repeated the effort two minutes later but for a great cover tackle by Nick Jackson.

"The gusty wind was making life a bit difficult at the line-out, and it also took two of Cusworths high kicks out on the full. The confident home side now thrilled the crowd, with its excellent handling, but the closing stages of the half saw Leicester coming back thanks to good work by the forwards, with Johnson, Redfern and Forfar storming in and Jackson and Adey doing well at lock. But the Fijians were more skilful at picking up the ball from the ground, and there lay the main difference at this stage.

"Half-time came with the scores level, but from Leicester's kick off the Services Number 8, Marika, raced up field through some weak tackling and covered 80 metres before Kevin Williams, who had raced back, was able to hack the ball into touch near the Leicester line.

"The conditions were now really appalling, reminiscent of last season's Barbarians match, and in the 55th minute Smith was taken off with an injured ankle, which later proved not serious, and Nick Joyce went into the second row to allow Adey to go to Number 8 and Forfar to flank.

"Leicester dominated in the final quarter of the match and, with the only really fluent and flawless handling move they had put together, they bewildered

Line-out action against Fiji Combined Services. Leicester players (L-R): Steve Redfern, Garry Adey, Ray Needham, Nick Jackson, Steve Johnson

the opposition and Cusworth scored in the corner to make the game safe. The Leicester pack had once again proved its great value as indeed had the fitness of the whole side, which once again had out-lasted the opposition. This was a good Leicester win although there had been some really anxious moments early on."

That evening, the touring Tigers were honoured guests at a reception organised by the British High Commission, before their final training session on Friday August 22, and the final game of the centenary tour on Saturday 23. Captain Peter Wheeler, now fully recovered from injury, started a game for the first time on tour

Reporting on the tour's final match, John Allen noted: "Leicester ended their six-match tour in the South Pacific with a really workmanlike victory when they beat the Fijian RU Chairman's XV, 12-0, at the National Stadium in Suva today. Once again, the palm must go to Leicester's pack for their skill and expertise, but praise to the whole team once again on outlasting the opposition because of their physical fitness. The heat here is not of the kind that English players are used to, but thanks to the skilful training programme arranged by coach Chalkie White, the Tigers have never been found wanting.

"The home side kicked off with a gusty wind at their backs and they were in running action in the opening minutes, trying to do what their coach had said they would, just 'run everything', but after these opening flurries the Tigers pack steadily and remorselessly took control and denied them good possession. At half-time there was no score.

Former Tigers forward Eric Lacey, one of the great personalities at Welford Road, as a player (1947-59) and as club President (1979-81).

"Two minutes into the second half, Dusty Hare put Tigers into a 3-0 lead with a simple penalty goal from 12 metres out. In the 50th minute, David Forfar was taken off with a cut ear, which necessitated stitches, and his place was taken on the flank by Angus Collington. Five minutes later, Wheeler took a tap penalty five metres out but dropped the ball over the line.

"A miss-kick by Hare was fielded by the Fijian left wing, but a great covering tackle by Cusworth prevented an almost certain try. When Leicester were penalised two metres out from their goal line, the Fijian hosts tried to run the ball but Cusworth intercepted and raced 70 metres up field only for his intended pass to Burwell to be knocked down by a defender. Merriman and Burwell were quick on to the Fijian full back who was forced to touchdown. From the scrum, first Johnson and then Redfern nearly got over, but after Dodge was tackled ten metres short, the ball came back sweetly for Cusworth to drop a neat goal in the 68th minute. Hare kicked two further penalty goals as Leicester kept up continuous pressure on a now well-beaten side.

"In their six matches, of which they won five and lost one, Leicester scored 99 points and conceded 54, with Dusty Hare top points scorer with 41, followed by Les Cusworth with 22. In 48 hours, we shall be home. What the tour has done for the players is of immense value."

20

The Tigers' Centenary Season – 1980-81

The defence of the Midlands Merit Table title was launched with victories over Bedford and Nuneaton before the first of three prestigious centenary fixtures at Welford Road, the visit of the Irish Wolfhounds. Like the Barbarians, the Wolfhounds were a nomadic club with no home ground. They were established in 1956 as an invitational side to spread the rugby gospel among the towns and villages of Ireland, and for younger players to have experience of playing with experienced internationals. Their final recorded appearance was in 1987, but the Wolfhounds name survives as the Ireland 'A' team, linking the past and future of Irish rugby.

Played on Wednesday September 10, Leicester got their centenary celebrations off to a winning, if not convincing, start with a 10-6 victory, as was reported by the veteran *Telegraph* rugby writer, John Mason: "Leicester, blowing fitfully as the gusting wind, cobbled together one of their less distinguished victories last night, beating the Wolfhounds by a goal and a try to two penalty goals in a centenary match at Welford Road.

"Despite five more changes to an already much revised team, the Wolfhounds settled swiftly to an attacking rhythm, following a penalty goal in the first minute by McNeil. The alphabetically – jerseyed Leicester scrambled anxiously and defensively deep in their own half. There was a heel against the head as well, and the Wolfhounds' backs used their possession effectively

"But at Leicester it is never long before Hare is busily involved in one way or another. Attack is his forte, defence a necessary chore. A miss-move in the centre brought Hare dashing into the line, and Williams, the right wing, gathered the kick ahead at speed. When checked, Williams worked the ball back inside as his colleagues converged, and the man at the bottom of the pile was Hare, the try scorer.

"McNeil kicked a second penalty goal to restore the lead of the Wolfhounds. They continued to attack inventively, and the back row of Ripley, Uttley and Gareth Williams were always prominent, and twice, came close to scoring. But Leicester's team work, a prime strength, triumphed late in the half. Again,

Hare swept down the middle. Barnwell was on his left shoulder and when the tackle came Woodward was on the inside for the return pass and a gallop to the posts. Hare converted.

"The benefits of Leicester's August tour to Australia and Fiji were readily apparent, not only because of their sun tans. But there were disadvantages too. The assumption that someone would always be in support bred carelessness, and too often in useful attacking positions the ball was allowed to go astray. The Wolfhounds seized gleefully on these errors and were unlucky not to have drawn level when Hooks, Sparks and scrum-half O'Conner combined alertly in an attack covering 70 yards.

"Woodward, Leicester's third Lion, was hurt halting the raid and was replaced by Key, who at once had the unnerving prospect of confronting McNaughton and Irwin when they were in full flight. The strong running of both centres was the outstanding feature of a spirited second half. The wind upset the goal kickers, nor did a sharp shower of rain help Hare, unusually for him on this ground at any rate, missed three kicks at goal and at all times the Wolfhounds, scratch side or not were close to bringing down resplendent Leicester."

Next up, at the end of October, were the visits of Romania and Queensland, timing whose one downside was that the usual autumn visit of Swansea which might, for the second year running, have represented a clash between the best club teams in England and Wales, did not take place. Just as in the previous season, Tigers reached the end of October in fine form with their only defeat at Bath. The Romanians were at this time the strongest nation, other than France in continental Europe, building on a heritage dating back to 1909 and including participation in the 1924 Paris Olympics.

After the Second World War Romanian rugby took off spectacularly, supported by the newly installed communist regime. In May 1956 Harlequins visited Romania and were beaten 14-10. They came back full of praise for both hospitality and playing standards, and trailing the legend that a club official, mistaking the meaning of the words on a small roadside building, had begun a speech 'Urinals and Water Closets'. The RFU invited a Bucharest selection – the Romanian national team in all but name – to tour England. They drew 6-6 with Leicester at Welford Road on September 8 1956, the season before Chalkie's arrival, surprising many by using the full back as an attacking player

By October 1980 Romanian rugby was enjoying its halcyon days. Their six-match tour was essentially a visit to Ireland, with the visit to Leicester tacked on four days after they had played an Ireland XV at Lansdowne Road. Romania fielded an unchanged team for the match, played on Wednesday October 7, which resulted in a substantial 7-39 defeat for the Tigers

The Romanian journalist Chris Thau covered the Irish Test and the Leicester match: "The trip to Leicester, celebrating their centenary, came at the end of the 1980 Romanian tour of Ireland, for the up-and-coming East Europeans. It was their second tour to the British Isles, after the previous year's visit to Wales, and the second time the Romanians were visiting the Midlands club after their early tour in the 1950s.

The verdict of that year's *Rothmans Yearbook* columnist on the emerging rugby power was satisfying: "Any lingering doubts about the abilities of the Romanians to pose a challenge to the home countries were dispelled, when the touring team gained a 13-13 draw with an Ireland XV at Lansdowne Road in their fifth and final match. Following their narrow 12-13 defeat the previous season against a Welsh XV at Cardiff, it underlined that the Romanians now have to be taken seriously."

"Some felt that the addition of the Leicester match to a rather demanding tour was a step too far for the Romanians, especially since they had celebrated the drawn match in Dublin until the early hours of the following morning. The team manager, Viorel Morariu, a former international himself, was concerned

Four Romanian players who played against Leicester in 1980, (L-R): Captain Mircea Paraschiv (scrum-half), Mircea Munteanu (hooker), Dumitru Alexandru (fly half) and Man of the Match, Florica Murariu (flanker). (© Chris Thau)

that a possible drubbing at the hands of the Tigers, at the time the holders of the John Player Cup, would spoil the good impression left in Ireland, and could undermine their future progress. Others, including the Head Coach, Valeriu Irimescu, himself one of the stars of the great Romanian team of the 1960s, begged to differ. Irimescu, the architect of Romania's ascension on the international stage, felt that the team had just peaked the previous weekend and that a match against the Tigers, devoid of the pressure of the 'international' tag, may just release his players from the 'must win' shackle. The accommodation of the players, a large dormitory in a former gym within the Granby Halls, adjacent to the stadium, was far removed from the standard offered during the Irish tour, added to the informality of the occasion.

"Just before the players left the dressing room, Irimescu told them again: 'Listen guys, this match has no real bearing on your achievements. It is an opportunity to make a statement about how good you are. Show them what you are capable of. Just go for it. Use your head and do not exhaust yourselves,' he said. Romania fielded the same XV that started the game in Dublin. There were six England internationals in the Leicester line-up, including two Lions, centres Paul Dodge and Clive Woodward.

"Within twenty minutes of kick-off, Irimescu's premonition proved right. Leicester were facing annihilation as the Romanian pack tore into the hosts with relish. Murariu had scored a couple of tries, Fuicu added a third, and Ion Constantin landed a penalty and two conversions, for an early 19-0 lead. Dusty Hare landed a penalty, 19-3, but 'the penalty king' Ion Constantin re-established the margin 22-3. With the half nearing the end, at a scrum near the Leicester line, Romanian hooker Munteanu won a ball against the head, and flanker Stoica scored the fourth Romanian try for a half-time score of 26-3. 'We made them mincemeat in the scrum,' recalled prop Ion Bucan. 'We dominated the scrum and the line-out with authority and, to be honest, all areas of the game'.

"After the break outside-half Dumitru Alexnadru landed a drop goal, only for his opposite number Les Cusworth to launch a brisk counterattack, finalised by Williams' try, 29-7.

Kevin Williams scored Leicester's only try against Romania

"The Romanian pack increased the pace and the range of their attacks, and the sensational Murariu, playing like a man possessed, went over for his third try from a rehearsed 'bulldozer' move with scum-half Paraschiv leading the charge and full back Codoi converting it to increase the margin 35-7. The Romanians played flankers left and right (similar to the French).

"As the match had been inexorably moving towards the closing stages, the astonishing Murariu, scoring his fourth try, at the end of a blistering attack, which had featured in the early stages both Number 8 Bors and skipper Paraschiv. Final score 39-7, the largest margin of the tour. The following morning the headlines saluted the Romanian recital: 'Powerful Romanians silence Tigers Roar', 'Rampant Romanians humble Leicester', 'Tigers find Romanians are a different class'. 'Impeccable Romanians deserve more tours'. Four weeks later on November 23, with one change in the line-up, Romania demolished France in Bucharest 15-0."

Florica Murariu scored four tries against Leicester Tigers. Regarded as one of the outstanding forwards of his generation, Murariu, a serving officer in the Romanian army, became a national hero during the 1989 Revolution; tragically he was shot and killed at a road block in Bucharest

Martin Johnson reported for the *Mercury* that:

"Leicester Tigers must pick themselves off the floor after last night's shattering defeat by Romania, and prepare themselves both physically and mentally, for Queensland's visit to Welford Road on Saturday. The players will train as usual tonight and apart from any tactical considerations, coach Chalkie White must attempt to restore some self-belief that could have drained away against Romania.

"The defeat by Romania was a short sharp shock admitted Leicester Secretary Jerry Day. Even if our hooker Peter Wheeler had been fit, I don't think it would have made much difference. The tourists were so fit and powerful that Leicester were physically unable to compete 'some people seemed to forget that they were a national side and a very good one at that,' said Jerry Day, 'they would have made mincemeat of any club pack in the country last night.

"Leicester had hoped to hold their own in the set scrums but, said Day 'the soft conditions prevented Tigers forwards getting any traction and allowed their far

Queensland and Wallaby captain Tony Shaw

heavier opponents to shove them about.' Coach Chalkie White last night started the task of getting his players back on their feet after Wednesday's thrashing by the touring Romanians. Leicester will not face the same overwhelming power against Queensland, held 9-9 in an exchange of penalties in the Bristol mud on Wednesday, as they showed in Brisbane when they beat Tigers 22-12. Queensland can run the ball adventurously in good conditions. Leicester's four England backs form the nucleus of another attractive line up, so it will depend on possession and how the Australian pack play."

Still reeling from the hammering by Romania, Leicester faced Queensland on Saturday October 25 and ensured a much more respectable result – a 21-9 victory – as reported in *The Telegraph* by Michael Austin: "Leicester's recuperation, to borrow the words used by Chalkie White, their coach, was blissfully swift at Welford Road on Saturday. Their heaviest defeat in almost six years, by Romania, three days earlier seemed a distant echo.

"The past week has been a pretty exacting one for Leicester after taking on the full Romanian team on Wednesday. They faced two thirds of the Australian national side yesterday as Queensland ended the British section of their tour. Leicester had no answer to the Romanian drive and in the light of the heavy defeat I was looking for signs of self-doubt in the home team, where before this season there has only been absolute confidence.

"As it turned out, if Leicester were affected by the mid-week hammering, it didn't show. They held Queensland at arm's length and adapted their normal running game to suit the occasion. The display of the Leicester forwards against a pack which was 75 per cent international was remarkable. Leicester won more ball and made better use of it.

"Joyce, not exactly in the gazelle class as a line-out jumper, had the better of Australian lock McLean, and Cowling, returning after his harvest made a considerable difference to Leicester's scrummaging. When Queensland did manage to win the ball there was always that fine home back row to cover and the bonus of some aggressive tackling by Dodge and Williams.

Paul Dodge's huge influence on the Leicester team was such that Chalkie nicknamed him 'The Colossus'.

"Williams had caused Queensland problems by moving in from his position on the wing to tackle the Australian centres before they could develop moves. He had his reward when his tackle created a loose ball which he acquired gratefully and ran 22 metres for the clinching try.

"Hare was the only other Leicester scorer and his right boot made its usual contribution. Yet he also missed one or two easy kicks when Leicester led 9-3 and desperately needed another score.

"The game was not quite the spectacle which two running sides might have produced. Queensland will be disappointed to lose their unbeaten tour record and Australian rugby in general will not be too pleased at the prospect that many will return with the 1981-82 Wallabies.

"In this connection, it was a strange spectacle when the current Australian full back Gould, missed the target with a penalty attempt in front of the posts. It was also frustrating that the pace of Slack and Moon only surfaced in Queensland's consolation try at the end."

The special matches done, Tigers set about replicating their triumphs of the previous season. A 31-4 hammering at Gloucester the week after beating Queensland suggests a sense of anti-climax, and was also in keeping with a season when defeats were rare, but sometimes resounding. It was followed by a 16-match run in which the Merit Table was sewn up; only a draw with Moseley depriving them of a 100 per cent record, revenge taken on Gloucester, and the only defeat by 28-24 in a nine-try season romp with the Barbarians. That run ended resoundingly, however, with a 46-10 loss at Old Deer Park.

By then, the all-important cup defence had begun with a 34-3 defeat of Roundhay, Hare scoring 16 points and Cusworth seven, including the drop-goal seemingly mandatory on cup days. Next up, and only a week after that hammering at Old Deer Park, was the fourth-round match at home to Bristol.

"The press were saying that we were going to be steamrollered in the forwards," recalls Peter Wheeler. "On the day of the game I saw Jerry Day as I drove through the old gates on Aylestone Road. When I'd parked up, I spoke to Jerry and asked him to get the trophy and bring it into the changing rooms to remind everyone what we were playing for."

Martin Johnson reported a match limited by both nerves and mud, ultimately settled by the boot of Hare whose 19 points included a late penalty and conversion to stretch Tigers' winning margin to 27-14. They were at Welford Road again, in another sea of mud, for the quarter-final, Hare contributing 14 more points to the 21-7 defeat of Sale.

The run of home draws ended when Leicester had to travel to Richmond for the semi-final against London Scottish. Wheeler, Woodward and Cusworth had returned only 24 hours earlier from helping the Barbarians win the Hong Kong Sevens, and Scottish battled all the way, taking Tigers into the uncharted territory of extra-time when no side was blown at 12-12.

Woodward, concussed during the match, ended it believing he was still in Hong Kong, but no such disorientation afflicted Cusworth whose two drop goals, combined with another 12 points from Hare, took Tigers to the final.

Easter victories over Neath and Pontypool would have been the highlights of most Tigers seasons, but faded into near-insignificance compared to the last two matches of the season. The first, on April 25, was the visit to Moseley, always a challenging occasion even if this time there were no Merit Table percentages on offer. This was where Dusty Hare's 14 points made him the highest scorer in the history of first-class rugby, with 3,658. The opposition could not have been more appropriate since the record Dusty took had been set by Moseley's much-loved and mourned Sam Doble, who had died in 1977 aged only 33. Formidable as this feat was, Dusty was not even quite halfway to his final tally of 7,337 – widely regarded as unbeatable.

Three months later, an oak tree was planted on the village green in Hare's native community of South Clifton to mark the feat. The planting was attended by teammates Peter Wheeler, Tim Barnwell, Terry Burwell and Paul Dodge. Chalkie, who presented Dusty and his wife with a piece of Wedgwood pottery, later paid for the plaque which stands in front of the tree to this day.

The victory at Moseley set Tigers up well for the cup final at Twickenham, the first to be played as the final match of the

Chalkie watches Dusty Hare plant the oak tree on South Clifton village green – July 1981

Dusty Hare with the mighty oak in 2023

season, against Gosforth. In the week in between they received the 'Team of the Year' trophy award at an event held at the Dorchester Hotel.

Tigers went into the match knowing it would be the last for Cowling and Adey who were both retiring. Adey, who had quit in January due to an injured ankle, returned as an emergency replacement for Angus Collington and played so well that although Collington was fit by the time of the final, Adey retained his place.

Tigers had more than just hope to see old colleagues out with a victory to motivate them. Wheeler had been promised by cup sponsors John Player that they could keep the trophy if they won for the third time in a row.

"This helped galvanise the team and was a real added incentive," said Wheeler. "It was something in the club's history at that period to win the trophy again. In those days you didn't get a cup to retain, it was kept for a season and returned to be played for the following year. The importance of the John Player Cup had grown on everyone at the club over the years. The cup epitomised what people associated with Leicester Tigers, a team that regularly delivered success. It was a key competition to Chalkie, the players, supporters and everyone involved with the club."

Nor was Chalkie taking any risks with preparation. Notes in his distinctive handwriting show his analysis of Gosforth – in particular that scrum-half Malcolm Young was 'their key man', their scrum very strong, England lock Steve Bainbridge reminiscent of former Tigers stalwart Eric Bann, flankers Anderson and Butler both 'flashers' with Butler further noted as 'not agile' but 'all teeth and elbows'. He noted particular moves such as Bainbridge peeling off from number 6 in the line-out to link to Roberts then Bell, and weaknesses such as gaps inside outside-half Johnson as 'Anderson plays wide'.

But, unlike some coaches with a predilection for detail, he did not load his players down with directions. Nick Joyce, playing his fourth consecutive final, remembered: "Chalkie White coached the Leicester team but specifically the backs which was his own expertise. He was happy to be in the background

Photo Leicester Tigers John Player Cup final 1981
Back Row (L-R): Ian Smith, Paul Dodge, Angus Collington, Steve Johnson, Wayne Richardson, Nick Jackson, Garry Adey, Steve Redfern, Chris Tressler, Brian Hall, Nick Joyce, Chalkie White (coach)
Middle Row (L-R): Andy Key, Les Cusworth, Dusty Hare, Peter Wheeler (captain), Robin Cowling, Clive Woodward, Kevin Williams
Front Row (L-R): Steve Kenney, Tim Barnwell, Mike Merriman

and to let Peter Wheeler and Robin Cowling run the forwards. Importantly, with the right players, the system he put in place worked. My favourite of his sayings was "fatigue makes cowards of us all."

Tigers fans were reckoned the majority, probably about 15,000 in a 24,000 crowd, for a match which *The Guardian*'s David Frost reckoned: "Perhaps the most exciting and certainly the fastest final in the ten years of the Cup."

John Player had to find a new trophy, reckoned by Frost to cost around £4,000, as the current one was clinched for good by Leicester. In spite of Gosforth enjoying the bulk of possession, he reported, "As soon as it was clear that Leicester had managed to slip back into their sharp form of a few months ago, there was never much doubt about their winning."

Tigers led all the way from an early Hare penalty, and try by Kenney, whose sharp combination with Cusworth contrasted with the manner in which Young was kept shackled. Both Frost and Reason, acknowledged Leicester's Paul Dodge, who "played like a lord", reckoned the decisive period came after

Steve Kenney scores Leicester Tigers' opening try against Gosforth

Peter Wheeler and Robin Cowling hold the John Player Cup aloft at Twickenham

Gosforth fought their way back to 12-9 after half-time, when, as Wheeler conceded "it was anyone's game".

However, tries by Barnwell and Hare, who set yet another new club record with 358 points for the season, were a triumph for Chalkie's mantra of 'Pressure, Patience, Ploys' – his plagiarized version of 'Pace, Possession, Position', a formula devised by New Zealand coach Charles Saxton and much cherished by the Leicester coach.

Referring back to underwhelming performances, even in the finals they had won, Frost concluded that, "It was good that Leicester, who for years played better quality rugby than any other club in England, should at last do themselves justice in a cup final ... It was the ideal climax to Leicester's centenary."

The trophy is, Wheeler notes: "Still at the club today as a reminder of our three consecutive cup wins, in perpetuity for Chalkie and the achievements of the Leicester players."

Leicester Tigers Extras and Swifts Tour to Florida, USA
Back Row (L-R): Colin Dexter, Vendis Afflick, Wayne Richardson, Kelvin Wilford, Bob Watson, Dean Waddingham, Duncan Black, Jim Watts, Mick Newton, John Murphy
Middle Row (L-R): John Cooke, Paul Gamble, John Dakin, Jez Krych, Dave Manship, Phil Smith, Ian Dodson, Chris Tressler, Dave Gavins
Front Row (L-R): Dave Williams, Alistair Deas, Peter Riley (Team Secretary), Graham Willars (Tour Manager), Eric Lacey (President), Steve Solomons (captain), John Jolleys (doctor), Rod Oakes (coach), Dave Thomas, Neil Hartley, (insert – Stuart Redfern)

Steve Solomons (left) with Garry Adey (right) at the opening of The Droglites (an anagram of Old Tigers) bar at Welford Road

For Chalkie, though, the celebrations were short-lived and rapidly overshadowed. His mother Annie had a stroke on the day of the final and was admitted to hospital. The family didn't tell him until after the game. He had always been close to his mother, and she was very proud of him, writing to him every week throughout her life. Chalkie took the John Player Cup to the hospital where the family hung Tigers scarves on her bed and her photograph was taken with the cup.

Sadly, Annie had a series of strokes and died on June 11 1981. Chalkie headed up to Carlisle to be with his brother and sister and help with funeral arrangements, while Doris stayed at home with Nick, as he focused on exams. Typically, for men of his generation, Chalkie largely concealed his grief, but daughter Stella remembers one occasion, a few months after Annie's funeral, which made him very emotional, when he saw one of her letters while tidying his desk. In later years, he often told Stella about Annie's working life.

Meanwhile Tigers were showing that great clubs extend beyond their first team elite. Fringe and youth players were given their own centenary tour, the Extra 1st and Swifts, captained by Steve Solomons, winning all four matches without conceding a point in Florida.

21

The Final Season – 1981-82

As Chalkie approached what would be his final season at Leicester, a young Yorkshireman was looking forward to his first season as a Tiger. The author of this book, Martin Whitcombe – the grandson of Wales and GB rugby league international, Frank Whitcombe, and son of the Bradford, Keighley and Yorkshire rugby union prop, Frank Whitcome Jnr – sets the scene on that fateful season: "My introduction to rugby came from two different grass roots environments. I first learnt to play rugby union with the 'Bantams' (the junior section at Keighley RUFC), in addition to playing rugby league at junior school. My journey between the two codes was somewhat moulded by my secondary school, Bingley Grammar, a rugby union playing school and so union ultimately became my game. It was when I was at school that I first heard about Ray Needham, a former pupil at Bingley Grammar, who was playing for Leicester Tigers, and would later become a teammate.

Ray Needham served Leicester as a player, coach, and kitman for over 40 years

"In 1980 I met RAF Officer, Roger Hill, at a school careers convention at Belle Vue in Manchester. Roger, who had succeeded Dickie Jeeps as scrum-half in the Northampton team, told me about the opportunity to join the RAF as a Physical Training Instructor (PTI). I also met Wing Commander Leighton Jenkins, a former Wales and Leicester Tigers forward, who recommended me to Tigers, and also helped me with my posting to RAF North Luffenham. I owe these two men a lot."

At his first Leicester Tigers training session, Whitcombe met Barry Evans from Hinckley, a winger whose sprinting pedigree had made him

Leighton Jenkins, and Chalkie playing against Harlequins at Twickenham – September 1958

Barry Evans playing against the Barbarians, keeping Mark Bailey and Richard Cardus at bay

Leicestershire county champion at 100 and 200 metres at various ages.

"When I left school to go to university," Evans explained. "I had not joined any rugby club and because I would be attending a teacher training site with more emphasis on athletics than team sport, my view was that I would concentrate on sprinting and get a game of rugby wherever I could in whatever teams were on site or close by. However, my girlfriend's mother taught at South Wigston, the same high school as Rod Oakes, coach of the Extras XV, who suggested that I have a go at training with Leicester in August before going to university. It turned out to be the best decision I ever made, as following one game in the Swifts, and the Extras the following week, I turned out for the 1st XV against Saracens away on the third week, and loved every minute. John Deacon, from London Welsh, and Nick Youngs, from Bedford, also joined Leicester at the same time as me. Nick was a farm manager at Bringhurst, and soon we started sharing lifts to training."

Scrum-half Nick Youngs joined Leicester from Bedford RFC

Speaking about his decision to join Leicester, Nick Youngs explained: "I joined Leicester because I came from Norfolk and there was no senior club I was tied to. I was a Norfolk born and bred lad and joined Bedford as it was my closest club. I had no allegiance to any club, although I thoroughly enjoyed playing for Bedford, but I wanted to play with Les Cusworth and the fantastic Leicester back line of that time, and of course work with Chalkie White who was the best coach in England."

After receiving a tetanus injection before training on the 'Rec', Whitcombe was given an introductory letter by Rex Skelton, which concluded: "Please make a note of your bar duty and do it! Your duty involves assisting the committee member in charge of the bar on training nights, Saturdays and mid-week matches if any occurs in your week of duty. The club provides facilities for you to enjoy yourself, please help to make it enjoyable for everyone else by fulfilling your responsibilities."

The Committee man in charge was Bob Beason and the players on the bar rota were Barry Evans, Vendis Afflick, Whitcombe and Mike Merriman.

"For my first match," recalls Whitcombe, "I was selected as a reserve for the Swifts on the Rec but, because we had no touch judge, I also ran the line.

For the following six weeks I played in the Swifts and then the Extras and got to know my team managers, Pete Riley and Pete Herbert.

"On October 16 1981 I made my home debut against Swansea. Arriving at the ground early I got changed into my kit, using my Tigers jersey to stand on instead of the cold changing room floor. Chalkie White walked in, saw me standing on the jersey and told me, in no uncertain terms, "No! You can't do that." He came across, sat next to me, and explained about being a Leicester Tigers player and how Robin Cowling – a man who refused to give in – had worn the letter 'A' on his shirt. I never stood on my jersey again. Knowing that I'd be nervous, just before kick-off Chalkie walked over to me and told me to take confidence from my new teammates."

The competitive highlight of the season was the visit of the Australian Wallabies, coached by Bob Templeton, as part their four month, 24-match schedule. In recognition of Leicester's achievement of winning three consecutive John Player Cups, Tigers became the first English club side to play a major overseas touring team since they had met the All Blacks in 1924. While Leicester Tigers undoubtedly deserved the accolade of the fixture, it also represented a minefield for the touring Australians who had been portrayed as spineless in a media onslaught.

When the 1981-82 Wallabies landed in England, two days early to be certain of shaking off any jet lag, they found themselves being accused of cowardice by Leicester Secretary Jerry Day, who was furious that the Wallabies had refused to play the match under lights at Welford Road on Wednesday November 25.

"We have spent £7,000 this summer improving our lights and an evening kick off would have guaranteed a full house of 17,500," Day was reported to have said by a local newspaper. "I think they are frightened. They know what we can do and are not prepared to take any chances."

The article further reported Day as claiming: "The Wallabies agreed to play two games under lights, against Devon & Cornwall at Exeter and the South West Division at Gloucester. But they are well aware of the Tigers' bite. On last year's South Pacific tour, Leicester lost 22-12 to the might of Queensland, who provide 15 of the current Australian touring party. They took Eastern Suburbs apart, 24-3, and then against Randwick, in a match billed by their Sydney hosts as 'The club championship of the world' they came back to win 31-19. Leicester avenged their Brisbane reverse by being the only British team to beat Queensland, 21-9, on their world tour last autumn. The Australian management have refused to budge for Leicester."

The Wallabies had already encountered Welford Road, and Chalkie, going down 16-10 to a Midlands team he had coached in their first fixture on October 17. He pledged attacking play, but previews noted that the presence of world

Leicester Tigers (15) v Australia XV (18) – November 1981
Back Row (L-R): Jerry Day (Hon. Secretary), John Allen (Hon. Treasurer), Ian Smith, Dave Forfar, Peter Wheeler, Nick Joyce, Nick Jackson, John Deacon, Steve Redfern, Duncan Black, Martin Whitcombe, Chalkie White (coach), Harry Sibson (President), Tudor Thomas (Team Secretary)
Middle Row (L-R): Paul Dodge, Dusty Hare, Les Cusworth, Steve Kenney, Steve Johnson (captain), Clive Woodward, Tim Barnwell, Barry Evans, Chris Tressler
Front Row (L-R): Kevin Williams, Brian Hall, Nick Youngs

record points scorer, Dusty Hare, and Wallabies full back, Paul McLean, who was already halfway to his 154 points total from his previous tour six years earlier, would make goal-kicking a major factor.

"We are representing English rugby," commented Chalkie, "and we've got to accept the challenge, even though we have been struggling for form lately. After a shaky start, Australia have got their game together and won their first international against Ireland."

"Leicester Tigers were, so to speak, a Hare's breadth from pulling off a well merited draw against the Australians at Welford Road yesterday," reported the *Leicester Mercury*. "The full back was, in fact, only the width of a goal post from

Australia captain Mark Loane

putting over a 45-yard penalty with the last kick of a pulsating match, but far from looking back with disappointment, Tigers should now look ahead with confidence. So far this season Tigers have only been identifiable by the colour of their jerseys. But in this game, they offered conclusive proof that they are anything but a spent force.

"True they never really came close to scoring a try, but the Wallabies, as fit and strong as a touring side should be after so much time together, were rock solid in defence. It was a cruel irony that Les Cusworth seemed to have capped a brilliant display with a winning drop goal seven minutes from time. Only to watch his opposite number, Mark Ella, who could barely have done more to explain why he is not in the Test team, do exactly that in the dying seconds of normal time

"Tigers gave blood in the forward battle, in Dave Forfar's case about a pint of it. He had to have ten stitches in an ugly leg wound after being trampled early on, and although he tried to bravely come back, the leg gave way almost immediately. What did not give way was Tigers' spirit. They tackled ferociously, and Cusworth, whose idea of a tackle used to be to hitch a lift on the back of someone's shirt, saved a certain first half try by crunching into big centre Mick O'Conner right on the line.

"Tigers led 6-3 at the break. Paul McLean, who had an impeccable game at full back, sandwiching a penalty in between Hare's superb 45-yard dropped goal with a simple under-the-posts penalty.

"Six minutes into the second half, the Wallabies scored the only try of the match, when the ball flew out of a ruck they had enough men there to argue about who was going to score, before Michael Martin did. McLean, the only man saving the torpedo kick from passing into ancient history converted from the touchline, but then Hare, whose own round-the-corner style was once regarded as a fleeting eccentric phase, levelled with a drop goal from fully 50 yards.

"A Hare penalty, again from long range, put his side ahead, McLean levelled immediately and then Wheeler took his third strike against the head to set up Cusworth's drop goal. Only two minutes remained when McLean made it 15-15 with his third penalty, but then came Ella's dropped goal, and in the sixth

Les Cusworth, Leicester's fly half, manages to off-load the ball despite the attention of the Australian defence. Steve Kenney looks on as Australia's Mike O'Connor covers back

minute of injury time, Hare's agonising penalty miss.

Following the game Australian Coach Bob Templeton said: "Leicester played a magnificent game of rugby. They are impeccably coached and encouraged to express their game within a well organised team pattern. We had great difficulty in overcoming them 18-15 half way through our tour."

Snow and ice meant only one match was played between early December and mid-January, the Barbarians clash among the games to fall victim to the weather, but that one game wrote a line in Tigers history as Chalkie selected Vendis Afflick, their first black player, for the 9-9 draw with Bath.

Mark Ella's late drop goal won the game for Australia

Wallabies goal kicker Paul McLean

The injury sustained in the Australia match meant it was Dave Forfar's final game after a decade-long career of 223 Leicester appearances, an England B cap against France, and two England final trials.

"I played in the youth team and the county colts with Vendis," recalled Paul Dodge. "A strong defender and good in attack, he was a versatile back who could play in the centre or on the wing. Vendis and Dusty had hilarious banter together whenever the West Indies and England played cricket. He was a great character and teammate."

A gifted rugby player who made 32 appearances, Vendis Afflick had been a footballer before Tudor Thomas introduced him to rugby at New Parks Boys School, and encouraged him to join Leicester.

Prop Wayne Richardson made his John Player Cup debut in the defeat at Moseley

For most clubs, a season of 27 wins in 40 matches, including a 36-32 romp against the Barbarians in more seasonal conditions when the match was replayed in the spring, and another shared Merit Table title, when defeat at Northampton led to a top-of-the-table tie with Coventry, would have been a decent return.

It had, though, something of an air of anticlimax, for Tigers, as the long run of cup triumphs came to an end after 18 matches. There were wins over Hartlepool Rovers, Northampton and Gosforth before the draw sent Tigers to the Reddings for a semi-final against Moseley. Les Cusworth scored the only try against his old club but this was a rare day on which Dusty Hare went pointless and Cusworth's successor in Moseley's number ten shirt, Mike Perry, landed two drops and two penalties for a 12-4 victory.

Chalkie complained of poor preparation, with players away at the Hong Kong Sevens, and other distractions: "It is no use saying we've had a good run and it was bound to end sometime. That's the sort of attitude that gets you beaten. You're only as good as your last game, and we were bad. Moseley went on to share the trophy with Gloucester after a drawn replay of their fractious meeting in the first-ever final a decade earlier.

The season was also memorable in the club's annals, however, for the start of one of the greatest of all Tigers careers, with Dean Richards joining the club in March from French club Roanne.

Speaking of his decision to join Leicester, Dean Richards explained that, "The fear of failure can make the hardest of individuals do things totally out of character, so when I was faced with knowingly failing all my A Levels before the results were revealed and having to face the most ferocious but devoted and religious of mothers, I chose what was considered the only option available to me, I left home.

"I returned a year later assuming the dust had settled, having spent a year brawling in possibly the world's toughest rugby arenas, the French Pro D2, and by chance was offered the opportunity to trial at Leicester in a training session, by our family neighbour Bill Brown, an ex-Coventry and Leicester Tigers player himself.

"I arrived at the club, was told to change and train with the youth team, none of whom I knew. We did a quick trawl of the pitch for dog muck and then got stuck in – scrum, maul, and ruck triangles for an hour and a half. We were totally abused by the first team but like all youth players, showed we had a bit of spunk and secretly enjoyed every bit of it. At the end of the session, Graham Willars, the then youth team coach, pulled me to one side and told me I'd be involved with the Swifts at the weekend and to train with them on the Thursday. A year fighting my way around France had matured me in a way probably playing youth rugby couldn't and it obviously showed. Having been abroad, and it being in the dim and distant past when there was no internet, I didn't really know any of the other players that evening other than my old school teammate, Barry Evans, so reputations and names really counted for nothing.

Dean Richards' baptism of fire at Neath

"As we returned to the changing rooms having walked back over to the main stadium, I went into the showers and started to wash when a small middle-aged figure came and stood beside me. He had a broad Cumbrian accent and wore a red polka dot neckerchief around his neck. After getting over my initial surprise, as I wasn't sure what type of person wore a scarf in the shower, we spoke about French rugby, where I'd been and what I was going to do in the future, and then he was gone. I neither knew his name or what he did. This was my first introduction to Chalkie.

"Three games for the Swifts, two for the Extras and then I found myself selected for the Easter tour and was starting against Neath on the Saturday. Having returned from France to unemployment, my income was restricted to a £19 social security payment, all of which I handed over as board and lodgings, so I went to Wales with a loan of £5 in my back pocket! As we boarded the bus I sat on my own, half way up on the left-hand side. There was a buzz about the bus, there always was when going on tour, but a tour and a free 'stash' being handed out, doubled the excitement. Chalkie was walking up the bus handing out kit but when he came to me he just paused and quietly said, 'You haven't earned anything yet lad', and just moved on. I got it, totally understood it, but it just doubled the agony, no beer money and no stash!

"The game itself was a blur. The things I remember well were Tim Barnwell returning the ball from the kick off, going to ground, being kicked in the head and having to leave the field to be stitched just 30 seconds in, and lastly, my good friend 'Dosser' Smith just guiding me through the game. Oh, and that we won. I spent my whole £5 that night!

"On Sunday we had a game of football between ourselves on the beach at The Mumbles. Bearing in mind I was the young pup on the block, and had seemingly pushed Duncan Black's nose out of joint by being selected ahead of him, it wasn't a surprise that five minutes into the game Duncan and I ended up scuffling amongst ourselves on the beach. As other players stepped in to stop the kerfuffle, all I heard Chalkie say was, 'Leave them to sort it out.' The scuffle, like all my on-pitch fights, didn't last very long, and like all of those fights, I most probably didn't win but it showed Chalkie at his best. The playground pecking order was so important in the contact sport that rugby was in those days, and Chalkie showed no allegiance to the established local player, he liked people to be challenged even though it was just an 18-year-old upstart that nobody knew anything about.

"When the Pontypool team was announced later that day, I was selected on the bench with Duncan starting. Thirty minutes into the game, he got one of the biggest 'shoeings' I have ever seen, from the Ponty pack, with the Welsh referee unsurprisingly 'tying up his shoe laces' with his back to it all. Chalkie told me to go and warm up. As I was jogging up and down the touch line, Ray Prosser, the Pontypool coach, said, 'Lad, what are you doing'. 'Warming up', I replied with a smile on my face thinking I was getting on, to which he replied in his quiet, deep Welsh accented voice, 'You'll not be on there long enough, now f**k off and sit down!" Thankfully Duncan got back on his feet and finished the game.

"I remember when Chalkie sadly passed away in 2005 and I attended the memorial service at Leicester Cathedral, along with Martin 'Whimp' Whitcombe and Vendis Afflick. Chalkie will always be remembered as the one coach who never told you how good a player you were but just how you could become a better player."

22

From Rhodesia to Zimbabwe – 1982

For most Tigers, the truly memorable event of 1982 was the tour of Zimbabwe. Not long independent, the country had previously been called Rhodesia, the name under which it had made a Unilateral Declaration of Independence (UDI) from British rule on November 11 1965.

Not since the United States in 1776 had a British colony declared itself independent, and the Rhodesian declaration was not dissimilar in language to its American forerunner. That afternoon Prime Minister Ian Smith addressed the nation. He assured them that Rhodesians remained 'second to none in our loyalty to the Queen', but 'the end of the road has been reached'.

Ian Smith, the former Prime Minister of Rhodesia

In response, Ndabaningi Sithole and Robert Mugabe's Zimbabwe African National Union (ZANU) and the Zimbabwe African People's Union (ZAPU) under Joseph Nkomo both declared breakaway governments. Back in London, Harold Wilson's government ruled out military action. Instead, Britain sought the imposition of sanctions. While the UN approved the suggested measures, they failed to end the 'rebellion' and the Rhodesian Bush War intensified. The war lasted from July 1964 to 1979 despite ongoing attempts at a settlement. In December 1966, Wilson and Smith famously met off the coast of Gibraltar aboard HMS Tiger, with another round of talks taking place in October 1968 aboard HMS Fearless. Rhodesia's leaders, however, continued to distance themselves from Britain. Withdrawal from the Commonwealth came in December 1966 and in 1970, Rhodesia declared itself a Republic. By 1978, all white men up to the age of 60 were subject to periodic call-up to the army; younger men up to 35 might expect to spend alternating blocks of six weeks in the army and at home. The Bush War affected every aspect of life in Rhodesia including its rugby team. In later years, Springbok Harry Roberts' stories from his military service in the late 1970s kept numerous Tigers teammates enthralled.

The author in the Welford Road car park – the legendary 'bank' in the background – ready to depart on the journey to Zimbabwe, with a new suitcase, a gift from his parents

During the talks which led to independence at Lancaster House in 1980, Smith, a rugby fan alleged in a Welsh urban legend to have played for Neath, came to watch a match between Richmond and Leicester and amid tight security visited the changing rooms where he invited the Tigers to tour, as recalled by Tigers' Ian Smith: "After the game Peter Wheeler told us that Ian Smith was coming to the changing rooms. Peter then introduced Smith to the Leicester team, and to some laughter Peter introduced him to me as, 'and this is our Ian Smith' to which he replied, 'well at least you've got a good name.' Ian Smith then spoke to the players and extended an invitation to visit his country."

The invitation was accepted and in July 1982 the Tigers toured Zimbabwe as only the third European team to visit the country since official independence was declared on April 18 1980. This would not be an easy trip. Swansea had toured Zimbabwe in May, winning their first game with Zimbabwe 26-6 but losing the second 31-30. In July, Romania toured the country and in their two Tests, Romania won the first 25-23 and the second 25-24.

By today's standards Leicester Tigers selected a small touring party of 23 players and five officials for the five-match schedule, a mixture of seasoned and upcoming young players, captained by Steve Johnson.

At the same time in Johannesburg, South Africa, Ellis Park stadium had been demolished and re-built. To celebrate the occasion the Transvaal Rugby Union organised a special game against an Overseas Invitation XV, assembled by 1974 Lions coach Syd Miller, to play Transvaal at the new Ellis Park. The

Leicester Tigers Tour to Zimbabwe 1982 – The Police Grounds, Harare
Back Row (L-R): Wayne Richardson, Rob Tebbutt, Duncan Black, Malcolm Foulkes-Arnold, Nick Jackson, Angus Collington, Martin Whitcombe, John Deacon, Vendis Afflick
Middle Row (L-R): Ian Dodson, Terry Burwell, Dave Thomas, Nick Youngs, Steve Kenney, Chris Tressler, Barry Evans, Mick Poulson, Ian Smith
Front Row (L-R): John Ford (physio), Nick Joyce, Chalkie White (head coach), Tim Barnwell, Harry Sibson (President), Steve Johnson (captain), John Allen (Tour Manager), Brian Hall, Rod Oakes (coach), Kevin Williams

Invitation XV included five Leicester teammates; Peter Wheeler, Les Cusworth, Paul Dodge, Dusty Hare and Clive Woodward, rendering all unavailable to tour Zimbabwe.

Reporting in the *Sunday Telegraph*, John Reason commented: "Leicester are conscious that without four of their top backs they would be an ordinary side, and to complicate matters further the club has not yet found anyone suitable who is available to manage the team. As if all that was not enough, there have been natural and persistent feelings of disquiet about the political situation in Zimbabwe. Leicester have now chosen a team for the tour, but I presume that there must still be a possibility that they will not go to Zimbabwe.

"Even that is not the end to the matter, because Chalkie White, the Leicester coach has been invited to coach the England Schools 19 Group in Zimbabwe at the same time as the projected Leicester tour. He has been offered this assignment because, John Elders, the former England coach, is about to emigrate to Australia and Ian Gibson is not available. 'I would really like to coach the England Schools team on a tour like this,' says White. 'But obviously my first loyalty is to my club and so I will have to see how that matter is resolved first'."

The last two Rhodesians to represent the Springboks – wing Ray Mordt (left) and centre David Smith (right), played for South Africa against the 1980 Lions

The Tour management problem was resolved with the inclusion of assistant coach Rod Oakes, as Tour Manager John Allen explained: "My father was unwell at this time, so to cover all eventualities, and in the event that I had to return to England, Chalkie would have stepped in as Tour Manager and Rod Oakes as Coach."

While the other political manoeuvrings were dealt with, the Leicester players concentrated on preparing for the tour. At the final training session at Ratcliffe College, John Allen reminded everyone that in August 1980 Leicester Tigers became the first English club team to visit the southern hemisphere and it was the players' duty to uphold the reputation the club had gained. Chalkie White ominously warned us that we would be playing against men who had been looking down the barrel of a gun for the past 12 years.

Arriving at Welford Road on Thursday July 22, the car park was a mass of kit bags and suitcases being loaded on to the team bus, with gathered family and friends wishing the players good luck as they embarked on what would be the trip of a lifetime. By Saturday Leicester would be playing their first tour game, 6,000 miles away from home.

Arriving in Harare, the capital of Zimbabwe, on Friday July 23 at 5.45am, where a State of Emergency had existed since July 1980, the tour party checked into the Monomotapa Hotel where a duty boy system was initiated along with a daily dress code; all players were given a tour number for roll call. Afternoon practice gave us just 24 hours to acclimatise before playing our first game against Mashonaland – at 4,865 feet above sea level – in the first of two provincial games before playing the Zimbabwe national team. While the new Zimbabwe strove to gain international acceptance as a rugby side, they no longer had teams playing in the Currie Cup and other South African competitions, and as of October 1980 their players were no longer eligible for the Springboks.

The players' first experience of training and running at altitude was a shock. Breathing was difficult to begin with but it got better with time, assisted by salt tablets, but within hours the team was facing its first opponents, who were no pushovers. Andy Tucker played for Zimbabwe in the inaugural 1987 World Cup and was in the Mashonaland pack against Leicester Tigers that day, he remembered: "We knew about the reputation of Leicester Tigers before they arrived here, but we had probably the best side ever that season, coached by former Rhodesia and Springbok centre Ian Robertson."

Played on Saturday July 24, Leicester Tigers were tamed 28-23 by Mashonaland, as was enthusiastically described by 'Rugby Correspondent' in his match report: "Rugby thrillers appear to be the 'in thing' at The Police Grounds these days and yesterday's match was certainly no exception. The score line suggests a great Mashona fight back. It was, but to be fair to the visitors, Leicester have not played a match for some time as it is their closed season and what with arriving the day before the game they faded badly in the second period.

"Mashonaland superbly led by Alan Mansfield turned a hesitant, fumbling first half display into a fine, cohesive power packed performance after half-time. It was a tale of two stars, Kloppers the forward and Mansfield the back. National lock, Neville Kloppers, clobbered unmercifully in the line-outs and made this his department – with the help of Pete Bristow and his fellow forwards – almost entirely his own, supplying scrum-half Brian Coghill with a stream of good ball.

"Leicester gave an indication of things to come with their deserved first half lead. They dominated the line-outs, won the loose ball with fly half Mike Poulson showing a fine boot and full back Kevin Williams a fine pair of hands, to add to a sharp turn of speed. There is certainly going to be some sad opposition when the visitors 'get it together' on their tour. They could have taken yesterday's tally in to the 30s had their handling and understanding been better, but they faded badly after the interval.

Under severe pressure, Nick Joyce delivers line-out ball for Leicester Tigers against Mashonaland in Harare

"The Mashona first half performance was poor. They were disjointed with no cohesion between backs and forwards, with too many kicks going astray. Immediately after the start of the second half, prop Martin Whitcombe burst away leading a great 50-metre forward rush, which ended just short of the Mashona try line and it looked as though the landslide was about to begin. But then came the 'revival' with Mansfield, and full back Kenyon Zeihl, tidying up the backs, the skipper exhorting his men to Herculean efforts and feeding his perfectly timed passes to his fellow threes."

It was not the ideal start to the tour for Leicester, but there were plenty of positives from what was for most of the team their first game in Southern Africa.

The following day the tourists were driven to Troutbeck in the Eastern Highlands for an overnight stop before travelling to Bulawayo, the capital of Matabeleland, where the Tigers would play both Matabeleland and Zimbabwe at the city's Hartsfield Stadium.

The Bush War may have been over, but peace had not yet returned to this troubled land. In February 1982 Joshua Nkomo, Robert Mugabe's principal political rival, was accused of plotting a *coup d'état,* and dismissed from the cabinet. More worrying for the Leicester touring party was the news that six

Not a typical rugby tour photograph. The Leicester Tigers team bus was stopped and searched several times at army road blocks during the tour to Zimbabwe

Hooker Dave Thomas made his Leicester Tigers debut against Matabeleland

foreign tourists had been kidnapped and held as political hostages by dissidents in Matabeleland the day the Tigers had arrived in Zimbabwe.

"The Leicester Tigers squad who are touring Zimbabwe have been caught up in a high security web after the abduction of six tourists," reported the *Leicester Mercury*. "Army patrols on the outskirts of many towns stopped the Tigers party as they made their way to Bulawayo. Team Physiotherapist Mr John Ford said, 'We have been stopped several times by the military, but once they knew who we were; they immediately allowed us to continue our journey. We have seen no signs of severe military activity, although most towns seem to have one or two military vehicles patrolling, rather like our own police vans'."

The six-day stopover in the Bulawayo was the longest leg of the trip, and after a defeat in the first match, the encounter against Matabeleland was now a very important match to win. Played on Wednesday July 28, Leicester recorded a relatively comfortable victory, 25-12, as was reported by David Fox in *The Chronicle*: "Leicester shrugged off the effects of a long trip to Zimbabwe when they proved the more consistent side in beating Matabeleland in a match marred by frequent stoppages at Hartsfield yesterday. The Leicester side looked jaded at times but their three tries were well deserved and they looked the better team throughout the match.

"The game started at an incredibly slow pace and the frequent whistle blowing by referee Kingsley Went, prevented the game from reaching any great heights. Referees are often criticised at Hartsfield, but after awarding four penalties and four free kicks in the first five minutes of the match, Went, was nearly a candidate for a lynching. But referees are also human and although the first half of the match was appallingly bad, he let the ball run much more in the second half.

"The visitors opened their account in the seventh minute after half the Matabeleland pack were caught offside in a loose maul. Fly half Ian Dodson, who had earlier missed a relatively easy penalty, confidently slotted the kick and for a while it looked like Matabeleland were in for another thrashing. Dodson had another attempt at goal five minutes later but missed and Matabeleland came back with a vengeance.

"The home team attacked like they have never done this season, and although the ball never reached the wings, centre Henry Rosser nearly stormed through his opposite line on two occasions. But in the end, it was Matabeleland's relentless attack that cost them the first try of the match, Leicester conceded a penalty under pressure, which was quickly taken by scrum-half Iain Buchanan who slipped the ball out. The ball passed quickly along the back line, but a poor pass by Mick Springer was intercepted and Leicester wing Tim Barnwell ran the length of the field to dot far out.

"Colin McIntosh pulled three points back for Matabeleland in the 16th minute, but Leicester fought back and were rewarded when Vendis Afflick received the ball and slipped under the posts to give Dodson an easy conversion. Tim Barnwell crossed the line again in the 36th minute to give Leicester a 19-3 lead which remained until the teams changed ends.

"The first half proved nightmarish for Dodson who, although he goaled two tries and slotted a penalty, he missed at least four easier attempts. But he came into his own in the second half and more than made up for his poor showing in the first 40 minutes.

Malcolm Foulkes-Arnold stretches every sinew to secure possession for Leicester

Bloodied but unbowed, a defiant Rob Tebbutt leaves the field in Bulawayo

"For Matabeleland, McIntosh slotted a penalty while Neville Parkin finished off a good forward rush to score and give McIntosh a conversion. Dodson grabbed two penalties in the second half to seal the game."

Many of the practice sessions started early in Bulawayo; some mornings at 7am. Chalkie told everyone to bring the hotel towels to practice, and working in pairs on the try line we tied a towel round our partner's waist to hold him back when running. Chalkie was doing his version of resistance training before it had been invented. His standard of professionalism was on another level. His constant attention to detail and his unbending principles of hard work and sticking to the basics was practised over and over again, and he left nothing to chance. A compulsive note-taker during training sessions and games, he used this information for analysing and mentoring his players. Chalkie White was not a big man in stature, yet he emanated great power.

Duncan Black, the Leicester forward, attested to Chalkie's man-management: "In Zimbabwe, Chalkie took me to one side and we had a heart-to-heart about what was blocking me from reaching my true potential. He said that if I played to please myself rather than trying to please others – which in my case was my dad, whose own father, Adam Black, was a famous Leicester City player and captain – I would go far. After that I had a great tour and played most of the next season in the 1st XV. Later, I studied psychology to HND level and understood what a great psychologist Chalkie was."

With a win and a defeat, Leicester now faced their most challenging opponent, Zimbabwe, and it would be, for many of the Leicester players, their first experience of playing against an international team.

Played on Saturday July 31, and without five of their strongest players, the Tigers recorded a famous victory, 18-22, as was reported in *The Chronicle* by David Fox: "Two early errors by Zimbabwe lock Ian Marais and centre Jan Pelser deprived the national team of victory in their match at Hartsfield Bulawayo yesterday. Zimbabwe had looked the better team throughout the game and until Pelser's mistake in the 25th minute looked set for victory.

"Zimbabwe scrum-half Brian Coghill had just slotted a penalty which had given the home team a 15-12 lead when Pelser attempted to catch their long range kick off in front of the posts instead of letting it go over to the dead ball area. Referee John Kennedy awarded a scrum to the visitors close to the Zimbabwe line and they quickly slipped it out to Duncan Black who, supported by the rest of the Leicester pack, went over to score.

"Coghill put Zimbabwe level only minutes later and the score remained at 18 all until five minutes before the final whistle when Ian Marais fluffed an off-the-line clearance. The English visitors were pressuring their Zimbabwe opponents when Marais received the ball inside his own goal area. He attempted to kick for touch but the ball skewed off his boot into the arms of

Tim Barnwell who just had to dot down to give his side their sought victory.

"The match was played at a cracking pace with most of the action amongst the forwards. Here Zimbabwe proved they were as good as their opponents and they won more than their fair share of ball. However, their pressure proved too great and in the tenth minute they were penalised for playing the ball on the ground.

"Mike Poulson made no mistake with the kick, but it was to be his last of the match. Soon after he attempted to intercept a pass and found himself sprawled on the turf with a pulled hamstring. A difficult penalty conversion by Colin McIntosh levelled the score line, but the visitors attacked with fury and were rewarded when Ian Smith went over for a try. Ian Dodson converted and Zimbabwe came back with a vengeance."

Matabeleland and Zimbabwe captain, prop Rob Halstead, who was tragically killed in 1985 when the aircraft he was piloting crashed in heavy mist in the Beza Range mountains

"McIntosh pulled Zimbabwe three back with a penalty in the 25th minute, but Dodson retaliated with a long penalty only two minutes later. Both teams then spent considerable time attempting to get their lines moving, but it was to be a day of kickers, and McIntosh once again slotted three points.

"The teams changed ends at half-time with the score at 12-9 to the visitors and it was a quarter of an hour before Brian Coghill booted a long-range penalty to put Zimbabwe on a level footing. The scrum-half put Zimbabwe ahead only five minutes later, but it was here that the tragedy of errors occurred.

"It was a deserved win for the visitors who showed more aggression for most of the match, and Coach Chalkie White must be pleased with his team's performance.

"For the visitors, winger Tim Barnwell once again turned in an outstanding performance. His strong runs and adept tackling relieved much of the pressure from his team and he was ably backed up by the hard-working forward John Deacon.

"For Zimbabwe the half back pairing McIntosh and Coghill again proved to be a feature of the national teams play. All in all it was a game in which

Zimbabwe should have won, but it seems that Bulawayo fans are to be deprived of a Zimbabwe win this season and once again it will be the Police Grounds crowd in Harare who are likely to see a great match next week."

After the game the Leicester Tigers team were entertained at The Queens Sports Club in Bulawayo. The next day they were treated to a 48-hour 'holiday' at Victoria Falls which for everyone was the highlight of the tour.

Tragically, the six foreign tourists kidnapped on the day the tour party arrived in Zimbabwe were slain by their captors. The hostages had been abducted by armed assailants as they were riding on a safari truck from Victoria Falls to Bulawayo – the very road the Tigers were due to travel on, but deemed too dangerous by the security forces, the Leicester team was flown to Victoria Falls in a Vickers Viscount, courtesy of Air Zimbabwe.

On arrival at the Victoria Falls Hotel, despite being winter, the players swam in the outdoor pool and enjoyed a *Braai* – a traditional Afrikaans barbeque. An early start was required the following morning when the touring party were driven in safari trucks to a local watering hole where they watched the local wildlife gathering at first light. Then, in groups of four in a Cessna light aircraft, the Tigers were flown over Victoria Falls.

"All aboard" – Leicester players Duncan Black, Steve Johnson and Nick Jackson boarding the unexpected flight to Victoria Falls

Heading for the Zambian border post – with Chalkie in charge it was normal to run everywhere (L-R): Martin Whitcombe, Nick Jackson, Vendis Afflick, Ian Dodson, Chalkie, and Ian Smith

"The flight consisted of four flyovers of the falls," recalled Steve Kenney. "Two with the left wing down and two with the right. We then flew at low level along the Zambezi river where we saw hippos and elephants on the river bank. This is the one thing I have seen so far in my life to stand out, head and shoulders above anything else."

Next stop was the Zambian border post on the far side of the Victoria Falls Bridge to have passports stamped as a souvenir just before it closed at 6pm, followed by a Sundowner evening cruise on the Zambezi.

At breakfast on the final morning, Chalkie White informed the players that everyone had been drinking and eating too much, and to meet him at reception in training kit. Led by Chalkie, who at 52 set the pace from the front, the players set off for a run along Livingstone Way and up the slow climb out of Victoria Falls, past the Sprayview Hotel and the other local landmarks for what felt like an age. By the time everyone arrived back at the hotel it had turned into a seven-mile run. Chalkie didn't say a word, but the players all got the message – the fun was over, the next game against the Midlands was in two days' time.

Tourists for a day at the Victoria Falls Bridge (L-R): Martin Whitcombe, Steve Kenney and Vendis Afflick, with Chalkie and Ian Smith behind.

After the flight back to Harare, the players were driven to Que Que – amid some confusion, as the city was in the process of reverting its name to the original KweKwe – for the final provincial game against the Midlands at the KweKwe Sports Club Grounds.

In a very one-sided affair on Wednesday August 4, Leicester hammered the Midlands 46-0, as reported by the rugby correspondent of the *Herald*: "The Leicester rugby machine moved into top gear at KweKwe Sports Club on Wednesday when the English visitors ran in eight tries without reply to thoroughly trounce the Midlands team. The English team ran the ball from the start and Midlands never looked like causing an upset.

"Leicester opened their account in the second minute when fiery winger Tim

John Deacon discussing tactics with the Leicester forwards. To the right, Chalkie White provides instructions to the backs

Barnwell scored after good three-quarter line movement. Midlands came back with some ferocity but were held by the adept tackling of centres Vendis Afflick and Terry Burwell. However, minutes later, the Leicester backs got moving and after a high up-and-under by fly half Ian Dodson, Afflick went over to score far out. Dodson was successful with the conversion and after a brief counter attack by the home team, it was all Leicester until the end of the game.

"Full back Kevin Williams grabbed the visitor's third try after he kicked through and beat Roy McFarlane in a dash for the line. Dodson converted once again and the writing was on the wall for the brave Midlands team. The final first half try came from scrum-half Nick Youngs who ran nearly the length of the field before dotting down under the posts.

"After the break, Midlands pressured the English team, but a penalty missed by Kevin Smith was the closest they came to upsetting the rhythm. Big lock forward Malcolm Foulkes-Arnold stormed over for the first try of the second half and Ian Dodson added his own four points to his team's tally after another fine run by the Leicester backs.

"Dodson played his best game of the tour and apart from a few missed conversions, he did not put a foot wrong. His intelligent touch kicks relieved the token pressure of the Midlanders. He was also responsible for the setting up of the visitor's final try when he received the ball in his dead ball area and decided to run the ball from there.

"In all, the visitors won by five goals and four tries, but more important was the fact that coach Chalkie White gave his men a good run for their return match against Zimbabwe at the Police Grounds, in Harare."

The final match of the tour was certainly concerning the Leicester coach, as the players discovered to their cost. Leicester hooker Chris Tressler takes up the story: "One of my most vivid memories of Chalkie while on tour in Zimbabwe was the day we had a day off but told to take our kit as we may be training later in the day. Everyone had a great day and we even saw Chalkie drinking from a wine glass. As the coach was returning to the hotel, we all assumed it was too late for training that day. How wrong we were! Chalkie had arranged for the coach to drive us directly to the training ground where Chalkie told us to get changed and be on the pitch in five minutes. When we got outside there was Chalkie with a fire hose in hand and he proceeded to hose us all down to bring us round, then made us train for an hour. He informed us that it was only water in his wine glass, and we needed to drink more water to keep hydrated and eat less meat because we were all putting on weight."

Back in Harare, and keeping in with the spirit of the times, 'Dosser' Smith, the author and the serving policemen in the tour party – Steve Johnson, Nick

Joyce and Nick Jackson – were invited as guests of the Zimbabwe Republic Police (ZRP) for an interesting morning at the ballistics department, which was good preparation for the shoot-out in the fifth and final game of the tour, the second match against Zimbabwe. After a very tough itinerary, travelling over 1,500 miles within the country, including five flights – one on a Second World War Dakota that had seen action at the Battle of Arnhem – and many bus journeys in the previous 12 days, the final game was probably one too many.

"Remember, 51% of the game is defence," said Chalkie as he ended his final team talk before kick off. "Get that right and you stand a good chance of winning." The Tigers took those words to heart when taking the field on Saturday August 7, but as 'Rugby Reporter' noted in his post-match article, Leicester held on for a 15-15 draw, and a creditable unbeaten record against their host nation: "Lucky Leicester! The English rugby union team were extremely fortunate to get away with a draw at the Police Grounds yesterday.

"Gaining a mountain of possession through the herculean efforts of Rob Halstead's powerful pack and the fine jumping of Neville Kloppers and Pete Bristow in the line-outs, the Zimbabweans held a territorial advantage throughout the match. However, there were too many mistakes, the most notable being Rob Greys 'gift' penalty with just ten minutes to go which allowed the visitors to equalise when fly half Mike Poulsen slotted the simple kick.

"The Zimbabwe backs did not have the pace to match their visitors, but they gave the one man who might have tested the opposition absolutely no ball. Right winger Jan Lock had a few opportunities to show his paces, but he had to do his own thing, gathering from broken play. One such attempt was a beauty; Leicester ran the ball along their back line. Tim Barnwell was tackled, the ball rolled loose and Lock set up a counter attack which took play within metres of the Leicester line. It was from this offensive, that Leicester won a scrum shortly after, but Zimbabwe wheeled and flanker Grey snatched up the ball and dived over.

Half-time at The Police Grounds, Harare. Exhausted Leicester Tigers player's regroup, as Chalkie White tends to Mike Poulson

"After an attack, Zimbabwe were rocked back on their heels by some superb running by the visitors who looked like they were going to chalk up another comfortable win with a 9-0 lead after 15 minutes. Captain Steve Johnson finished off a fine passing move just after the visitors had run the length of the field with a bewildering series of short passes and Poulson goaled to add to his penalty a minute earlier.

"Zimbabwe had missed a penalty attempt in the fourth minute when fly half Colin McIntosh hit the upright, an unhappy omen for the home team. Brian Coghill missed three kicks and McIntosh another. But despite these misses McIntosh proved the outstanding home player. His tactical kicking was superb, he got his line away smoothly, goaled a try by scrum-half Coghill, a beauty from the touchline and put over an easy effort when Grey had touched down under the posts.

"Coghill landed a 40-metre penalty at his fourth attempt and scored a first half try, but did not have his happiest match, while at full back young Kenyan Ziehl made a sound debut for Zimbabwe.

"Fly half Poulson looked as classy as ever, opening the scoring with a drop goal and converting Johnson's first half try. He had two attempts at the posts in the second half, and landed both kicks, missing only one kick at the posts, an off-balance drop kick in the 23rd minute."

After the game and much to the tour management's displeasure, most of the players skipped the dinner, in favour of the after-match disco where they celebrated their two undefeated games against Zimbabwe long into the night

However, at the same time, and unbeknown to us, a meeting took place that would shake Leicester Football Club to the core, as is explained by John Allen: "I had just taken over the role of Secretary from Jerry Day, and it was towards the end of the Zimbabwe tour that Chalkie informed me that he would be standing down as Coach, to take up a new position with the RFU. He told me this in confidence as the role would not become operational until January 1 1983. This was a surprise to me, especially him giving up his school teaching post at Nottingham High School. I thought he would be a school teacher until retirement."

Zimbabwe prop Keith Nicholson, a much-respected opponent

The author played in four of the five games on the tour and on three of those occasions he packed down against Keith Nicolson, a farmer who served in the Selous Scouts during the Bush War: "a humble man who made a big impression on me". After the tour the two exchanged letters and Christmas cards for many years until, tragically, Keith was shot and killed while trying to rescue a neighbour who had been abducted by armed men at his farm in 2011.

It's very doubtful whether any rugby team would agree, or be allowed, to visit a country during a State of Emergency. Leicester Tigers took

"Whatever Chalkie White said or did, there was a firm and good reason behind it, which made you question and look at yourself as a person and a player" – Leicester hooker Chris Tressler who played in both matches against Zimbabwe

a big gamble in accepting the invitation, and in sending so many inexperienced players on tour, but the gamble paid off

Assistant coach Rod Oakes, writing in the Leicester Tigers world tour brochure in 1987, remembered: "The trip to Zimbabwe was a real tour and despite all the marvellous times and visits we had, the rugby memories remain heavier etched. Arriving on the coach, slowly going by crowds of thousands all with colonial distrust in their eyes, stirred the blood. The togetherness, of the whole touring party of 30 versus the 13,000 spectators, with those of us in the stand fighting every battle alongside those on the field, and of course winning – that is what rugby tours are about."

Tour captain, Steve Johnson, added: "I had the greatest respect for Chalkie although we didn't always see eye-to-eye. He was an expert in building players' strength and endurance. He was able to organise the team to enable them to exploit their strengths, to cover each individuals' weaknesses and achieve success with a ruthless self-belief in our own ability.

"The Zimbabwe tour was a challenge as the country was still in turmoil after their war and the election of a new regime. It was a challenge in many respects, both on and off the field. We were unable to take a full squad because of international commitments but it gave great opportunities to some younger players to put down their markers for the future. They all stepped up to the plate and, without exception, gave their all, and would all feature in the future success of the club.

"Chalkie was a man who was rugby and Leicester through and through and should have coached England without a doubt, but I believe the RFU could not deal with his temperament and forthright way of expressing himself. To this day I don't think there has been a more deserving or qualified individual who never got his just deserts."

23

All Change – Chalkie leaves the Tigers

There was a strong sense of Tigers being a club in flux, with both Jerry Day and Chairman of Selectors Bob Rowell standing down due to pressure of business. There was a readymade successor for Jerry in Treasurer John Allen, whose service as Secretary would be one of the few things in club history to match his record-setting contributions as a player. But it was far harder to imagine how to replace Chalkie, who announced that he was leaving to fill one of the Rugby Football Union's newly-created Regional Technical Administrator posts, taking the South-West role based in Taunton.

Once the news of Chalkie's departure had broken, rumours were rife regarding a successor: "Chalkie deserves our congratulations, but it will be difficult replacing a man who has been with us for 15 years," John Allen commented in *The Telegraph*. "A lot of the style that people associate with the club can be put down to him."

"There is speculation in Leicester that Peter Wheeler, the club's international hooker, now nearing the end of his career, will take over," *The Telegraph* reported.

John Allen immediately implemented the process to find the new Head Coach at Leicester: "When I returned from tour, along with the committee, we had to start the process of replacing Chalkie and start planning for it. There were a few problems to overcome. Rod Oakes was the Extras' coach and Chalkie's Assistant Coach on tour; however we had to go through a process in order to find the right man. To continue the success of the previous five years, we didn't look outside the club and wanted to keep the post in-house. We didn't necessarily look for coaching qualifications, as you would today, but with his understanding of the traditions of the club, and his knowledge of the game. The committee eventually appointed the Youth Team Coach Graham Willars, to succeed Chalkie White, as the new Leicester Tigers Head Coach."

The new position with the RFU also meant leaving Nottingham High School, as his colleague Geri Thomas, explained: "Chalkie White's name is synonymous with rugby but his contribution to school life at Nottingham

Inspection Day at Nottingham High School, 1979 – Chalkie (right) in his Royal Navy uniform, with his wife Doris and daughter Stella in the audience

High School was much more than that. His professional approach and ability to motivate boys of all ages and abilities ensured the school's rugby team benefited. His work as a house tutor in Maples House was perhaps his finest work. Boys would stay in his care throughout their time at the school where they were dealt with by him with so much care and understanding. He was also a superb athletics coach as many javelin throwers and pole-vaulters will testify.

"He was Officer IC Naval Section, a role that was only a year old when he arrived at Nottingham High School. He built up a range of imaginative activities including night exercises on the River Trent, expeditions to remote areas of the country and visits to naval establishments. Chalkie's talents subsequently ensured that he was later appointed Commander in Chief of the Combined Cadet Force (CCF).

"He attended an Outward Bound leader's course in Scotland, and at some point, he had a window display in a shop in Nottingham extolling the virtues of Outward Bound courses. His enthusiasm for the great outdoors brought about his appointment as Nottinghamshire & Derbyshire Secretary for the Outward Bound organisation.

"Chalkie also contributed a great deal to the Old Nottinghamians RFC. He introduced them to circuit training and hard training, at the first session after they arrived, as usual, from The Vernon pub, oh did they suffer! However they soon got fitter and skilful, and as with the school teams they were transformed. He was held in such high regard by Old Nottinghamians."

Chalkie left at the end of 1982 with another Merit Table title all but secured with six wins, and only a meeting with Rugby – who would be beaten by 53 points in the spring – to come. His farewell supper on December 14 at Leicester's Grand Hotel was reported by Martin Johnson: "Leicester Football Club last night said goodbye to Tigers coach Chalkie White, and as the tributes poured in at his farewell dinner, there were quite a few lumps in rugby's most famous larynx.

"White who leaves on January 1 to take up a post with the Rugby Football Union watched films of Tigers' cup exploits on a BBC video screen and heard commentator Nigel Starmer-Smith tell him, 'It's a tragedy your talents were never used at international level'." Former skipper Peter Wheeler said, "In our quieter moments, the club internationals are saddened, that he could not share our England moments in the way he so richly deserved to. No words of mine," continued Wheeler, "can adequately express our gratitude towards him. We wish him and his family the success and happiness he has given the people of Leicester."

Club Chairman Kevin Andrews added, "Chalkie's commitment, dedication and integrity can never be questioned. White's successor as Coach, Graham Willars, told him 'We have memories of fun and hard work, and there's hard work still to be done'."

That night, the departing White, told Willars, "There have been one or two doubts over the past few years, over whether Tigers are the best. People say Tigers are the best, then add 'maybe'. I want Graham and his players to remove those doubts," adding, "but we are a championship club and I'm glad that I have been part of it."

Graham Willars – Chalkie's successor as Leicester coach

Les Cusworth kicks ahead as Leicester attack the Barbarians at Welford Road

Appropriately, he ended his involvement with Leicester Football Club facing the Barbarians on Wednesday December 29 1982. The match programme noted: "On this day, usually the highlight of the Leicester fixtures, it's sad to say farewell to Chalkie White after 15 seasons as the Tigers coach. The club and the players have already shown their appreciation of his talent last week, and it is fitting that he again received the Rupert Cherry trophy for the personality to have done most for the game. Leicester have a full-strength team on duty today, trying to give Chalkie a victorious send off."

"Leicester Tigers, proudly alert and richly successful, presented handsome farewells to Chalkie White the clubs coach for 15 seasons, with a superlative performance against the Barbarians at Welford Road yesterday," reported veteran *Telegraph* correspondent John Mason. "White, (who next week joins the RFU as coaching organiser for the South West), plus 17,000 others, all tickets were sold an hour before kick off, and the gates shut, were awarded a Christmas bonus.

"Victory by two goals, three tries, and four penalty goals represented a splendid cross section of the spoils that have allowed Leicester to become England's outstanding club in the past five years. The modest White described his part, 'The players put it together, not me!' is his perennial answer, somehow

Barbarians lock Donal Lenihan drags Nigel Gillingham through the line-out. Leicester players (L-R): Steve Kenney, Steve Johnson, Nick Jackson, Nigel Gillingham Steve Redfern. Barbarians players (L-R): John Scott, Nick Jeavons, Bob Norster, Ian Stephens

though I suspect he will have enjoyed what happened before a full house yesterday."

In a fitting and rousing send off, Leicester Tigers put a formidable group of Barbarians – Mark Wyatt; Trevor Ringland, Huw Davies, Dave Johnson, Mike Slemen; Oli Campbell, Robbie McGrath; Ian Stephens, Ciarán Fitzgerald (captain), Ian Milne, Bob Norster, Donal Lenihan, Nick Jeavons, John Scott, Jim Calder – to the sword by 36-16, with Barry Evans scoring a hat-trick, other tries from the half-back pairing of Kenney and Cusworth and 16 points from the boot of Hare.

24

On the Bus with (the other) Martin Johnson

Chalkie's legacy to Leicester Tigers, like that of any outstanding coach, was more than just the results he secured, spectacular as they were. Memories are also vital, and little from his time is more vividly remembered by the Tigers of his time than the coach trips which accompanied away matches.

On the outward coach journey, initial high spirits at Welford Road were steadily replaced with apprehension as you got nearer to the ground in either south Wales or the West Country. Often, on the last miles the bus would fall silent as everyone focused on the job in hand. If you got a message to go and have a 'chat' with Chalkie at the front of the bus, when you returned to your seat, particularly if you were a forward, he left you in no doubt about what he expected from you in the upcoming game.

Les Cusworth – a crowd favorite to a generation of Leicester Tigers supporters

The return journey was very different, sometimes bruised and battered, it was a chance to relax and enjoy your teammates' company. New and young players, initially reluctant to join in, would soon feel part of the team once they had been on an away trip, but there were rules.

Sharing his memories of a particular coach journey to a match in Wales, Les Cusworth described how Chalkie identified a potential problem that could impact his team's performance.

"Chalkie White was a disciplinarian, but you knew exactly where you stood with him," explained Cusworth. "Whenever we travelled away on the team bus he would always sit at the front. For a long time, we had a core group of players that formed a card school and at times there was some serious gambling. It was clear that Chalkie was a little uncomfortable with this and on our long journeys away, Llanelli was one of them, I lost a little more money than I should have, and as I got off the bus he asked, 'Are you ok, we have a big game today, you look worried and anxious'. He knew full well what had happened. Fortunately, we won the game and it came as no surprise when he banned the card school a few weeks later. No messing about for him, simply focus on the task that lay ahead; winning games of rugby playing to our optimum level. One of his favorite lines to the group was 'people in the bar will tell you all how good you are, all I will do is tell you how to get better'."

During the 1981-82 season, the club lost five out of six fixtures – between December 12 and January 15 – to frozen pitches, including the Barbarians match. With the first John Player Cup match against Hartlepool Rovers looming, using his initiative Chalkie decided that as the South Coast was free of bad weather the team should travel down to Torquay, to train there and play a Sunday fixture, still a rarity in those days, against Torquay Athletic.

There was quite a commotion, however, as the coach arrived in Torquay, where accommodation had been booked for Friday and Saturday night, when the storage compartments were found to be carrying not only the players' personal luggage and the team's playing kit, but two baskets full of racing pigeons belonging to the Welford Road groundsman, Derek Limmage, who was a keen pigeon fancier and who had been in great form on the journey to Devon.

The players had been puzzled as to why the groundsman had travelled, for the first time ever, with the team, and to much laughter the kit bags were unloaded and taken into the changing rooms while Derek's pigeons were loaded back onto the bus. Derek apparently wanted the driver to take them to a hilly part of Torquay, so they could then be released and fly back to Leicester, but when the storage compartment was opened the following day there were feathers everywhere and an awful smell. Apparently, the birds had gone crazy in the storage compartment overnight and left one hell of a mess behind them in the bus.

On the rugby field, Leicester enjoyed some frost-free training and their much-needed game-time, beating Torquay 44-4. That trip said a lot about Chalkie. It wasn't just his determination to ensure some quality training and competitive match practice, but also his recognition that the Tigers team was more than just the players, and that characters like Derek, who made everyone laugh, were essential contributors to team morale.

Robin Money echoes those memories with anecdotes from the Easter tours which were then an established part of the season. One tour took Tigers to the North West of England to take on Sale and Bill Beaumont's club Fylde.

Robin Money – the full back made 258 appearances for Leicester between1968-78, captained the club and was one of Chalkie's most consistent selections

"The thing that you miss most after retirement is the camaraderie of being in a team," recalls Money. "Chalkie made us, probably, the fittest team in England. We trained hard and played hard but on a Saturday night after a game we let our hair down. The Easter tour was always a great event and it was probably just as well there was no social media in those days. Easter Sunday lunchtime was always a big drinking session. We fell out of the Brunswick Hotel on Southport's High Street in a very lively mood and two of our forwards held me down and stripped me completely naked before running off with my clothes. Nearby Lord Street was somewhat busy but fortunately there were no police around. I found my clothes in a rose garden about half a mile down the road.

"On another tour, we socialised with the opposition on the Saturday and arrived back at our hotel on that night, very hungry. We asked the hotel if they could do some food but were told that the kitchen was closed. One of the guys spotted a three-tier wedding cake behind reception and told me to stand by as he sneaked over and threw the top tier of the cake to me. As a good full-back should, I caught the cake and ran up to one of the rooms where the boys satisfied their hunger. The next morning there was hell to pay when the hotel management informed the Tigers committee of our escapade. Everyone was deemed guilty but they could not punish us all."

Also, on those buses was whoever held the role as the *Leicester Mercury* rugby correspondent. Chris Goddard, who inherited the role after Chalkie's departure, and went on to cover the Tigers for more than 20 years before becoming sports editor, retains vivid memories of Chalkie's relationship with his immediate predecessor, Martin Johnson.

"I first met Herbert Victor White, better known as Chalkie, when I was second-in-command to the *Leicester Mercury* rugby writer Martin Johnson back in the early 1980s," explained Goddard, "and I know Martin liked and respected him a huge amount, which is not a surprise because both were geniuses in their own field. Mind you, it did not stop Martin, probably the funniest sports journalist ever, taking the mickey out of the man who built, arguably, the most entertaining Tigers side.

"When I asked Martin what Chalkie was like, he said: 'Well, you hear him before you see him, and you know you are within two miles of the Tigers' ground on training night when you hear this voice barking, 'Dodgy, Les, Dusty…' He makes Brian Blessed sound like Whispering Ted Lowe'.

"When Martin was on holiday or had a day off, I rang Chalkie every morning at Nottingham High School to try to get a Tigers story and, on the first couple of occasions, I took copious shorthand notes and thought I had a decent article to publish. It was only when I read my notes that I realised I'd not got a back page piece at all. Some of it made no sense. Chalkie, it seemed to me, was a bit of an intellectual as well as an academic and a rugby obsessive, so some of what he said would have gone right over the heads of your average rugby punter.

"He also had a twinkle in his eyes and a great sense of humour, which he needed after Martin was made rugby writer. 'I don't know anything about rugby,' protested Martin when the *Mercury* sports editor, David Welch, asked him to take over from David Hands, who had left for the *Times*. 'Don't worry, you'll be fine,' said David, and he was, although there was a minor hiccup early on when a Leicester Committee man, according to Martin, was dispatched to the *Mercury* to try to get him sacked due to his irreverent match reports.

"Before too long, however, Martin was travelling on the team bus to away matches, presumably with Chalkie's permission, and, in those days, everyone had a sit-down meal after the game. Once, after Leicester had played Blackheath, Martin ended up sitting opposite Tigers prop Robin Cowling, who had been on the receiving end of a few choice words from the *Mercury*

The Leicester Mercury sports desk circa 1981
Back Row (L-R): David Welch, Chris Goddard, Jon Culley, Tim Murray, Graham Melton, Ken Hoxley, Godfrey Tabiner
Front Row (L-R): Alan Parr, Martin Johnson, Jimmy Martin, Alf Perkins, George Nunney, Peter Grundy

reporter, and Sue Lacey, wife of the then club President Eric. Sue had become a big fan of Martin. 'Oooh, I do love your Monday match reports Martin, they make me laugh,' she exclaimed.

"Martin said this proved too much for Robin, who made a lunge across the table for him. Sensing he might not have too long to live, Martin high-tailed it out of the ground and caught a train home. On Monday morning, his telephone rang. It was Robin, who proffered an apology and invited him to his farm for a tour after which they became good friends.

"This was a regular occurrence early on in Martin's Tigers career. He once wrote a hilarious piece on Leicester lock Lord Arthur Hazlerigg, a mixture of praise for his rugby prowess and mickey taking over his title. After a game, we walked into the clubhouse and who should be standing near the bar but Arthur, who, upon seeing Martin, threw an entire pint over him. Minutes later they were laughing and joking.

"Chalkie would probably have laughed too, as I'm sure he did after we stopped for a drink at a country pub after a match in the West Country. On the way out I, fortunately, went to the loo and, when I got outside, I heard a commotion on a nearby bridge. On approaching, I saw that the front row had Martin by his ankles, dangling him over the side. His car keys and money ended up in the river.

"Drink was usually the cause of the mayhem, and after a boozy Easter tour to Wales, Martin told me he went to bed but forgot to lock his hotel door. He had not been asleep long when the door opened and a bucket of water drenched him. After drying himself, he clambered into the other bed but, still worse for wear, forgetting to lock the door. Sometime later, another bucket of water drenched him again. With the sun coming up, he decided to make an early start for home. So he went to the foyer, ordered a cup of tea and started to read a paper. Suddenly he heard footsteps and giggling but, before he could react, a bucket of water came crashing through the paper. Thoroughly wet and fed up, he set off for home and pulled into a petrol station to fill up and, as he emerged from the kiosk, he spied Peter Wheeler parking his car. So he got a bucket of water and poured it over Braces' kit in the boot: 'It wasn't me,' protested Brace.

"Even on the bus, things were never dull. On one trip home on the M5, the banter was such that the players stripped Martin of all his clothes, including his shoes, one of which Eric Lacey, who I think had had a few, threw out of the skylight: 'You bugger,' said Martin, 'they're brand new shoes'.

"On another occasion, during a stopover at a steakhouse, he sent a steak back three times because it wasn't cooked properly after which he was invited to the kitchen to cook it himself. When he returned, to thunderous applause, his attention was distracted and when he found his steak had disappeared, he looked up to see one of the props standing on the table with an exultant glint in his eyes. He swallowed the steak with a single gulp.

"These are just a few of the, printable, funny anecdotes from Chalkie's time as Tigers coach, a time that can only be described as the halcyon days of Tigers-*Mercury* relations, which is saying something because Martin did not hold back when it came to criticism of the team or the club, or indeed taking the mickey. It was his nature but also a product of the Tigers environment under Chalkie. Having fun and banter was mandatory.

"When Chalkie left Leicester in 1983 to take up a post with the Rugby Football Union he wrote a letter to me and Martin thanking us for 'what you have done over the past few years'. He signed off with: "I would like to thank you for your patience in the face of intolerance, for your persistence in the face of obstruction, and a willingness to understand the irrational obsession of a grey-haired old man. You have both made your contribution to my time at

Journalist Martin 'Jonno' Johnson (1949-2021) – with (1987-89) club President Kevin Andrews (centre) who captained Leicester in 1969-70, and former England and Lions centre Mike Weston (right) – had a unique relationship with the Tigers players and officials in a way that would never happen today

the Tigers, a period beyond comparison anywhere in the world. For your help, thank you very much. Good luck'.

"It was a sign of the kindness and class of a man who became synonymous with Tigers and attacking rugby, and I treasure the letter. I doubt if we will ever see the likes of Chalkie or Martin again. Both were one-offs."

In *A Tribute to Peter Wheeler* in October 2014, on the occasion of Wheeler's retirement from Leicester FC's Board of Directors, Martin Johnson summed up his love for the club and for his profession with the comment: "I remember my time as rugby correspondent at the *Leicester Mercury* (1979-85) with a fondness others might find curious, considering this was an era when a local paper's rugger reporter was not so much in the running for a journalistic award as a Victoria Cross. A posthumous one, of course."

25

Part of the Union – 1983-94

In January 1983 Chalkie moved from Nottingham to Somerset to take up the role as RFU Divisional Technical Administrator (DTA) for the South & South West, one of four DTAs appointed to help develop English rugby. Initially, Chalkie lived alone, in rented accommodation – while Doris and Nick stayed in Nottingham until Nick's exams were finished. In September 1983, they moved into 'Penshurst', their final family home together – in Wellington, Somerset.

That he was the choice of RFU Technical Administrator Don Rutherford, an England full back in his playing days, came as no surprise to Robin Cowling,

Chalkie and Doris visiting Land's End while 'house hunting'

Don Rutherford initiated coaching and playing programmes which were emulated by rugby playing nations across the world

who knew them both. He recalls: "Back in my own playing career, I remember Chalkie got along with Don Rutherford at Gloucester, who took on a captain / coach role; they were the first coaches I knew. Don introduced a training schedule to Gloucester which made him the most unpopular man at the club. The players had been used to meeting up on training nights for a few pints before going home!

"Chalkie and Don got on very well, and together they wrote the RFU Level 1 coaching programme. I don't think Don ever got the recognition he deserved in England, he was more highly thought of in New Zealand, where they took on many of his ideas. Don became the first paid coach at the RFU, when he became RFU Technical Administrator. Some years after his appointment and once he had established a coaching structure, he then appointed the first Divisional Technical Administrators, which is when Chalkie left Leicester to take on the role of DTA for the South West. Chalkie, along with Frank Butler, who Chalkie appointed as Youth Development Officer for Cornwall, encouraged me to get involved in coaching. Both were very instrumental in me getting involved with Exeter Chiefs – they dragged me along to everything."

Three of the four new regional administrators were former Leicester Tigers players. Among them was Alan Old, who remembers: "Barrie Corless, for the Midlands, was first. I, for the North, second. Then Dave Shaw took on London & South East and finally Chalkie the South West. We were managed by Don Rutherford and were tasked with developing the playing, coaching and refereeing of rugby on a regional basis, working with clubs, schools, colleges, local authorities, counties and divisions – a wide brief and a lot of travelling."

Chalkie's own view of the job was explained in an interview with the *Cumberland News* in August 1982: "This is a new position, and the RFU were anxious that it should have some credibility. I was reading England soccer manager Bobby Robson say that the schools no longer provided as many good players as they used to. It's a similar situation in rugby. The schools are no longer a great breeding ground, so that's something I will be trying to put right in the South West. That's not to say that the standard of club rugby has declined over the years. People play the game because they love it and they get a great deal of enjoyment out of it. For instance, I have just toured Zimbabwe with Leicester, the club has also been to the USA and Fiji, the player of 20 years ago couldn't hope to see those places."

Former Leicester Tigers lock Dave Shaw became Divisional Technical Administrator (DTA) for London & South East

"Chalkie doesn't share the prejudice of some union people to rugby league," continued the article, "and was even an interested spectator at Carlisle's match with Wigan last weekend. He says he has always enjoyed the commitment of the professionals and will be monitoring Carlisle's progress this season. His job in the West Country will be to install a similar level of commitment, 'I'm looking forward to putting across my ideas' he adds, 'I hope they will listen'."

Alan Old pointed to a single event as epitomising his approach: "We had been at Twickenham for a meeting, and to be introduced to a very well-respected New Zealand coach, Bill Freeman. I was ferrying Bill to the North to take some coaching clinics and offered Chalkie a lift to Nottingham as there were problems with the trains. From Twickenham to Nottingham Chalkie interrogated Bill – in the nicest way – on the All Blacks' methods, philosophies and organisation of all aspects of rugby. As the weather was bad I concentrated on driving and had little input, however, after dropping Chalkie off, Bill sighed, sat back in his seat and said what a pleasure it had been to discuss things with Chalkie, and he felt that both had appreciated and enjoyed the expertise, enthusiasm and passion of the other. It was a privilege to be a colleague of his in the RFU coaching organisation."

In his new role, Chalkie crossed paths again with another former Tiger, Terry Burwell, who remembers: "In 1990 I was appointed Director of Coaching at Newbury RFC, a professional position five years before the game went open. By now, Chalkie was the Divisional Technical Administrator for the RFU in the South West and so he became my mentor, again, helping to shape my personal development and eventually guiding me to success on and off the field, in Newbury and then my career at the RFU. In amongst a myriad of coaching sessions and matches, some stand out more than others, but I will

Bob Reeves gave over 50 years' service to student rugby in England

never forget the January Monday nights at Bisham Abbey with Alan Black and HV White ... the Black and White coaching evenings when in excess of 100 coaches came to gain insight and understanding of the game through their eyes."

Future RFU President Bob Reeves remembers the annual coaching conferences with particular fondness: "I had known Chalkie for many years prior to him coming to the South West, being a senior and then staff coach of the area, and seeing him every year at the coaches' conference at Bisham Abbey. I was also one of the coaches, when the infamous photograph was taken at Lilleshall, when Chalkie sat on the front row with his private parts showing.

"From the early days, he often called me 'Preston', it being my home town, but where I had not lived for years! When he left Leicester it was a bit of a surprise, but in the South West, Chalkie quickly established himself and he was hugely respected and liked. My main contact with him was via what became the South West Coaching Conference, held annually at the University of Bristol's Coombe Dingle facility.

"For a number of years, I had organised what was initially the Gloucestershire RFU Coaching Conference, then combined with Gloucestershire and Somerset. Chalkie suggested that it should become a full South West affair, and was prepared to find some RFU money towards it. Over the next years to his retirement, we had some wonderful weekends. From the start, I had wanted the weekend to be a bit different, and to get visiting coaches in from all over the place – such as Pierre Villepreux from France, Brian O'Shea from Australia and Bill Freeman from New Zealand.

"Chalkie fully supported this, and our regional affair was always different to what went on in other parts of the country. This of course suited Chalkie, as he was always a bit of a rebel, and not necessarily inclined to follow the RFU path. This may have been because he genuinely was different, but even though he was working for the RFU, I suspect he was always quietly disappointed by the fact that he had never had the chance to coach England, something he certainly had deserved.

"Our coaching weekend was not for any qualification and we welcomed coaches with different levels of experience as well as players interested in coaching. We had over 100 every year, staying on Friday and Saturday nights, with a dinner on the Saturday. Chalkie loved all of this, and I recall fondly us all sitting at the bar, in the university's Badock Hall, into the early hours sorting out the world of rugby. He was a friend and guide to all, and I felt very close to him."

Chalkie wearing his RFU senior coaches' tracksuit

However, when Chalkie attended representative squad sessions, it was no longer as Head Coach, it was as Divisional Technical Administrator for the RFU. A point not lost on Bath's international forward Gareth Chilcott, who recalls: "I remember going along to squad sessions at Taunton School where Chalkie was based when we had the old Divisional Championship. Jack Rowell was our coach at the time. Chalkie was never introduced to us a coach but he did help out and work with the players. He was never going to tell Stuart Barnes how to make an outside break, but he would talk to him and make him think about when he would do it. I personally liked Chalkie and got on with him very well. Without a doubt, Chalkie's best work in the South West was done working in the clubs and bringing on the next generation of coaches where he influenced many."

His impact on individuals within the system was epitomised by Will Feebery, from Chalkie's old stomping ground in the Royal Navy. He joined up in 1965 and served until 1990, including 13 years as a Warrant Officer, then spent eight years as the RFU's Regional Development Officer for Hampshire followed by 12 years as Training Manager at the RFU Coaching Development Department based at Twickenham. A full back or wing for ships, establishments and United Services Portsmouth RFC until he was injured playing against the South African Army in Cape Town in 1975, he began coaching in 1977 at US Portsmouth and qualified on the RFU Preliminary Coaching Course in 1981. He remembers: "At the time of my first meeting with Chalkie in 1983, I was coaching HMS Collingwood and the Royal Navy Colts. In the following season HMS Collingwood won the RN Cup and the RN Colts beat the Army. A year later, whilst serving on HMS Illustrious, we won the Big Ships Cup. I put this success down to the confidence that Chalkie gave me. He filled me with

Will Feebery, one of many coaches to be inspired by Chalkie

self-belief and he set me free as a coach with his emphasis on individual skills, free running and finding and exploiting space.

"I realise I was a small fish in a big pool but the effect that Chalkie had on me, prior to and whilst he was working for the RFU is something I will be forever grateful for. With his wisdom and guidance, he helped me to change my career path from serving in the Royal Navy to one of working in rugby. The opportunity therefore to share my thoughts on this great man is something that I never envisaged, yet on reflection it is not often you come into contact with a master of his craft, a maestro that inspires you, changes the course of your life and probably without him even knowing."

The big moment came in 1983 when he was asked to coach Royal Navy Colts and, facing a fixture list of county colts teams leading up to the Inter Services Colts Championship, realised he needed to supplement the skills acquired on the Preliminary Coaching Course. He took a weekend course run at his own home base, HMS Collingwood in Hampshire, by Rutherford and his assistant Ron Tennick, with Chalkie in attendance.

Chalkie led on several practical sessions, as Feebery explains: "What stood out was his clarity of purpose for each session, coupled with an almost forensic method of questioning. At first, we all thought that he came across as being dictatorial and it took time to get used to his technique of detailed question after detailed question. We also considered, at times, that he was not sure why he was asking so many questions without offering any notion of what the answer was. How wrong could we all be?"

That evening, Feebery found himself sitting next to Chalkie at supper and, "realised how adept he was at asking questions about our families and backgrounds. It turned out that we had three things in common; we both served in the Royal Navy, we both had Ménière's disease (an ear related problem leading to a loss of balance), and we both shared a love of coaching." Over the weekend, further, broader lessons emerged: "Chalkie emphasised that coaches should spend more time on running with the ball and evasion skills. With lots of handling and passing activities, finding space and beating defenders was key. Less time should be spent on scrum and line-out without undermining their importance."

"Never having played in the forwards, or any other position, should not prevent you from gaining as much knowledge as you can about game management, team dynamics and to be really honest about what you didn't know. He emphasised the point in improving your questioning skills, to ask the right questions of the players who probably knew more about their position than you, and to use them wisely in sharing and demonstrating to others.

"Despite the above I was still left a little bewildered by the tough approach Chalkie took when challenging individuals through his persistent questioning of players and coaches alike. I was about to be tested further. However, we came to realise that there was no pretending with Chalkie, he told it how it was and most of the time he was right."

Further exposure to Chalkie's methods came the following year at a level three course held at Rugby School that Feebery attended with his close friend Mike Heffield, Chief Petty Officer from the Royal Navy Physical Training Department: "Affectionately known as 'Scouse', Mike was a no-nonsense tight head prop from the old school and his rugby knowledge of forward play was immense. He always joked that, as a result of a field gun accident, his face was so pock marked you could throw a handful of peas at him and non-would drop off. He called the backs piano players and the forwards piano shifters. However, my time with Mike listening to his love of scrummaging was about to pay off."

Both were scheduled to deliver a 20-minute presentation, Heffield on the role of the front row at scrums, Feebery on the fly half in attack, but that was before Chalkie, waiting outside the classroom, asked what they were going to do: "To our astonishment, Chalkie took my presentation notes and handed them to Scouse and handed his notes to me, saying that we were to deliver each other's session. We were both gobsmacked and not very happy. Later, after we both managed to get through our presentations, we realised what Chalkie had done. He had challenged us both to find out how we dealt with what we felt we didn't know, he took us outside of our comfort zone and judged us on how we dealt with it. We learnt from him that not knowing is ok, but trying to hide or to flannel is not acceptable.

"I'm happy to report that I just about qualified from the course, having learnt a valuable lesson that it's only when you are outside your comfort zone that you really learn who, and what you are. It was Tony Biscombe who assured us not to take it personally and that it was customary for Chalkie to liven things up and to test candidates whenever he got the chance."

A few years later, Feebery saw Chalkie's questioning methods at their most effective at a session in Oxford with his colleague Lynn Evans, previously Oxford University coach and now RFU Youth Development Officer (YDO) for Oxford. Chalkie was assisted by All Black scrum-half Dave Loveridge, "now retired but nonetheless extremely skilful."

"Chalkie asked Dave to demonstrate the scrum-half's pass from the base of the scrum," recalls Evans, "and to explain to the coaches how he managed to not use any back lift yet still be so accurate. Dave addressed a dozen balls placed on the grass and quick-as-a-flash delivered the balls so fast that the receiving young fly half, standing some 20 metres away, only had time to catch and drop each ball before the next one was on its way.

"A perfect demonstration from Dave was followed by a question form Chalkie, 'How did you do that Dave?' Dave again demonstrated the passing technique but with little verbal explanation of how he did it. Chalkie asked again: 'Now, Dave, how did you really do it? Can you break it down for us?" Dave replied, 'I've just showed you'. 'I know,' said Chalkie 'but you still haven't told us how you did it'. 'Are you dumb?' said Dave to Chalkie, 'I've just showed you?'

"Chalkie took a deep breath and said, 'Yes, ok, but let's break it down together. Look at your feet position; what is your stance and why is your left foot pointing that way?' After a moment's thought, Dave Loveridge said, 'I don't really know, I've been doing this since I was 15.' By the time we'd finished, Dave fully understood where Chalkie was coming from, and made an excellent contribution to the session. Dave realised that he had never analysed or broken the skill down in such detail before."

This did not mean New Zealand players were deficient in their understanding of the game, quite the opposite, as Chalkie had realised on visits there.

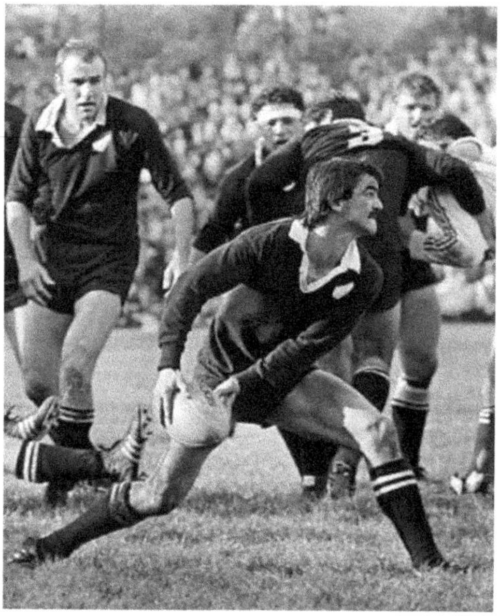

Former New Zealand scrum-half Dave Loveridge

"He realised that players in NZ were almost all technically more developed than their British counterparts," Feebery explained. "He concluded that in NZ the players' early learning had been instilled with the focus of countless sessions covering the basic skills of running and handling, that so many of their movements were automatic and would be done without really understanding the 'why' of the technique or skill."

This changed in the late 1980s and early 1990s when coaches like Lee Smith and Wayne Smith used questioning of players to great effect, consciously or not echoing the example Chalkie had set at Leicester since the late 1960s. His impact on New Zealand thinking was acknowledged at the 1991 World Cup coaching conference by Lee Smith, National Director of Coaching from 1988 to 1995, as Feebery continues: "After an excellent practical session, based mainly on basic skills under pressure, Lee went on to present on the principles of play for New Zealand rugby, which came under the following headings: (1) Win the ball, (2) Go forward, (3) Support, (4) Continuity, and (5) Pressure. The room went silent because many attending from the RFU knew that (2), (3), (4) and (5) were the four principles of play laid down by the RFU Technical Director, Don Rutherford, and his Divisional Technical Administrators (DTAs).

"Before anyone could say anything, Lee Smith went on to add that New Zealand rugby had for some time been using the excellent coaching manuals, written by the RFU during the late 1970s and early 1980s, as a guide to their technical programmes. Lee and his coaches had simply added 'Win the Ball' to their version. Then he congratulated Don Rutherford and his good friend Chalkie White for their vision and expertise. Don wrote some great stuff on coaching in the '60s, '70s and '80s, and NZ recognised that because it was new and ground-breaking. Chalkie was similar and he gave Don a lot of support and new ideas."

Chalkie nurturing the next generation of coaches

Another coach strongly influenced by Chalkie was Bob Hood, a graduate of Carnegie College and holder of the Level 3 coaching award, whose career in West Yorkshire, as a player, rugby coach and mentor spans more than four decades. He progressed through the Rugby Football Union's coaching awards and now holds the Level 4 award.

"After completing the RFU Level 3 award," explains Hood, "I was asked to staff a L3 delivery session at Trent College in Nottingham. It was on this occasion that I met Chalkie White. I had heard a lot about him and felt a sense of trepidation and a certain amount of fear at meeting this legendary rugby personality.

"Whilst delivering the session my heart skipped a beat as the door opened and Chalkie White, appeared without any notice. He arrived just as a candidate was in full flow, regarding the tackling qualities needed by a right winger. Chalkie listened with avid intent and as soon as the individual paused for breath, Chalkie pounced on the unfortunate candidate who had been in waffle mode for some time. Now a recipient of Chalkie's famous probing questions, it wasn't a pretty sight and after his verbal dismantling, I quickly dismissed the group to break.

"However, Chalkie remained behind. He began to question me and was particularly interested in the work I was doing on mini-unit formations I had been discussing with the group. Then, suddenly out of the blue, the question 'what are your coaching ambitions' boomed from Chalkie's mouth. Completely flustered I answered nervously and definitely too spontaneously, 'to get as far as I can as quick as I can'."

Hood remembers that after listening intently, Chalkie vanished as quickly as he appeared, but he clearly gave that answer serious thought, and acted upon it: "From that day on I noticed that I was starting to get some fantastic coaching opportunities from the RFU to develop my coaching. I was appointed the first Head Coach to the England Senior Counties XV with Test matches in Chile, Romania and France. Although I can't prove it, I am absolutely certain that Chalkie White was responsible for my coaching career changing direction in those early days, and that his opinion of me that day at Trent College was a positive one. It was like being guided by a rugby genius who started me on the incredible journey that I am still on today."

Chalkie's impact was also felt by coaches who never met him personally, through publications such as *Start Rugby* co-authored with Tony Biscombe, *Skills Practices for All* and *Coaches Handbook*, as well as an academic article 'Teaching Rugby Football – Using the Ball', published in the *British Journal of Physical Education* in 1984.

He had an impact on coaching for schoolchildren through the courses organised by future Tigers chief executive Simon Cohen, who utilised many of the top Leicester players as coaches – Peter Wheeler, Dean Richards, Ian Smith, Les Cusworth, Paul Dodge and John Wells were all involved. Simon applied for RFU approval and was invited to a meeting with Don Rutherford and the development officers, of whom Chalkie was one. The expectation was that the discussion would evolve around how much money should be paid for RFU approval but Chalkie's idea was that approval should be given if Simon provided every child with a free rugby ball. His initiative led to tens of thousands of rugby balls entering playgrounds all over the country.

Sat on the bank – Chalkie casting a watchful eye at a training session

He then, as part of the coaching programme, decided to put his ideas into practice and Simon marketed a 'Chalkie White Academy' which was extremely popular. Chalkie introduced a programme that, both on and off the pitch, set high standards for skills and behaviour, but the youngsters responded wonderfully to the charismatic coach. Many top players went through the programme and had their eyes opened by a youth coach who taught them to think for themselves but also what the parameters were for a successful team.

He also took part, alongside veteran Jeff Butterfield and members of the England touring team – including Mark Bailey, destined for a distinguished teaching and academic career – in the 'Ford Coaching Clinics' held in association with England's tour of South Africa in 1984. This was not his only overseas venture as he, Rutherford and Alan Black attended the coaching conference in Brisbane, organised in associated with the first World Cup in 1987.

This enabled him to watch the matches played in Brisbane at either end of the week in which the conference took place, and it is a fair bet that he enjoyed the epic semi-final in which France finally saw off Australia with Serge Blanco's magnificent try, more than the previous weekend's quarter-final between England and Wales, which saw an English performance so abysmal that it helped spark wholesale reforms at national level over the next few years.

A few years earlier, Chalkie might have been prominently involved in such changes. Instead, it was Geoff Cooke who proved to be England's agent of

Former RAF PTI Paul Hull enjoyed a stellar career with Bristol and England

change as national team coach. Nor was he particularly strongly involved with the South West regional team.

Paul Hull, the brilliant Bristol and England full back who was appointed the RFU's Head of Professional Game Match Officials in 2021, recalls that: "He was respected and liked by all, but suffered from not being Head Coach and was seen as the man from the RFU. It probably did not help that he still wore his Leicester Tiger's tracksuit at times!"

By the late 1980s, times had changed and a new generation of players had come through who knew nothing of his achievements. He had great success developing coaches and improving standards, but basically his team coaching days were over.

This need not necessarily have been the case. Tigers, who had dropped back into mid-table after winning the first RFU League title in 1988, made a serious attempt to persuade him to return as the first professional Director of Coaching in the early 1990. John Allen's approaches, which came in three letters between December 1989 and the end of January 1990, were sufficiently discreet not to be mentioned in Stuart Farmer and David Hands' comprehensive and well-informed 1993 club history, and also unsuccessful.

Chalkie applied for the new position of Director of Coaching at Leicester Tigers and was interviewed at the Hinckley Island Hotel on Sunday January 21 1990. Following his successful interview, Chalkie was offered the position in a letter from John Allen on January 31. However, Chalkie later declined the role and Tony Russ was appointed to the post, the following summer, on a reported annual salary of £20,000, as Chalkie's son, Ged recalls: "I can remember Dad telling me that senior members of the club had encouraged him to apply to return to Leicester as coach. I remember him telling me that he'd told Leicester it wasn't a one-person job – it was a three-person job – telling them they needed to employ three people: one to coach, one to look after recruitment and one to do the admin. And, that he'd told them that the total cost to the club would be close to £100,000."

'No injuries sustained'

One factor in Chalkie's refusal may have been concern over his health, with a diagnosis of Inclusion Body Myositis, a rare muscle-wasting disease, in the late 1980s. Also, in the late 1980s, he contracted a significant dermatological illness after driving through Gloucestershire during crop-spraying. He was interviewed on local television about the condition and continued involvement with Pesticide Action UK Network well into his retirement.

His life was not all rugby, although the game was sufficiently dominant for him to reply good-humouredly when invited to a Royal Garden Party in 1985 emphasising, "My wife's and daughter Stella's delight at the chance of accompanying me to something other than a rugby match". Stella had also not long before appealed successfully to the intrepid side of his nature when she won a parachute jump and, with one brother unwilling and the other living in Florida, persuaded him to join her in the adventure at Shobden airfield near Leominster.

Retirement came in 1994 when Chalkie turned 65. His departure from the RFU was marked warmly by his boss, Don Rutherford, who wrote: "It seems incredible that Chalkie now qualifies for his bus pass and cheap travel on

Chalkie delivering a coaching session to young rugby players at Brixham RFC

British Rail, but he has reached a milestone which hopefully we will all reach one day, even if not in his pristine condition.

"No one who knows Chalkie would ever describe him as an 'establishment' man. He was always and remains a man of strong views and never one to be shy of expressing them most forcefully. Some on the receiving end of his views have not taken them very kindly, but the more discerning have realised that what he had to say has always been thought provoking, and on more occasions than not, absolutely 100% correct. It was with some difficulty that Chalkie was persuaded to join the RFU, the mythical beast, that temple in the sky, that frequently used waste bin of glib comment or frustration. Yes, he committed the ultimate rugby sin, he became one of them, an RFU man.

"Chalkie's patch stretched from Penzance in the South West to Slough in the East, and a more parochial area it would be difficult to imagine. It's one thing to imagine the rivalries between Bath and Gloucester, but also as all visitors to Cornwall will recognise, it is not uncommon for locals to refer to holiday makers as 'emits' and dismiss events taking place north of the river Tamar with the phrase 'Up country in England'. It's as though 'emits' and 'new ideas' were being delivered by Martians from outer space. The welding together of this disparate group of people to give them a sense of purpose was Chalkie's challenge, and it speaks volumes for his tenacity that the South West are the current holders of the Divisional Championship, a position they have enjoyed for the last two years. This is no mean achievement.

"There is little doubt that Chalkie is a charismatic character, a man who can light a flame and persuade others to carry it. Players always knew he would give them an honest opinion and for that they respected him. Some coaches have been known to seek popularity with players and in so doing, have dismissed their effectiveness. Chalkie never fell into this trap, first came respect, then understanding – of the man, his commitment, his ideas – then, and only then, through the respect and understanding came real fellowship.

Chalkie and Doris at the Paris Hilton March 1994. "This was Mum's first visit to Paris with time to relax, socialise and inevitably, watch rugby. They had a wonderful time." – Stella

"On a personal level, Chalkie was a most agreeable travelling companion and all those who bumped into him will have their own special stories. Some 20 years ago at Lilleshall, I remember we took a marvellous photograph of all the coaches present. Only when the photograph was developed was all revealed. Sitting proudly in the front was Chalkie wearing his wide legged shorts minus jock strap – and a very fine display it made! I had the good fortune to travel with Chalkie from Brisbane to Sydney on June 13 1987, to watch the semi-final of the inaugural World Cup between Australia and France. Chalkie described this as a golden wings trip because not only was the flight and companionship quite excellent but the game was one of those really outstanding matches which will live long in the memory. France won in the dying moments with a Serge Blanco try.

"No one better epitomises the phrase the 'age is in the mind and not in the calendar'. I think that I can safely say that Chalkie was never one for waiting for the ship to come in, but was more prepared to row out to meet it. I know when I speak on behalf of the technical staff and say he will be sorely missed; I also echo the thoughts of many coaches and players who have the good fortune to come under his spell.

"Behind every good man is an even better woman. We wish Chalkie and Doris a long and extremely happy retirement."

On Wednesday April 27, he returned to Leicester for the 'Special Tribute to Chalkie White Dinner' at the Grand Hotel. With Les Cusworth as Master of Ceremonies, Tigers Chairman Peter Tom gave the Loyal Toast and there were tributes from, Brian Hall, Clive Woodward, Eric Bann, Don Rutherford, Robin Money and Peter Wheeler.

Club President Tudor Thomas farewelled him in writing: "When I watched HV White play his last game for Leicester against Cheltenham in October

A Special Tribute to Chalkie White

1963, little did I think I would be attending a retirement dinner here in Leicester this evening. On behalf of the players, committee, members and supporters of Leicester Football Club I am honoured and privileged to welcome Chalkie back 'home' tonight. This remarkable philosopher, who once worked on a farm in Cumberland, has enriched the lives of most people who have enjoyed the privilege of his company. Light years ahead of his time, Chalkie has upset people, educated people, improved standards and made a greater contribution to the game of rugby football than anyone I know.

"Respected throughout the world for his knowledge, for the clarity of his thinking and for the honesty of his expression, he has become a legend in his own right.

"Chalkie, thank you for all you have done, not only for rugby football, but also for the society in which we live. You epitomise what is good in life. In particular, thank you for what you have done for so many players at Leicester Football Club, and for the foundations you have laid on which we can continue to build in the future. It is gratifying to know that you are only one expensive phone call away.

"In conclusion may I say thank you to Doris, without whose love and devotion, you would not be where you are today. When you return to Wellington, please give her our love. Enjoy your evening and your possible but very improbable retirement."

26

The Final Years – 1994-2005

Chalkie was never likely to be a man for the pipe-and-slippers variety of retirement and neither was he. Speaking on behalf of the family, Chalkie's son Ged describes his father's latter years:

"Since moving to their Somerset home, and with help from local builders, he had replaced the Crittall windows; added a unique porch; re-fitted the kitchen, creating a kitchen-diner; added a utility room – and extended the second living room, 'the barn', providing access to the gardens. He had changed the approach pathway to the garage and to the front door and transformed the gardens, with help from the local workforce. Their Somerset home also saw the acquisition of a summer house – and now, in retirement, he and Doris had more time to enjoy it.

"During his retirement years, family and friends phoned regularly and continued to visit – with Doris always ready to greet them with tea and cake. There were frequent excursions to the nearby coast, with Chalkie determining the destination according to wind direction – not wanting to have the wind blowing in from the sea, sending sand into their faces! They were members of the National Trust and would travel by car to look around stately homes and castles, with many visits resulting in 'another souvenir'.

"In 1995 he went to South Africa to see the third, extremely memorable World Cup. Ged and Di were there too, on a separate tour. They met up on a couple of occasions and recall Chalkie's view of a sponsor's jingles being played again and again while injured players were being treated, as being 'unseemly'. Active involvement was maintained until 1997, through Simon Cohen running coaching holidays for children.

"Wedding anniversaries had always been important celebratory occasions for Chalkie and Doris. In 1977, Chalkie's mother Annie, brother David and sister Margaret – with their partners Phyllis and Dennis – had joined them for their silver wedding celebrations. Now, in retirement, Chalkie and Doris organised family weekends away for their ruby and golden wedding anniversaries. Their ruby celebrations were based at Lynch Country House,

Doris and Chalkie celebrating at their 50th wedding anniversary dinner

Allerford, Somerset. Their golden celebrations weekend was in Sidmouth, a popular destination for visits since his retirement. Ged, Stella, Nick and their partners Di, Nick and Melissa were there for both – while David and Phyllis were at the ruby celebrations.

"Retirement left more time for them to travel to visit their children and other family members. They continued to visit relatives in Carlisle and holiday in Silloth, and attended the weddings of Margaret's son and daughter in Cumbria. They travelled to Florida in 1998 and 2000 to visit their youngest son, Nick, and his family, and visited old rugby acquaintances such as John Lockyer in Devon.

"Chalkie also spent a lot of time during his early retirement on the phone – 'talking rugby'. Coaches would phone to seek his advice, while Ged sent rugby news clippings to read and discuss with him on the phone, but his interest in the game and in his garden waned as the illnesses which clouded his later years took hold. He was diagnosed with Type 2 diabetes after his retirement and the muscle wasting effects of Inclusion Body Myositis progressively eroded his physical ability and mental enthusiasm.

"His past achievements continued to receive recognition. On August 21 2000 he was made an Honorary Life Member of Leicester Football Club, a distinction shared only with Jerry Day and John Allen.

"Fifteen months later, on December 6 2001, he received The Geoffrey Dyson Award for his significant contribution to the development and management of rugby coaching. Accompanied by Ged, and joined by former Leicester Tigers players and RFU officials: Peter Wheeler, Dean Richards, Ian Smith, John Wells, Dusty Hare, Brian Hall, Paul Dodge, Garry Adey, John Elliott, Barrie Corless (RFU DTA Midlands), David Shaw (RFU DTA London & SE) and Chris Spicer (RFU Director of Performance), Chalkie was clearly thrilled to be invited to the awards evening.

HRH Princess Anne presents Chalkie with The Geoffrey Dyson Award

"I met Dad at Paddington Station," recalls Ged, "and we jumped in the back of a black cab over to the Café Royal. Mum told me later that Dad had been up for hours, dressed and ready to go at 3 o'clock in the morning. He was starting to struggle by then. Once we got to the Café Royal we went to scope out where the awards were going to take place. The room was set out with a stage running along one side. This was obviously where the awards would take place. As well as steps up to the stage, there was a ramp. We tested out dad walking up the ramp. It was a slow process, as he was quite unsteady on his feet by now – plus the fact that he was probably tired having been up half the night.

"As people started to arrive, Peter Wheeler was the first of the Tigers group to get there and he and dad immediately started chatting. When Dad was announced as one of the award winners, I helped him to his feet then, stepped aside and he set off towards the ramp. It was at this point that Princess Anne said: 'That's OK, Mr White, I'll come down to you' and stepped off the stage to present his award. A lovely and caring touch to someone she could see was unsteady on his feet. Dad described the whole event as 'a wonderful experience'."

"However, his unsteadiness was symptomatic of his progressive deterioration, as was his waning interest in and ability to talk rugby. He was no longer

In February 2003 Chalkie returned to Leicester for the last time to attend a special dinner where he was presented with a Leicester Tigers '100' game cap

interested in talking to coaches who called, so they stopped calling. Dementia was diagnosed by a doctor who came to the house to examine him in 2002 and, as his condition steadily worsened, he was admitted to the local cottage hospital, Stratfield House, while Doris was in hospital – in February 2003. "He was not forgotten by English rugby. Mike Catt and Alan Black defied official regulations to bring the World Cup to him at Stratfield House after England's victory, led by Tiger Martin Johnson, in the 2003 tournament.

"There was one final move, to Orchard Court Care Home in Taunton. He was there for only three weeks before dying of vascular dementia on January 24 2005, eight days after his 76th birthday. Stella and Nick were at his bedside – Nick had come over from Florida. Doris, who lived until July 2015 was in hospital herself when he died.

"His funeral was at Taunton Crematorium on February 2 2005. Among a mass of tributes and more than 100 letters received by the family following his death, perhaps the most evocative was from a former Nottingham High School pupil, who wrote: "I remember him with fondness and awe as one of the great and formidable characters of my youth who inspired me to do things which I had not thought possible. I have remembered one of his half-time talks for over 30 years and in recent years have passed it on to my son. I was amused to hear one of the Leicester World Cup winning players repeating it for the benefit of world TV last year, and knew exactly from whom it had been learnt."

That touching tribute from a former pupil spoke for the thousands of former pupils and rugby players, whose lives he affected. That impact, along with many of their names, is summed up in the section which follows.

His most profound effect was perhaps on Leicester Football Club. No great institution, least of all one built for so collaborative an enterprise as rugby union, can be the work of one man. Tigers had been a great club before Chalkie arrived at Welford Road, as the most imposing of English club grounds stands as a monument to that status. His own work was buttressed by allies and collaborators – club officials, players and other coaches – so numerous that singling any out would be invidious.

In 1995 Tigers would enter the transformative era of professionalism better equipped than any other club. It was the sole English club with sufficient support to handle the transition without being subjected to the erratic mercies of rich men, and would dominate the league so completely that it was forced to introduce play-offs to inject unpredictability into the destination of its championship.

Chalkie's contribution to that achievement was commemorated on May 26 2005. It was 12 days after Tigers had played yet another Twickenham final. It was not among the most fondly remembered, following defeat to Wasps – who were to master the play-offs as much as Tigers dominated under the league format, which remains the fairest test of quality across the season – but it is also remembered as the last of the 362 matches played by the defining figure of that Tigers era, Martin Johnson.

If further evidence for Chalkie's longer-term impact is needed, no witness could be more compelling than arguably the greatest of all Tigers. His debut was not until 1989, seven years after Chalkie's departure, but England's 2003 World Cup winning captain leaves no doubt, in the Afterword that follows, of the former coach's continuing influence on Leicester Football Club.

AFTERWORD

I'm often asked who has been the biggest influence on my career. The person asking is inevitably looking for a person, a mentor, but the answer I've always given, ever since I can remember being asked, is not a *who* but a *what*. It's an institution, a rugby club and that, unsurprisingly, is the Leicester Football Club as it was called officially when I joined, but known to everyone in the game as The Tigers.

I'd first watched a game there in 1981, clutching my free schoolboy season ticket that had been distributed through the local schools, and very quickly fallen in love with the whole thing. Welford Road seemed a huge stadium but friendly and welcoming, the team was full of star names – Paul Dodge, Clive Woodward, Dusty Hare and Peter Wheeler – I'd heard my rugby savvy friends talk about but had never seen play. We went to watch as often as we could, and couldn't get enough. I can still vividly remember many of those games. I was hooked and wanted to one day run out there myself in the green, red and white hooped jersey.

Six years later I walked through the front gates to take part in my first training session for the Tigers' youth team. We trained on the not so glamorous Welford Road Recreation Ground behind the stadium but I didn't care. Paul Dodge, Les Cusworth and Dusty Hare were still playing, now joined by Dean Richards and Rory Underwood, and I was rubbing shoulders with the best players in the game and trying to prove my worth.

In the Tigers' youth team, I joined a group whose senior players were fiercely loyal to the club and its players and immensely proud to be Tigers – we thought that by winning our games we were doing our part in maintaining Leicester's proud history.

That history for me started in 1981, but I was aware that the club had just completed a run of three successive cup wins, captained by Peter Wheeler and coached by a man called 'Chalkie' White. That cup sat in a cabinet above the bar in the clubhouse, and that was the standard – Leicester were winners and nothing else was good enough.

Martin Johnson captained Leicester Tigers to unprecedented success

Chalkie had retired by the time I arrived but very quickly you became aware of his achievements. When we trained, we were surrounded by international players and British and Irish Lions, and the large crowds that watched games not only expected winning rugby, they expected exciting, running, winning rugby.

Chalkie White left an incredible legacy for those that followed to aspire to. The numerous trophies and future internationals that came from the club and its youth system in the following years is no coincidence. We had fantastic role models and success to emulate, along with huge expectations, and they had all been shaped and influenced by Herbert 'Chalkie' White in some way.

So, when I'm asked in the future who has been the biggest influence on my career I'll answer the 'Leicester Tigers' and when saying it I'll regret that I only got to meet him a couple of times, the man probably more than any other that makes that statement true – Chalkie White.

Martin Johnson
July 2025

APPENDIX

(i) The 195 Leicester players selected by Chalkie White: 1968-82 (by appearances)

376 Garry Adey, **333** Bleddyn Jones, **320** Bob Barker, **311** Peter Wheeler, **302** John Duggan, **298** Brian Hall, **295** John Allen, **258** Nick Joyce & Robin Money, **238** Bob Rowell, **236** Steve Kenney, **227** Paul Dodge, **223** David Forfar, **207** Graham Willars, **193** Dusty Hare, **187** Steve Johnson, **184** Robin Cowling, **182** Steve Redfern, **172** Ian 'Dosser' Smith, **171** Tim Barnwell, **162** Eric Bann, **159** David Matthews, **155** Mike Yandle, **145** Roger Grove, **139** Les Cusworth, **132** Mike Mortimer, **126** Ray Needham, **119** Angus Collington, **116** Chris Baynes, **114** Terry Burwell, **111** John Elliott, **109** Kevin Andrews & Jim Kempin, **98** Nigel Gillingham & Arthur Hazlerigg, **95** David Bird, **90** Kevin Williams, **89** Clive Woodward, **86** Bob Beason, **84** Nick Jackson, **76** Ray French, **75** John Dawson & Graham Pulfrey, **73** John White, **70** Bob Watson, **69** Mike Harrison, **57** Peter Nicholls & Dave Shaw, **56** Paul Ringer, **51** John Reeve, **50** Roy Sleigh, **48** Mike Evans, **47** Phil Vesty, **46** Trevor Spence, **45** Dave Whibley & John Ingleby, **44** Steve Betts & Chris Tressler, **43** Graham Jackson, **42** John Deacon & Roy French, **41** Barry Evans, **40** David Beaty, **39** Ted Holley, **38** John Mawbey & Chris Owen, **35** Duncan Black, **34** Larry Parkes, **33** John Quick, **32** Nick Youngs & Mike Marshall, **31** David Berry, Alan Raine & Malcolm Sayer, **30** Ian Dodson, Andy Key, Mike Brownhill & Tim Walley, **29** Malcolm Foulkes-Arnold & Ken Bracewell, **28** Jez Krych & Field Walton, **27** Martin Whitcombe & Mike Poulson, **26** Mark Duffelen & Mick Newton, **25** Dick Cooper, Rodger Arneil & Jock Millican, **23** Bob Smith, **21** Graham Horner & Peter Tom, **20** David Pickering, **19** Bill Reichwald & Marcus Rose, **18** Alan Old & Mick Merriman, **17** Richard Berry & Arthur Chapman, **16** Rob Tebbutt & Wayne Richardson, **15** Peter Aldwinckle, **14** Mike Gavins, Frank Jones & Dave Truman, **12** Bev Bedggood, **11** Mac Knowles, Vendis Afflick, Peter Edwards, John Hill & Steve Solomons, **10** Alistair Grocock, Danny Kirk & Dave Williams, **9** John Flint, Dave Manship, Steve Newsome, Bob Small & Paul Stone, **8** Dean Richards, **7** Andy Beevers, Ted Edwards, Tim Ringer, Mike Thomas & Rod McMichael, **6** David Harris, Guy Millar, D. Morley, Andy Northen, Dean Waddingham, Adey Marriott & Gary Weinberg, **5** 'Thumper' Dingley, Stuart Redfern, Terry Roberts, Tim Cooke, Dave Hanna, Andy Matthews, Peter Riley, Kelvin Wilford, Malcolm Bussey & Chris Holroyd, **4** Jess Glover, Neil Holloway, Dennis Sobey & Vic Wigley, **3** Jeff Denner, Neil Hartley, Chris Hemsley, Dave Macey, David Perkins, Rex Skelton & Paul Strickland, **2** George Allen, Mark Churchward, Pete Clements, J. Golding, N. Haines, Cliff Hilliker, Tommy Lawton, Mike Lockett, Dick Peters, Dick Royce, Graham Smith, Dave Thomas, Jim Watts & Alan Whitehall, **1** Colin Dexter, Nick Drake-Lee, Keith Fielding, John Wells, Dave Gavins, John Berry, John Broome, Peter Broadbent, Ian Bridgwood, Chris DeLuca, Keith Freeston, Nick Humphries, Alan John, John Lacey, Brian Llewellyn, Alistair Meldrum, Mike Nangreave, John Rawes, Mike Ryan, Phil Smith, Charlie Tassell, Ian Tomalin, George Walton, Dave Webb, Bob Williams, Jeff Young & Kevin Steptoe

(ii) Leicester players capped during the Chalkie White era: 1967-82

Year[1]	Player	Country	British Lions[2]
1969	Rodger Arneil[3]	Scotland	1968 & 1971
1973	Alan Old[4]	England	1974
1975	Peter Wheeler	England	1977 & 1980
1976	Garry Adey	England	
1977	Robin Cowling	England	
1978	Dusty Hare[5]	England	1983
1978	Paul Dodge	England	1980
1979	Les Cusworth	England	
1980	Clive Woodward	England	1980 & 1983

[1]Year of first cap while a Leicester player
[2]The name British Lions was adopted in 1950, changing to British & Irish Lions in 2001
[3]First capped in 1968 while with Edinburgh Academicals FC, winning seven caps before moving to Leicester
[4]First capped in 1972 while with Middlesbrough RUFC, winning five caps before moving to Leicester
[5]First capped in 1974 while with Nottingham RFC, winning one cap before moving to Leicester

In November 1983, just 11 months after Chalkie had left Welford Road, six Leicester Tigers players he had coached – Dusty Hare, Nick Youngs, Peter Wheeler (captain), Les Cusworth, Paul Dodge, Clive Woodward – all played for England in an historic 15-9 victory against New Zealand at Twickenham. This photograph was a gift to Chalkie from Dusty Hare.

(iii) Chalkie's achievements as coach of Leicester Tigers
John Player Cup Finalists 1977-78 v Gloucester (Lost 3-6)
John Player Cup Winners 1978-79 v Moseley (Won 15-12)
John Player Cup Winners 1979-80 v London Irish (Won 21-9)
John Player Cup Winners 1980-81 v Gosforth (Won 22-15)
Winners 1980 *Sunday Telegraph* English Champions
Winners 1981 *Sunday Telegraph* English Champions
Winners 1981 *Daily Express* Team of the Year

Leicester Tigers – Team of the Year 1980-81
New club captain Steve Johnson (centre left) holding the Team of the Year trophy awarded to Leicester Tigers by Dan Keough of Victoria Wine, with retiring captain Peter Wheeler (right) holding the Sunday Telegraph Trophy. Dusty Hare (centre right) also received a silver plate for setting the world record for points scored in first-class rugby.

(iv) Chalkie's Individual Achievements

Winner 1979 *Rugby World* - Services to rugby award
Winner 1981 Rugby Union Writers Club - Rupert Cherry Prize
Winner 1982 Rugby Union Writers Club - Rupert Cherry Prize

Chalkie with the Rupert Cherry Prize

(v) Representative teams coached by Chalkie White

Year	Team	Opponent	Venue	Score	Win / Loss
1973 (13 Jan)	Midland Counties (East)	New Zealand	Welford Road	12 v 43	L
1975 (12 Nov)	Midland Counties (East)	Australia	Welford Road	11 v 8	W
1976 (9 Oct)	Midlands & North of England	Argentina	Welford Road	24 v 9	W
1978 (18 Nov)	Midlands	New Zealand	Welford Road	15 v 20	L
1979 (3 Nov)	Midlands	New Zealand	Welford Road	7 v 33	L
1981 (17 Oct)	Midlands	Australia	Welford Road	16 v 10	W
1982 (6 Oct)	Midlands	Fiji	Welford Road	25 v 16	W

(vi) Match Statistics: 1967-1982

Season	Played	Won	Lost	Drawn	Pts For	Pts Against
1967-68	41	23	14	4	484	338
1968-69	43	27	12	4	657	461
1969-70	44	26	15	3	651	563
1970-71	45	23	20	2	654	495
1971-72	41	26	12	3	789	505
1972-73	46	29	15	2	988	683
1973-74	43	24	16	3	739	607
1974-75	40	19	20	1	542	598
1975-76	45	23	21	1	758	733
1976-77	39	26	13	0	752	424
1977-78	41	27	12	2	849	573
1978-79	34	24	10	0	784	372
1979-80	42	33	9	0	980	420
1980-81	41	33	7	1	940	527
1981-82	40	27	11	2	925	512
1982-83	21*	15	6	0	499	317

*Chalkie coached for half the season: September 1 to December 31

(vii) Midlands Merit Table: 1976-83

Season	Competing Clubs	Final Position	Played	Won	Drawn	Lost	Win %
1976-77	9	2nd	8	6	0	2	75%
1977-78	9	5th	8	5	0	3	62.5%
1978-79	9	2nd	7	6	0	1	85.7%
1979-80	9	1st	7	6	0	1	85.7%
1980-81	9	1st	7	6	1	0	92.9%
1981-82	9	1st	7	6	0	1	85.7%
1982-83	9	1st	7	7	0	0	100%

BIBLIOGRAPHY

Books

Allen, Fred & McLean, Terry: *Fred Allen on Rugby* (Cassell New Zealand, 1970)
Dewhirst, John: *Life at the Top - The Rivalry of Manningham FC and Bradford FC and their Conversion from Rugby to Soccer* (Bantam, 2016)
Evans, Steve: *Majestic Cov - Once the Kings of English Rugby* (Takahe Publishing, 2021)
Farmer, Stuart & Hands, David: *The Tigers Tale - The Official History of Leicester Football Club 1880-1993* (ACL & Polar Publishing (UK) Ltd., 1993)
Hands, David: *Leicester Football Club 1880-1980 - One Hundred Years of Rugby from the 'Death or Glory' Boys to the Present Day 'Tigers'* (Leicester Football Club, 1980)
Hare, Dusty W.H. & Norrie, David: *Dusty* (Queen Ann Press, 1985)
Hopkins, Sidney Ifano 'Van': *Leicestershire Rugby Union 1887-1987 - One Hundred Years of Rugby Development in the County* (Leicestershire RFU, 1986)
Jenkins, Vivian (Ed.): *Rothmans Rugby Yearbook* (Queen Ann Press, 1972 to 1982)
Johnson, Martin: *Rugby And All That - An Irreverent History* (Hodder & Stoughton, 2000)
Jones, Stephen (Ed.): *Rothmans Rugby Yearbook* (Queen Ann Press, 1983)
Mace, John: *The History of Royal Air Force Rugby 1919-1999* (Royal Air Force RU, 2000)
Owen, O.L. (Ed.): *Playfair Rugby Football Annual* (The Dickens Press, 1957 to 1964)
Ross, Gordon (Ed.): *Playfair Rugby Football Annual* (The Dickens Press, 1965 to 1972)
Salmon, Tom: *The First Hundred Years - The History of Rugby Football in Cornwall* (Cornwall RFU, 1983)
Thau, Chris: *Rothmans Rugby Yearbook* (Queen Anne Press, 1980)
Thomas, J. Tudor: *John Tudor Thomas - A Farmers Boy at Heart* (self-published)
Wheeler, Peter J.: *Rugby from the Front - An Autobiography* (Hutchinson, 1983)
Whitcombe, Martin & Bridge, Bill: *The Indomitable Frank Whitcombe* (St. David's Press, 2016)
Winch, Jonty: *Rhodesia Rugby - A History of the National Side 1896-1979* (The Zimbabwe-Rhodesia RFU, 1979)
Woodward R, Clive: *Clive Woodward - Winning!* (Hodder, 2005)

Newspaper & Magazine Articles

Austin, Michael: *The Telegraph* (October 25 1980)
'Cherry and White': *The Camborne and Redruth Packet* (1957)

Hands, David: *Leicester Mercury* (April 17 1978)
Fox, David: *The Chronicle* (July 27 1982 & July 31 1982)
Frost, David: *The Guardian* (October 24 1960 & May 4 1980)
Johnson, Martin: *Leicester Mercury* (April 7 1979, October 7 1980, November 25 1981 & December 14 1982)
Lander, Chris: *Daily Mirror* (April 20 1979)
Mason, John: *The Telegraph* (September 10 1980 & December 30 1982)
Matthews, Mike: *Nottingham Evening Post* (1976)
Neal, Paul: *Leicester Mercury* (1973)
Reason, John: *Sunday Telegraph* (July 1982)
'Rugby Correspondent': *The Telegraph* (July 31 1980)
'Rugby Correspondent': *The Gloucester Citizen* (April 15 1978)
'Rugby Correspondent': *The Gloucester Citizen* (April 17 1978)
'Rugby Correspondent': *The Courier-Mail*, Brisbane (August 1980)
'Rugby Correspondent': *Newark Advertiser* (July 1981)
'Rugby Correspondent": *Cumberland News* (August 1982)
'Rugby Correspondent": *The Herald*, Zimbabwe (August 4 1982)
'Rugby Reporter': *The Herald* (August 7 1982)
Silver, Eric: *Cumberland News (1962)*
Todd, Ian: 'On the Blind Side', *The Sun* (1976)

Other Resources

A Special Tribute to Chalkie White (Leicester FC, 1994)
British Newspaper Archive: www.britishnewspaperarchive.co.uk
Centenary Brochure (Camborne RFC, 1977-78)
Chalkie's Farewell (Leicester FC, 1982)
Cumberland & Westmorland RFU, match programmes
Cumbria's Museum of Military Life, Carlisle
England Rugby - The RFU Technical Journal (Rugby Football Union, 1994)
Kendal RUFC, match programmes
Keswick RFC, match programmes
Leicester FC, match programmes
Leicester FC World Tour Brochure (Leicester FC, 1987)
Old Creightonians RFC, match programmes
Rugger & Rugby World
Stafford RUFC, match programmes
Touchline (Rugby Football Union, 2002)
Workington RFC – match programmes

Interviewees

Marcia Abel-Smith
Garry Adey
Vendis Afflick
John Allen
Rodger Arneil
Tim Barnwell
Bruce Barritt
Bob Beason
Simon Bennett
Duncan Black
John Blondin
Terry Burwell
Gareth Chilcott
Tony Cliff
Merrill Clymo
Philip 'John' Collins
Professor Tony Collins
Fran Cotton
Robin Cowling
Sean Cusack
Les Cusworth
Mike Davis
Gwynne Day
John Dewhirst
Paul Dodge
John Duggan
Brian Eddy
Jeff Edgar
Barry Evans
Stuart Farmer
Keith Fielding
Will Feebery
Jack Forfar
Malcolm Foulkes-Arnold
Ray French
Nigel Gillingham
Ged Glynn
Chris Goddard
Darren Grewcock
Roger Grove
Brian Hall
Dusty Hare
Bob Hood
Phil Horrocks-Taylor
Paul Hull
Nick Jackson
Martin Johnson
Steve Johnson
Geraint Ashton Jones
Nick Joyce
John Kaye
Steve Kenney
Andy Key
Maurice Key
Jez Krych
Adam Lubbock
Dave Lyons
David Matthews
Robin Money
Ray Needham
Mick Newton
Alan Old
John Owen
Mike Poulson
Cristian Răducanu
Steve Redfern
Bob Reeves
Dean Richards
Wayne Richardson
Mark Ring
Harry Roberts
Brian Smith
Ian 'Dosser' Smith
Steve Solomons
Chris Thau
Geraint 'Geri' Thomas
Peter Tom
Chris Tressler
Andy Tucker
Peter Wheeler
Ged White
Nick White
Stella White
Stephen White
Kevin Williams
Les Williams
Nick Youngs

Father and son, Maurice and Andy Key – both of whom played full back for Leicester. Maurice (right) and Chalkie were teammates in 1957, while Andy (left), a product of the club's youth team, was coached by Chalkie when he made his debut for the Tigers in 1978.

"Let others tell you how good you are. I'll tell you how to be better."
Herbert Victor 'Chalkie' White
(16 January 1929 – 24 January 2005)

INDEX

www.ingramcontent.com/pod-product-compliance
Ingram Content Group UK Ltd.
Pitfield, Milton Keynes, MK11 3LW, UK
UKHW050342061025
463584UK00003B/7

9 781904 609261